Self, Attitudes
and
Emotion Work

Self, Attitudes and Emotion Work

Western Social Psychology and Eastern Zen Buddhism Confront Each Other

Anson Shupe and
Christopher Bradley

Routledge
Taylor & Francis Group

LONDON AND NEW YORK

First published 2010 by Transaction Publishers

2 Park Square, Milton Park, Abingdon, Oxfordshire OX14 4RN
711 Third Avenue, New York, NY 10017

Routledge is an imprint of the Taylor & Francis Group, an informa business

First issued in paperback 2017

Library of Congress Catalog Number: 2010012590

Library of Congress Cataloging-in-Publication Data

Shupe, Anson D.
    Self, attitudes, and emotion work : Western social psychology and Eastern Zen Buddhism confront each other / Anson Shupe and Christopher Bradley.
        p. cm.
    Includes bibliographical references and index.
    ISBN 978-1-4128-1348-8 (acid-free paper)
    1. Zen Buddhism--Psychology. 2. Social psychology--Western countries. 3. Psychology and religion--Western countries. 4. Religion and sociology--Western countries. I. Bradley, Christopher (Christopher S.) II. Title.

BQ9265.8.S58 2010
294.3'365--dc22
                                                          2010012590
ISBN 13: 978-1-4128-1348-8 (hbk)
ISBN 13: 978-1-138-51446-1 (pbk)

Dedication

To Master Ed Johnson and Master Roy Kurban, who taught me Zen in my head before I ever knew it.

-ADS

This book is dedicated to Marcie and Misty.

-CSB

The man who has not contemplated the mind is unable to give a reason of those things that have reason.

—Plato (427-347 B.C.E.)

Know the essence of mind. Its intrinsic essence is pure clarity.

—Tao-hsin (580-651)

There is a plurality of reflections of the moon but no plurality in the real moon.

—Ma-tsu (709-788)

When the mind is not aroused, this is discipline:
when the mind is unmoved, this is concentration;
when the mind is not obscured, this is insight.

—Hsueh-yen (cir. 1253)

Buddhi, the intuition ... is as different from intellect as intellect is from sensuous experience.

—Daisetz Teitaro Suzuki (1870-1966)

Only in action can you fully realize the forces operative in social behavior.

—Stanley Milgram (1933-1984)

Contents

Acknowledgments

A small number of persons have patiently listened to me meander verbally about my "take" on Zen regarding the behavioral sciences, my life, and life in general. Some have steered me toward extremely useful sources where I found kindred authors and ideas. I express appreciation, in no particular order, to Dick, Dr. Sam, Alan, Abby, Mieko, and Bobbi. Also, to ILH, whose penetrating insight into our project was invaluable.

—ADS

Ask anyone who has done it, without the support of other people, it's damn near impossible to write a book. Many thanks to my mentor Mike Nusbaumer and my beautiful wife Marcie Bradley, each of who provided me with the help and encouragement I needed while I worked on this manuscript. A special acknowledgement goes out to my coauthor Anson Shupe. I am deeply grateful to you for including me on this project and for always believing in my writing abilities, even though I kept blowing through deadline after deadline. Andy, you have been a true friend.

—CSB

Preface

This book is about Western social psychology interfacing with an Eastern Zen Buddhist perspective, a meeting that, to the best of our knowledge, has never systematically taken place prior to this point. Our work is neither a purely Zen Buddhist critique of the former, nor is it merely a social psychological interpretation of Zen. Rather, it is an attempt to create common ground between each via the systematic comparison of certain shared fundamental concepts and ideas.

Anglo-American social psychology, as we shall briefly review in Chapter 1, is not much more than a century old despite having its roots in a broad philosophical tradition. Alternately, the Zen version of Buddhism can trace its historical origins to roughly 1,500 years ago in China. At points, we will argue that even though the two arose at different times and appear to be stridently antithetical, they actually share considerable areas of overlap. Moreover, we will show how each can benefit from the various caveats one could suggest to the other, despite their separate beginnings, assumptions, and occasional rhetorical excesses.

For instance, Zen writings have few positive comments (at least at first glance) about the cultural blinders placed on every one of us via the process of socialization that begins at infancy, a process that Zen argues culminates in the Western obsession with individuality. In other words, what to most social psychologists are the results of "natural" or "normal" learning processes are for Zen distorting, constraining, and possibly even damaging to the individual. An example of this line of thought can be found in the writings of Belgian scholar Robert Linssen (1958: 113). He begins his essay on self-awareness and identity with a Zen vision of memory:

> The automatisms of memory constitute the most subtle and overwhelming conditioning factor of the human being. This chain reaction is so subtle and so delicate that at present nearly all men are totally unaware of it. The shadow cast by old mental habits darkens the light of each present moment.

As Linssen's last sentence implies, the results of collecting memories can be pernicious. The logic of Zen sees consequences of the "taken-for-granted tyranny" created by our personal memories and culture—every culture—including hubris, greed, self-centeredness, distrust, prejudice, hatred, fear, anxiety, and violence. Indeed, Master Hui-neng, Sixth Chinese Zen Patriarch and founder of modern Zen, warned during the seventh century:

> In the exercise of our thinking faculty let the past be dead. If we allow our thoughts, past, present, and future, to link up in a series, we put ourselves under restraint. (Price and Mou-lam, 1990: 96)

Other Zen authors and practitioners echo these sentiments in more or less hostile terms, referring to memories and ordinary thoughts as "mental objectivization of the world," "fabricated artificialities," "contrivances," and "the monkey mind." A ninth-century Chinese Zen master, Ta Hui, even referred to ordinary memories that influence our thoughts and impressions as "the stains of afflictions from alien sensations" (Cleary, 1977: 1).

In contrast, social psychology, which leans more toward the "nurture" rather than "nature" end of social maturation and identity formation, places a tremendous emphasis on the phenomena of socialization and the formation of the self via memory accrual and retention (areas of research that are firmly rooted within the domain of sociological social psychology), processes that are also sometimes referred to as "learning" or "conditioning" (terms that are more familiar to psychologically-oriented social psychologists). Regardless of nomenclature, social psychologists see memory as an important key to self-concept formation, but not the only key: equally important are a host of external stimuli or interested agencies. These include direct socialization influences, such as parents, families or schools, as well as more indirect ones, such as language, media, and the more implicit cultural messages that shape personality, memory, and even conscious thought.

While social psychology would dispute the Zen assumption that socialization and memory are always pernicious or negative in their effects, most social psychologists would certainly acknowledge the Zennist point that these forces are staggering in terms of the imbalance of influence they have on a person, especially with respect to the markedly profound effects that language and culture have on identity formation. Indeed, Zen likely overstates its case in condemning language, memory, and socialization processes, but for good reasons we will later explore. Suffice it to say here that Zen is not simply some exotic Asian brand of psychology, nor does it treat as disposable (at worst) or simplistic (at best) the sociological insights of cultural influence, interpersonal relationships, institutions, morality, authority, and language. Without those social processes Zen could not have thrived to become, by the year 1000, an enormously large and influential religion of Imperial (and peasant) China and then within another century an equivalent influence in medieval Japan. Such rejections of sociology would, practically speaking, render Zen ill-fitted for anything other than a monastic tradition, which it has certainly possessed, but which could not solely account for its wide practice among laity in Japan and, increasingly, among both North Americans and Europeans.

It is true that Zen often challenges in radical terms (at least from an initial pass through its doctrines) key assumptions of both sociology and psychology concerning individual identity, human nature, and human motivation. But it more often than not proffers these challenges in an effort to unnerve and "shake up" unreflective persons, much as did the work of the ancient Greek Stoics, the more contemporary ethnomethodologists of late twentieth-century American sociology, and the satirists and tricksters of every age. Their collective mission has always been one of reconsidering taken-for-granted assumptions of everyday life and social order, a mission shared by Zen Buddhism.

We offer two caveats about the text to follow:

First, as scholars who have taught and researched in the field of social psychology for a total of over forty years between us, we have not sought to construct "straw man" portrayals of either social psychology or Zen Buddhism. We have not been deliberately cavalier in applying Zen criticisms to social psychology, nor have we been equally disdainful by dismissing out of hand or debunking any insights Zen would have for social psychology. Instead we have attempted to offer a deeper illumination of the underpinnings of both social psychology and Zen Buddhism through the art of contrast and comparison.

Second, as we note in Chapter 1 where we briefly review Zen history and perspectives, there are two predominant modern approaches to Zen: *Rinzai* and *Soto*, both of which trace their antecedents to T'ang China of the seventh century. On a personal note, one of us follows the *Rinzai* path for reasons discussed later, and this bias may be apparent to Zennists through our choice of citations and interpretations. Yet it is fair to say that between these two methodologically-different approaches to Zen (*Rinzai* emphasizing explosions, both major and minor, of mental Awakening; *Soto* maintaining that Awakening proceeds in far more gradual levels cultivated by progressively deep meditation exercises over time) there is nevertheless considerable overlap. Certainly they promulgate the same end state of personal liberation.

It is our greatest hope that the readership of this volume will gain a deeper appreciation of the realms of both social psychology and Zen Buddhism, though we admit that our conceptualizations, data, and referencing are geared more towards the former discipline. Thus much of our writing is predicated on the assumption that you will be more familiar with the social psychological portions of our arguments. We further assumed that many readers would only have a modest-to-minimal familiarity with recurrent Buddhist terminology. In order to assist readers who have little knowledge of Zen Buddhism, we have provided a short glossary that is largely made up of terms (Japanese—Jp; Chinese—Ch.; and Sanskrit—Skt.) within mainstream Buddhism and Zen. That said, we acknowledge that it can sometimes be tricky in nuancing Zen definitions, since Japanese Zen terms are usually translations (and pronunciations) of older Chinese translations of what were originally much older Indian *Sanskrit* concepts. There was a lot of cultural filtering understandably going on during the transitions from one language to another. In the glossary after the text we have attempted to be as orthodox in our definitions as a Western Zen observer can be. Note that throughout the text and glossary we omit accent marks that would ordinarily signify long vowels in Sanskrit, Chinese, and Japanese words. For speakers and scholars of these languages the pronunciations are already known; for non-speakers we recommend *The Shambhala Dictionary of Buddhism and Zen*.

In the following integration of two related but very different worldviews we are mindful of the words of Catholic Christian mystic Thomas Merton (1968: 3); to wit, "Zen is not something which is grasped by being set within distinct limits or given a characteristic outline or easily recognizable features so that, when we see these distinct and particular forms, we say, 'There it is!'" Or, as one ancient Zen teacher wryly put it: "Talking about Zen all the time is like looking for fish tracks in a dry riverbed" (Cleary, 2000: 25).

1

Approaching the Zen-Social Psychology Nexus

Before embarking on an analysis of the common (and sometimes uncommon) ground pertaining to Zen Buddhism and Western social psychology, there must be some cursory review of the salient subject matter of each. Zennists (i.e., Zen followers) will appreciate that their "denomination" or "take" on a much older Buddhism is only one of many variations in existence. For understandable reasons of economy, we have tried to summarize only the most fundamental, un-nuanced points of larger Buddhism and then of Zen's rather unique perspective. This is done for the sake of readers generally unfamiliar with either Zen or Buddhism, and we have sought succinctness rather than breadth. Alternately, social scientists may commiserate with our undertaking the rather formidable task of even modestly trying to reduce a voluminous literature and sea of concepts that straddle the disciplines of Zen Buddhism, sociology, psychology, and even at times anthropology into anything manageable for presentation.

Thus, mindful of all the limitations inherent in such efforts, we provide in this chapter brief primers on general Buddhism and its Zen variant, followed by an overview of social psychology that highlights its definition, recent history, and subjects of concern. More details on each perspective will unfold in subsequent chapters. We acknowledge that we err initially on the side of allotting more words to Zen Buddhism than social psychology on the assumption that fewer social scientists will be familiar with Zen's origins, assertions, and style of perceiving interpersonal life. Within each chapter, however, we have attempted a more even balance of Zen and social psychology. Further, at times we happen to veer into other academic fields, such as philosophy, history, or anthropology. That shift will be unavoidable since social psychology, as with all the behavioral science disciplines, has its roots sunk deep in the Western philosophical tradition. Likewise, in South and Far East Asia one cannot, in historical terms, smoothly demarcate religion from philosophical practice or from anything resembling empirical science. There is one commonality we wish to remark on at the outset: both social psychology and Zen put a premium on empiricism and the experiential, even if carried out in different ways.

The Finger and the Moon

There is a hoary Zen Buddhist aphorism about the act of observing the moon as opposed to the moon's essential, distinct existence, to the effect:

> When you extend your arm and point your finger at the moon, do not end up confusing the tip of your finger with the moon itself.

Students of modern behavioral science often by necessity have to settle for "the tip of the finger" rather than the presumed moon in their conceptualizations and measurements of an incredibly complex, continuously-in-flux phenomenon usually called interpersonal behavior, or social interaction. Social psychologists become routinely accustomed to assigning proxy numbers and scores to represent rather abstract notions like the self-concept, self-esteem, self-efficacy, personality, locus of control, and by extension schema, attitudes, and person-other perceptions. As these working constructs are often given confirmation or perceived validation by numbers, there is always the danger that these numerical representations will then become reified as if there *really* are such absolute things as self-concepts, personalities, attitudes, and the like. A self-fulfilling prophecy can and often does then ensue. Constructs and the scores that measure them may take on lives of their own and be attributed to individuals and/or aggregates of persons, with these attributions taking on real consequences. A case in point would be the usage of IQ scores to discriminate against minorities for a host of social purposes, beginning in the early twentieth century against Southeastern European immigrants and again later throughout the last half of the century against African-Americans and other minority groups within the United States (we will offer more on the concept of IQ later).

Conflating constructs and scores is a slippery trend that has, in part, accelerated during the past half century with the increasing sophistication of inferential statistics for gauging ever more complicated multidimensional analyses, with these analyses being facilitated through the widespread availability of computers. Generally speaking, however, no competent social psychologist would seriously conclude that the social reality of measurement scores as proxies for concepts are exact equivalents to objects of physical reality in the same way that biologists, chemists, and physicists do when they deal with their subject matters. Since these two terms, physical reality and social reality, are as important to Zennists as they are for social psychologists, it is worth briefly distinguishing each at the outset, and in doing so, provide something of a prolegomenon to Zen thinking.

Physical Reality and Social Reality

Physical reality, in an ontological sense, simply *is*: undifferentiated by typologies or categorizations, undelineated by human thought, without an identity or existence predicated on the classifications and measurements to conceptualize and operationalize it. In other words, physical reality *as ordinarily understood* by most persons exists in fathoms of depth, lengths of meters and miles, or degrees of Celsius or Fahrenheit temperature. But these units are our impositions of human specification on physical reality. Laws, trends, and generalizations are simply the way we think of reality. Thus we search with only partial success for the regularities that nature is not bound by, as nature frequently demonstrates in spectacular "disasters" (our term, not nature's) like typhoons, tsunamis, and earthquakes.

British Sinologist and philosopher Alan Watts, in *Nature, Man and Woman* (1958b: 54), addresses the uniquely human conceit that the natural world actually exists as we parcel it up for our predictive, manipulative convenience. For example, we learn to screen out many aspects from the plethora of details in any situation, or field of interest, and extract or focus only on those ones relevant for our purposes. Thus

we feel in better control of a situation to the degree that we can bring it under conscious scrutiny ... things appear to the mind when, by conscious attention, the field is broken down into easily thinkable unities.

We do this in daily perceptions (of how parts of our bodies feel to us, or of all the stimuli facing us simultaneously in congested traffic, and so forth) as well as in periods of deliberate contemplative study and mundane reflection. But that a physical reality exists *as* broken down into our analytical terms of focus and measurement, and not as an indivisible unity, is ultimately an illusion. Continues Watts (1958b: 55):

We are also able to predict events and manage the external world by breaking down distances into feet and inches, weights into pounds and ounces, and motions into minutes and seconds. But do we actually suppose that twelve inches of wood are twelve separate bits of wood? We do not. We know that "breaking" wood into inches or pounds is done abstractly and not concretely. *It is not, however, so easy to see that breaking the field of awareness into things and events is also done abstractly, and that things are the measuring units of thought,* just as pounds are the measuring units of weighing. But this begins to be apparent when we realize that any one thing may, by analysis, be broken down into any number of component things, or may in its turn be regarded as the component part of some larger thing [emphasis ours].

The fact that we can achieve such prodigious feats as sending spacecraft accurately to land on other planets in our solar system or architecturally design and then construct a multi-tiered shopping mall with pragmatic reliability makes our discursive view of physical reality no less an artifact of the mind. This is essentially a Zen (and as we shall see, an older Taoist) criticism of everyday problem-solving, as well as a Zen critique of Western scientific thinking. Because of their utility and the unquestionably impressive achievements following from them, however, we unconsciously allow abstractions to substitute for actual physical reality as it is before discursive, linear conceptualization. The physical reality we measure is therefore a reconstructed reality in our minds.

Ultimately Zennists would say this is all a conceptual "trap," along the same lines when astronomer Thomas Kuhn (1962) called such models of thinking, with their built-in presuppositions and limitations, "paradigms." Watts refers to this Western style of approaching physical reality as "a fractured way of experiencing the world" that renders reality seemingly complex and not otherwise easily "felt" or experienced except in terms of "abstracted marks of difference." Human beings want the events of their physical world to be comprehensible, predictable, and ideally malleable on their terms, and not a world that is unfathomable, unforeseen, and therefore fearful. That modern science has been so relatively successful in fulfilling the human desire for quantified stability testifies to why most of us do not ordinarily think of physical reality as anything *but* broken down into measurable constructs.

Matters are more complicated, however, in the case of *social* reality, as social scientists—particularly anthropologists and sociologically-oriented social psychologists—have long recognized. Social reality lacks much of the apparent objectivity by which our constructs have rendered physical reality understandable and malleable within limits.

Social reality can be defined as an agreed-upon set of definitions, assumptions, and explanations about aspects of social life. Social reality represents a group consensus as to what characteristics—individual and group actions, ideas, and attributes—*mean* to human beings in those groups. An extreme cultural relativist position is that no action of individuals or groups or their perceived attributes has any intrinsic, absolute meaning; rather, meanings are conferred upon a situation through negotiated agreement by persons who experience (directly or indirectly) or observe them. But extreme position or not, these meanings are grounded in personal and group interests, fears and concerns, hopes and expectations, and even word-of-mouth in the form of socialization from presumed reliable others. The dynamics of this process have been thoroughly explained by symbolic interactionists, phenomenologists, and cultural anthropologists, so we will not belabor the point unnecessarily.

More importantly, it should be made clear that meanings, understood here as constructs, can shift with time and circumstances and in hindsight can be seen to have been unrealistic or even false. But at any given moment these social abstractions can carry the taken-for-granted, even authoritative weight of actual existence to the same extent that abstract measurements of the physical world carry validity for, say, astronomers and engineers.

Only in the case of social reality the metaphoric confusion of the finger with the moon can enjoy a smoother morphing process. Several twentieth century examples will illustrate what we mean:

- Despite a lusty history of alcohol consumption, various forces coalesced in the early 1900s to convince the U.S. Congress and then two-thirds of the states to pass the Eighteenth Amendment in 1919 to the Constitution (otherwise know as Prohibition). This law made the production, distribution, and (with a few exceptions) consumption of alcohol (regarded by many as antisocial and evil) illegal. But after fourteen subsequent years of a policy that failed to enforce sobriety and generated much popular resentment, another series of votes to repeal the illegality of alcohol occurred with the Twenty-first Amendment in 1933. Alcohol itself could not have changed all that much in fourteen years—only its social meaning or label was renegotiated.
- Traditionally the majority of psychiatrists considered deviance (nonconformity) in sexual orientation to be a form of mental aberration or emotional disorder. Homosexuality was therefore seen as a mental condition worthy of therapy in order to "cure" those who (supposedly) suffered from this malady. Thus homosexuality, as well as other forms of sexual expression, was defined as a mental pathology in early editions of the *Diagnostic and Statistical Manual*, a sort of *Physicians Desk Reference* encyclopedia cataloguing the categories and symptoms of mental problems. Then, in 1973, after considerable lobbying efforts by homosexual advocates within and outside psychiatry and clinical psychology, the American Psychiatric Association *took a vote* and

reclassified homosexuality from mental illness to a functional lifestyle or preference, and not pathology worthy of treatment. Gayness, in other words, was consensually removed from the DSM's "scientific" scheme of things as a disease.

- During the 1980s one of us had the opportunity as a sociologist who had researched the dynamics of family violence to appear in several Texas criminal courts in the role of expert witness for the defense. The cases involved battered women who eventually killed their abusive husbands or boyfriends during acts of violence toward the women. The defense attorneys claimed the acts were justifiably committed in self defense, and this coauthor was enlisted to explain to juries why, despite previous abuse, *this time* each woman suddenly felt things had escalated and her life was in danger. The prosecutors reliably claimed that violence had occurred before without the women resorting to killing, so there was no need this time either; hence it was premeditated murder. The physical facts of the cases, i.e., the corpses, the weapons, the women's admissions and so forth were never in dispute. But what the men's deaths *meant* legally were up for definition, to be argued over by lawyers and finally decided by jurors. The consequences were stark: acquitted (which meant the women walked out of the courthouses free and honorable citizens) or guilty (in Texas, which at that time executed more persons per year than any other state, it meant the electric chair). Jury deliberations were therefore conscious efforts to construct a social reality out of the physical evidence. All but one woman was acquitted; the exception appealed her conviction to a higher court where she won on appeal and was relabeled from guilty to acquitted.

The moral is that social reality is made up of ideas, not things. Shifting definitions of reality usually work better in dealing with the social, rather than the physical, world.

The Issue of Platonicity

In his book *The Black Swan* (2007: xxv), economist/uncertainty mathematician Naseem Nicholas Taleb coins the term "Platonicity" in his critique of social scientists (particularly market economists but also psychologists). Platonicity, as he defines it, is "our tendency to mistake the map for the territory." (Or the finger for the moon.) His use of the term is a reference to the metaphor used by Plato at the beginning of Book Seven of *The Republic* in which the Greek philosopher is trying to convey to his listener how little we actually understand of the world around us, and how we often misperceive it.

Imagine, says Plato, a tribe of cave-dwellers, fastened all their lives by chains in such a way that they can only face toward the rear wall of the dim cave. Behind them is a fire at the cave's mouth, with a parade of people carrying objects and driving vehicles past the fire. All the cave-dwellers know of life at the edge of the cave and of their own confined world is seen as shadows of figures projected onto that wall. They see imperfect reflections of the reality beyond, not the reality itself. Zen Buddhism essentially employs the same metaphor as Plato, and it is one that social psychologists can readily acknowledge.

Taleb uses the logic of probability theory and the presumed random distribution of most phenomena (from, say, women's shoe sizes to intelligence test scores in a population) in the shape of the "bell curve" well-known to most social scientists. The average score or value is found precisely under the hump of the curve and the majority of other scores can be found within a certain determinable distance (expressed in standard deviations) of slope downward on either side toward the ends of the curve.

Taleb's argument is that most common forecasters rely on the familiar, known, and expected averages found under the center area of the bell curve for their predictions, thereby ignoring or missing the "outliers" or really deviant, uncommon developments at the ends of the curve. In the process Taleb is highly critical of the general linear modeling techniques preferred by social scientists and economists (such as the various forms of correlation and multiple linear regression); but these concepts, and the logic behind them, are also mainstays of social psychological analyses. However, notes Taleb (2007: xxiv):

> Almost everything in social life is produced by rare but consequential shocks and jumps; all the while almost everything studied about social life focuses on "the normal," particularly with "bell curve" methods of inference that tell you close to nothing. Why? Because the bell curve ignores large deviations, cannot handle them, yet makes us confident that we have tamed uncertainty.

We are not interested here in pursuing the logic of Taleb's criticism of statistical use, but his point is well-taken, for Zen Buddhism itself is an outlier perspective in a world (regardless of the particular culture) that operates on the more taken-for-granted "normal" assumptions of social reality. This last world is the one in which Plato's unfortunate cave-dwellers live, beguiled by the shadowy distortions on the wall. Plato, of course, suggests we all live in our separate, often group-shared cultural caves and are equally victims of shadowy distortions.

A black swan is an anomaly, once thought impossible (hence the title of Taleb's book). Taleb claims that ignoring outliers leads to a form of bell curve thinking that he caustically dubs *Mediocristan* (after a hypothetical realm where everyone reasons comfortably within the conventional "box"). In Mediocristan there is the sense of safety from surprise or novel interpretations and conclusions.

Many social psychological constructs have become part of the discipline's norm, so much so that it becomes difficult for social psychologists to think of any individual as existing without such things as self-concepts or attitudes. Statistical operationalizations only reaffirm and perpetuate the "wisdom" of continuing to conceptualize social psychological subject matter in such terms. To a Zennist there is grave danger of a comfortable slide into objectivizing or reifying and further obscuring the relative nature of everyday social reality.

The Mental Trap of Language

There is another source of abstractions problematic to social reality and indeed to any systematic study of human beings: language.

All higher animals communicate, though not necessarily in the same way. Insects, reptiles and mammals use a variety of mechanisms to converse, whether through noises (and the tones of noises) issued from the throat, body posture, changes in skin coloring, or even odor and urine. All of these devices can be used to convey emotions and messages of affection, alarm, territoriality, and aggression. Every dog owner knows what we mean. So do those who have worked with chimpanzees, a close biological cousin of *homo sapiens*. The psychological literature on primates' use of sign language in different forms is too vast and reliable to need even summarizing here; suffice it to say that this literature alone bears out our point.

But indisputably human beings display the most sophisticated use of language of all creatures. For humans the spoken language is a rich set of phonetic symbols articulated most importantly via the larynx and tongue, but also through the use of the hard and soft palates, teeth, lips, and facial muscles. Moreover, speech can be further symbolically transcribed by physical marks to represent actual sounds (and what they mean to listeners), with these physical marks in turn having the power to be saved indefinitely and communicated to other persons, thus initiating them into the same symbol system (for example, see Gordon, 1982).

Because language as a symbol system conveys meanings about the world around us, it is also the most important source of socialization and hence is a most salient factor in how we describe, interpret, and respond to social reality. Because language (not to mention physical reality) comes in so many varieties, it is the basis of a cultural anthropological axiom termed the Sapir-Whorf hypothesis (after Edward Sapir and Benjamin Whorf). This maxim states that the people who employ different languages also do not share identical social realities, a point which is eloquently articulated by Sapir (1949: 64):

> Human beings do not live in the objective world alone, nor alone in the world of social activity as ordinarily understood, but are very much at the mercy of the particular language which has become the medium of expression for their society. It is quite an illusion to imagine that one adjusts to reality essentially without the use of language and that language is merely an incidental means of solving specific problems of communication or reflection. The fact of the matter is that the "real world" is to a large extent consciously built up on the language habits of the group. No two languages are ever sufficiently similar to be considered as representing the same social reality. The world in which different societies live are distinct worlds, not merely the same world with different labels attached.

Moreover, while language as a set of symbols sometimes substitutes for direct experience, "it does not as a matter of actual behavior stand apart from or run parallel to direct experience but completely interpenetrates with it... it may be suspected that there is little in the functional side of our conscious behavior in which language does not play its part" (Sapir, 1949: 8, 15).

To this point, Zen and social psychology, as well as the disciplines of cultural anthropology and linguistics, are of one accord. Yes, language and social reality are two sides, if not the same side, of the coin. Language *is* indispensable for human life. But Zen, and to perhaps a lesser extent social psychology, explicitly regard it also as a mental trap that limits our understanding of the physical and social worlds. That is to say, language literally entraps us through conditioning in cultural blinders, just as the carbon deposits in a car engine's firing cylinders impedes our potential to reach what should be our goal: a true Awakening to all that is as it is. This Awakening or realization of the world, both physical and social, uncorrupted by cultural accretions of the meanings language imposes on our very modes of consciousness, is called in Buddhism *prajna* (from the Sanskrit words *jna*, or non-reflective, holistic, intuitive knowledge, and *pra*, or awakened) as opposed to *vijnana*, meaning ordinary, linear, discursive subject-object knowledge.

Contrary to the position of many social psychologists and anthropologists who matter-of-factly accept the role of words and definitions in human life and concentrate on how language is learned and used, Zen deals harshly with the negative role language plays in foisting Platonicity on us. Roshi Philip Kapleau (*Roshi* is Zen Japanese for "old one" who went before, or Master teacher—more honorific than *sensei*) was a former

U.S. military officer stationed in post-World War II Japan who went on to study, experience, and Awaken to Zen. This Awakening led him to become one of twentieth century North America's greatest expositors of Zen Buddhism. Like most Zennist spokespersons, Kapleau (1997: 35, 29) refers derisively to "the snare of language" and credits it with fostering in most persons the "habitual disease of uncontrolled thought." A foremost Japanese Zen expert and scholar, fluent in numerous sacred and modern languages and at home in Western philosophy, Daisetz Teitaro (D.T.) Suzuki (1964: 61, 58), similarly maintains that "we are too much slaves to words and logic" and condemns the "one-sidedness of our every day phraseology."

Zen, as will be described, is almost totally experiential in its methodology and regards language at best a useful, if limited, tool and at worst a pernicious impediment. Paradoxically, however, Zen castigates language but nevertheless relies on it. We quote from Suzuki's *The Field of Zen* (1970b: 50, 82) at length:

> When we point to the moon with a finger, others are apt to take the finger for the moon. Yet without the finger the moon is not recognized, and when the moon is recognized the finger can be thrown away. In the same way we cling to language and think that it is the thing which it represents. This habit of taking the symbol for reality does a great deal of harm in our daily life. Language is a most useful instrument, perhaps the most important means of communication that we humans have ever invented, but we frequently fail to understand that because of this usefulness language enslaves us.... When we try to express ourselves in language, we are apt to take that language as reality itself. But language is nothing but symbols, and behind that language there is something higher which makes use of language. Buddhist literature is filled with this caution not to take languages, words, concepts, names as reality itself. Reality itself is that which transcends dualistic understandings of subject and object, self and not-self.

Even Alan Watts, sympathetic to the Zen perspective but a Westerner nonetheless, refers to language as a hindrance as much as a facilitating medium:

> The spell of words is by no means an enchantment to which only the intellectual is disposed. The most simple-minded people are as easily its prey, and it would seem that, at all levels of society, the cultures in which Christianity has arisen have been particularly confused by the powerful constraint of language. It has run away with them like a new gadget with a child, so that excessive verbal communication is really the characteristic disease of the West. (1958b: 35)

It will be apparent from just the previous few citations that language, any language, comes in for a hard time in Zen teachings. Unlike linguists and anthropologists who professionally come to grips with the dynamic impact of language, Zen presents itself as angry, sometimes vehemently so, and often with belligerent defiance. Zen masters and teachers uncompromisingly refer to language in terms such as confusion; illusion; tyranny; slavery; harmful; corruption; an accretion, a blinder, and an impediment; a snare, trap, and disease; and, of course, the source of Platonicity. For those who take a more conventional view of language as a valuable and fascinating medium, and for those who enjoy its diversity but also appreciate the insight of the Sapir-Whorf dictum, the classical Zen perspective may seem unduly harsh. Make no mistake: it *is* harsh, even unforgiving.

Thus far, the reader now has been exposed to a preview of what Zen Buddhism seeks: to unravel the effects of every social reality as handed to persons by their culture and liberate individuals in order to transcend ordinary thought or consciousness. This is not a direct goal of mainstream social psychology so far as we understand it. Zen's critique of this point may seem mystical and appear anti-rational, but it is led by a systematic down-to-earth methodology. Zen accomplishes its unraveling by attacking first and foremost language, so fundamental is the latter to Platonistic ways of reasoning. The previous quote from Suzuki is meant literally. Zen's methodology does not rely on the discursive thinking we were all consciously taught to master in school and unconsciously in our daily absorption of socialization. The path of Zen is intuitive and experiential.

An Overview of Buddhism

Below we turn to an overview of the histories and doctrines of original (or "Primitive") Buddhism and then the Zen innovation. Some disclaim Zen as a revisionist offshoot; Zennists, however, say it represents the heart of the Buddha's message from 2,500 years ago.

Origins

Siddhartha Gautama (Gautama was his family name) was born in 563 B.C.E. during an era of other great religious leaders: Zarathustra, Lao Tzu, Confucius, Mahavira, to name a few. His family belonged to the Kshatriya (warrior/aristocracy) caste of the Shakya clan in the city of Kapilavastu, capital of the kingdom ruled by his father, Raja Suddhodana. His mother was a reportedly extraordinarily beautiful woman named Maya. All dates and numbers in the legendary account of the Buddha's life are approximate, disputed by the different geographic and theological divisions within the faith. Like Jesus of Nazareth, the Buddha wrote down nothing of his life or teachings. In fact, as Humphreys

(1951: 30) observes, no biography of Siddhartha Gautama was set down for several hundred years after his death. Indeed, "As the centuries rolled by, each version of the Life acquired an increasing garland of fabulous adventures, miracles and heavenly assistance." Much of such accounts have to be located within the dense framework of Hindu metaphysics, symbolism idiosyncratic to that tradition, and the panoply of popular Indian polytheism.

According to the generally agreed historiography, however, before Siddhartha's birth Brahmins (members of the elite holy caste) were summoned to Suddhodana's palace to prophesy on the child's future: they predicted he would become either an important political leader (perhaps emperor) or a supreme religious figure. Preferring the former, his father successfully managed to sequester the child, then the boy, then the young man within the royal grounds until Siddhartha (by then married and a father) in his late twenties prevailed upon his servant/charioteer Channa to take him outside into the city. There he saw four key reminders of the realities of life: an old man (age), a sick man (illness), a corpse (death), and a holy renunciate (piety), the sights of which introduced him both to suffering and to a possible path of salvation. At twenty-nine Siddhartha left home; embarked on several years of severe physical mortification, joining with other renunciates in living the life of mendicants; came eventually after almost dying to believe that a Middle Way, eschewing extremes of lifestyle, was a more feasible path; and finally planted himself beneath a Bo (or *bodhi*) tree for (some variously say) days, weeks, or months to seek Enlightenment. During that time he was rejected by fellow seekers for having abandoned the rigorous ascetic spiritual means of self-mortification and tempted by Mara The (archetypal) Evil One with, first, beautiful seductresses, then with visions of promised power and wealth, if he abandoned his spiritual quest. Siddhartha persevered nonetheless. Then under the Bodhi tree (*bodhi* in Sanskrit means wisdom), at the age of thirty-five, Siddhartha Gautama became Awakened as the Buddha The Enlightened One (*buddhi* in Sanskrit means intuition) and soon after began his ministry.

Without trying to put too fine a point on it, the legend of Buddhism's origins parallel in certain ways the stages of myth-making in Western Christology. For example:

- There were the prophesies of the Brahmins (the wise men).
- There was the Annunciation portending Siddhartha's birth (in a dream to Maya his mother).

- There were the earthly temptations by Mara, equivalent to the Christian Satan, to induce Siddhartha to abandon his quest for Enlightenment.
- There were the childhood miracle stories of Siddhartha, collected early in the faith tradition in a work of mixed verse and prose entitled *The Jataka Tales* (see Stryk 1969: 1-46 for examples, such as the newborn infant immediately taking seven steps to North, East, South and West, proclaiming his incomparable wisdom and eventual enlightenment). Further, the man Gautama acknowledged as the Buddha was believed the end product of many previous Enlightened Beings reincarnated through 550 states of animal and human existence (hence he was called "Tathagata"—successor to those who came before).
- There were countless exaltations and acts of obeisance paid by numerous Hindu gods acknowledging the Buddha's superiority upon Enlightenment along with the inevitable apotheosis (deification) by his followers soon after the Buddha died. (Later Buddhism was to draw a sharp distinction between Buddha the man and the eternal Buddha principle or Buddha nature.)
- There was the rich scriptural tradition that emerged within a few centuries based on the older techniques of detailed memorization of the Buddha's teachings, sayings, and sermons.

And there was the sociologically-inevitable sectarian divisiveness, which produced theological "lineages" or schools ("inevitable" due to geographical expansion and sheer membership increase). This transformative growth is briefly discussed below. (For excellent succinct treatments of "Primitive" or early Buddhism, see Humphreys, 1951: 25-43; Watts, 1957: 29-56; Linssen, 1958: 32-9; Suzuki, 1959: 31-7; Snelling, 1991: 11-33; and for longer histories, Conze, 1967; Mizuno, 1980; and Gethin, 1998).

Essential Doctrines

The Buddha's initial statement of the principles of his Enlightenment can be summarized in the Four Noble Truths:

Life is filled with pain and anguish, or suffering:
The source of suffering is desire;
It is possible to extricate oneself from the endless round of desires;
The method to do this is found in the Noble Eight-fold Path.

At first glance this concise syllogism may seem like a coping strategy more appropriate for a preindustrial, severely-hierarchical society filled with brutal warfare, extreme poverty, and mass deprivation in health and longevity. But the Buddha's message was intended to be universal, irrespective of time and place. We consider the first three truths with slightly expanded comments.

Noble Truth Number 1. Suffering can indeed be the three forms that young Gautama witnessed with his charioteer outside the royal grounds: disease, old age and infirmity, death. But suffering includes many other things, from anxiety and angst to the everyday setbacks, disappointments, heartaches, injuries, fears and depressions, dashed aspirations, and so forth familiar to modern Westerners and people everywhere.

Noble Truth Number 2. Desire encompasses not only greed or lust for physical comfort, sexual and emotional happiness, and material possessions but also psychological needs such as ambition, quests for security and acceptance from others, raises in salaries, better jobs and promotions, or power and prestige. Steve Hagen (1997: 30-1), a North American Zen priest, writes of the frustration we feel when we want stability and predictability in our lives but find ourselves continually stymied, in these words:

> [W]e magnify our problem by longing (and trying) to stop that change, to fix things in their places.... Even if we manage to make our situation comfortable for the moment, it can only be temporary. All circumstances surrounding this momentary situation will inevitably change.... This attempt to nail down the world is a profound, if subtle, manifestation of the second form of [suffering]. It is so painful and disturbing because it's nothing more than our desperate attempt to defy Reality. We may long for an other-worldly abode, a place where such pain and vexation will never strike. We may even try to create such a place, internally or externally. But no such place exists, or ever has, or ever can (Inserted brackets ours).

Attachment is a word often used as a synonym for desire. The attachment to wanting to achieve satisfaction, which we enjoy or anticipate or even imagine (including relative deprivation where we invidiously compare what we have achieved to what others have achieved) is what the Buddha meant. Thus desire is a disease universally endemic to human beings, paupers as well as kings. (In the Buddha's culture part of this desire was also to escape the travails of reincarnation, not a significant issue for most Westerners.)

Noble Truth 3. The cessation of desire is the hopeful third truth: one can escape the endless lattice of wanting, never having, having but not having enough, fear of losing what one has, and so forth. There is a plan one can follow diligently to extinguish those desires that consume so much psychic time and efforts. Put another way, the Buddha pointed to an alternative path, a perspective of living, that can destroy these insidiously endless, even self-destructive preoccupations, or at least pragmatically preserve some serenity while holding the demons of desire at bay. This is done by exposing suffering's true cause (desires and the impermanence of satisfaction) and then expunging them with a new perspective.

Noble Truth 4. Thus the Buddha's final truth is literally a prescription for removing the desires and the ignorance, thereby achieving an Awakened state of mind to perceive Reality beyond the ephemeral thinking around us. Breaking down the strategy of the Noble Eight-fold Path into its traditionally separate tactics, they are (in step-wise order):

(1)   Right Belief (View)—to accept the fact that life is constant flux, a key element in why people experience suffering.
(2)   Right Thought (Intention)—to commit or resolve to escape desire and suffering.
(3)   Right Speech—to be deferent, polite, discreet, and honest, thus avoiding double-dealing and back-biting gossip that distracts from Right Thoughts.
(4)   Right Action—to seek to engage in behavior (originally strictly ascetic) that reflects (1), (2), and (3).
(5)   Right Means of Livelihood—to follow an occupation that does not put one in opposition to (1), (2), (3), and (4).
(6)   Right Exertion (Effort)—to push oneself *continuously* to identify and militate ignorance about suffering and thereby counter desire.
(7)   Right Remembrance (Mindfulness)—to keep these precepts uppermost in one's consciousness at every moment.
(8)   Right Meditation—to avoid distraction in focusing and concentrating on this path. (The word "Right" used before each part of the method indicates its ultimate value leading toward Enlightenment. "Right" is not culturally relative but rather means efficacious.)

From the Four Noble Truths and the Noble Eight-fold Path flow all other important ideas and elaborations of Buddhist thought. Three of the more significant ones follow:

The first doctrine is *anitya* or impermanence and change. (Note: Here we are using only Sanskrit, not Pali, spellings.) This is an axiomatic fact of Life and Reality, both at the levels of personal material and nonmaterial wants and also for every social order and political structure. Human typifications and conceptualizations can only inadequately point to an understanding of the scope, complexity, and evolving immanence of impermanence. As Watts (1957: 46-7) observes,

The *anitya* doctrine is ... not quite the simple assertion that the world is impermanent, but rather that the more one grasps at the world, the more it changes. Reality in itself is neither permanent nor impermanent; it cannot be categorized. But when one tries to hold on to it, like one's own shadow, the faster one pursues it, the faster it flees.

Impermanence is the source of every major suffering and minor dissatisfactions. Hagen (1997: 18) explains:

[W]e try to make Reality into something other than what it is. We try to rearrange and manipulate the world so that dogs will never bite, accidents will never happen, and the people we care about will never die. Even on the surface, the futility of such efforts should be obvious.

The second doctrine following from *anitya* is *anatman*, or no-self. It maintains that the so-called personal self (so fundamental a concept in Western social psychology) is also impermanent. Worse, said the Buddha, self is a beguiling illusion, a chimera. Self-identity is a transitory convention employed on a taken-for-granted basis by consciousness. In reality fleeting consciousness imagines a continuity or stability where there is only ongoing electronic renewal of thoughts in our brains (like a motion picture projector creating for the viewer a sensation of continuous flowing movement by passing still frames successively over a light).

Coomaraswamy (1943: 59) explains by a famous analogy:

... the chariot, with all its appurtenances, corresponds to what we call our self: there was no chariot before its parts were put together, will be none when they fall to pieces; there is no "chariot" apart from its parts; "chariot" is nothing but a name, given for convenience to a certain percept, but must not be taken to be an entity; and in the same way with ourselves who are, just like the chariot, "confections."

The third doctrine, also an extension of *anitya*, is *sunyata*, realized or surrendered to when one enter into Nirvana, a state of awareness of All being, or Reality as it is undifferentiated. *Sunyata* is often translated in English as The Void, and unfortunately early translators (some of them with a missionary bent to disparage, not fairly interpret, Buddhism) implied that it, like Nirvana, represents an extinction or obliteration of mind/individual self/reality. Buddhism is not nihilism. Far from it, The Void means that all culturally-derived mental limitations of imperfect categorizations and form are dissolved and Reality is clearly seen in its complexity and *interdependence*, or *tathata* (Sanskrit for "thusness" or "suchness," i.e., *as it is*, not as it is merely conceived). Perceived holistically, Reality is like an immense ocean, and events, what appear to be discrete things, whether others or ourselves, are really transitory whitecaps and ripples on the surface. Consciousness, a useful enough day-to-day tool for coping in the conventional world, is the culprit. "Consciousness is nothing more than the splitting of reality into this and that [including ourselves as apart from others]" (Hagen, 1997: 140—Inserted brackets ours).

Humphreys (1951: 17) describes *sunyata* as:

All things are One and have no Life apart from it; the One is all things and is incomplete without the least of them. Yet the parts are parts within the whole, not merged in it; they are interfused with Reality while retaining the full identity of the part, and the One is no less for that fact that it is a million-million parts.

Appreciation of *sunyata*, claims Watts (1957: 63), means that one sees that "all things are without 'self-nature' ... or independent reality since they exist only in relation to other things. Nothing in the universe can stand by itself—nothing, no fact, no being, no event—and for this reason it is absurd to single out anything as the ideal to be grasped."

Belgian scholar Linssen (1958: 15) prefers the term The Plenitude, rather than The Void, as best expressing the rich multiplicity (rather than suggesting some obliteration) of *sunyata*. He employs the metaphor of a prism to convey the same sentiments as Humphreys in the previous description of *sunyata*:

White light, streaming through a prism is split up into a spectrum of seven different colours. If they were to be transposed to a swiftly turning disc, in the correct proportions, we would get an impression of whiteness ... we could say that this white light is neither blue, nor red, green, nor yellow. It is *void* of the distinctions inherent in the particular colours but is in itself the pure principle of brilliance.

Thus, if anything, *sunyata* expresses (and this expression has to be realized by *bodhi*, or intuitive wisdom, since all other analyses using words are poor substitutes) reality. *Sunyata* is not a spiritual "mystery;" rather, it is an experiential new perception and awareness of Reality, shorn of cultural discriminations. It is grounded in *prajna*, the original "pure" realization of Reality, which we possessed at birth before cultural categorizations corrupted our perception of it.

Sectarian Developments

Within a generation following the Buddha's passing, a council of *arhats* (enlightened followers) was called for the sociologically understandable purpose of defining standards of orthodoxy in what had been a purely oral tradition. There were to be a series of councils—some contentious—as the faith spread, and the initial challenge of *objectification*, i.e., translating the original essential truths and opinions into formal scriptures and commentaries, quickly turned the search for orthodoxy into heterodoxy. On issues of the means for achieving Buddhahood, the role for lay believers, how strict an observation of rules in the *sangha* (monastic order) was required, and so forth, disagreements arose. The word "heresy" began to be used by some against others. Conze (1959:

125-6; 1967: 119-58), by diagram and text, has charted the growing divisions, called ultimately schools or sects. There were at least eighteen Buddhist schools within the first five centuries (see also Snelling, 1991: 81). Yet as the faith spread north (to China, Vietnam and Korea, Tibet, Japan, Mongolia, and what is now Russia) and south (to Sri Lanka, Burma, Thailand, Laos, Kampuchea, and Indonesia) two distinct metalineages had emerged.

One lineage was termed *Hinayana* (called "The Small Wheel"). Hinayanists became known as conservative literalists and wrote their scriptures and liturgies in Pali, a now-dead dialect of Magadhi (the language which the Buddha most likely spoke—Stryk, 1969: xiv). They emerged out of the Theravada school and emphasized personal piety and salvation by strict discipline through individual ascetic efforts.

The other lineage was *Mahayana* (called "The Great Wheel"). Mahayanist scriptures and sacred liturgies built on the Pali texts but were written in Sanskrit, another now-dead literary sacred language and itself a removed dialect of Pali. Mahayanists were more speculative, metaphysical, eclectic, and in their expanding literature came to stress faith in the efficacy of apotheosized bodhisattvas (interventionist merciful divine beings who delayed their own entrance into Nirvana for the sake of saving all sentient beings), among many other things. (Mahayanists also can take credit for rather imperiously bestowing the name "Small Wheel" on their sectarian brethren.)

Buddhism was thus a missionary faith, and like Christianity, developed theological variations that came to be fused with the native beliefs preexisting in the regions of the world to which it spread. Humphreys (1951: 12-13) refers to Buddhism's malleability as the consequence of an "excess of tolerance": "As it gently flowed into country after country, whether of a higher or lower culture than its own, it tended to adopt, or failed to contest the rival claims of, the indigenous beliefs, however crude." These beliefs might be ancestor and/or spirit worship or sorcery and magical practices, as often happened in both the northern and southern "transmissions" (Snelling, 1991). This syncretism was particularly true of the Mahayanists who began to move into China early in the Christian era. It is out of this particular geographic movement that Zen originated.

The Zen Innovation

Alan W. Watts (1957:3) has described Zen:

Zen Buddhism is a way and a view of life which does not belong to any of the formal categories of modern thought. It is not a religion or philosophy; it is not psychology or a type of science. It is an example of what is known in India and China as a way of liberation....

Zen's primal presupposition, which it shares with Primitive Buddhism, is that the world most of us "know" is merely a social reality seen through a superficial consciousness predicated on the dualistic notion of subject and object. Says Suzuki (1970a: 38):

> This world we naturally see is intellectually reconstructed; it is not the real one. We have re-formed it through our senses and our intellect working at the back of those senses. We reconstruct this world and proceed to believe our fabrication is the real thing.

Zen has retained from the Buddha's original message the belief in universal, endemic suffering resulting from ignorance (*avidya*) of the impermanence (*anitya*) of the universe and life, including the funda-mental doctrine of the illusion of a personal self (*anatman*) that blinds human beings to their indivisible inclusion in a Reality (*sunyata*) both sensate and material. This reality is beyond discursive description and can only be intuited but not understood (though it can be appreciated) intellectually. Zen also has retained Indian Buddhist beliefs such as the law of the effect of deeds, or *karma* (in Sanskrit, *karman*) and, in some cases, reincarnation/transmigration (a subject dealt with more closely in Chapter 2).

But to understand what has become unique in the Zen perspective of Buddhism, and what came to separate it from its convoluted Indian metaphysical roots with innumerable deities, levels of heaven, alternative worlds, and so forth, one first needs to consider the latter's encounter with premodern Chinese culture and Taoism.

The Legacy of Taoism

Sinologist Ray Grigg (1994: xiii-xiv) bluntly asserts: "Zen is Tao-ism disguised as Buddhism" and (almost regretfully) that "Buddhism is the historical wedge that has separated Zen from its Taoist source." An extreme statement perhaps, but Buddhism was unmistakably altered by Taoism and recast in important ways.

Taoism is a practical, experiential, and yet mystical Chinese approach to living in and with the world of nature, including the cosmos, with its roots stretching back into prehistoric shamanism. There is evidence of it in religion as early as the Shang Dynasty of the Second Millennium B.C.E. (Palmer, 1991: 20). *Tao* (pronounced *Dao*) means in its narrower sense a road, path, or way. More broadly, *tao* may be a method, system, or doctrine. Often it means all of these things simultaneously. (In Japanese it is pronounced *doh*, with a long o, and is the do in the martial arts judo, kendo, and aikido.)

The *Tao* manifests itself in every living and non-living thing, especially in their interpenetrations. In Taoism there is no personified Divine Creator. "Tao is the ultimate source of all, the origin before origins, and the uncreated which creates everything ... the Unity and interrelatedness of life.... The Tao creates simply because it is the actual essence of all things" (Palmer, 1991: 3-4). Wright (1959: 29) characterizes the Tao as "the principle of vitality which infuses all phenomena."

Yet the Tao cannot be intellectually grasped. It discourages definition. The very first lines of the seminal *Tao Te Ching* (*ching* in Chinese means "classic"), dating back to the Han Dynasty (206 B.C.E. - 220 C.E.), states:

> The Tao that can be stated is not the Eternal Tao.
> The name that can be named is not the Eternal Tao.
> The Unnameable is originator of Heaven and Earth.
> The nameable is mother of the ten thousand things. (Wei, 1982: 129)

Wei (1982: 10-11) succinctly "summarizes" the Tao (insofar as words can) in commenting on the *Tao Te Ching*:

> It conceives Tao as all-embracing, as both immanent and transcendent, and as eternal and infinite, preceding the Creator of Heaven and Earth and continuing to sustain Heaven and Earth. It characterizes Tao as a profound mystery, immutable, subtle, elusive and ineffable, yet vital, Creative, pervasive, and powerful.... Furthermore, it leads man to realize that, willy-nilly, he has to depend and obey Tao for his life and happiness.... Tao cannot be expressed in words, but this does not mean that Tao cannot be encountered and experienced by the human spirit.

The *Tao Te Ching* was allegedly written by a contemporary of Confucius named Lao Tzu (alternately meaning Old Man, Old Master, or even Old Son) who allegedly lived sometime during the fifth, sixth, or seventh centuries B.C.E. (Wei, 1982: 1-5). Or perhaps he never existed except as a personified compilation of a Taoist corpus of (eventually) over 4,000 scriptures and treatises (Grigg, 1994: 13). But Lao Tzu is recognized as the titular spokesperson for classical Taoism; indeed, the *Tao Te Ching* attributed to him is sometimes also referred to as the *Lao Tzu*.

Taoists seek "Realization" just as Buddhists synonymously seek "Enlightenment" and Zennists "Awakening." A "realized" Taoist recognizes three primary guiding principles:

(1)   The dynamics of *yang* (active stimulating male force) and *yin* (passive receptive female force) which can be thought of as poles not existing in any complementary harmonious way but rather in a perpetual dialectic. Their struggle in turn generates all phenomena by creating *ch'i* (*ki* in Japanese), itself the purposeless, formless, but pervasive energy flowing within human beings as well as throughout the earth and universe (Page, 1988: 23). If *yin* and *yang* together generate all things, *ch'i* awakens them. Only in infants and very young (unsocialized) children do *yin* and *yang* exist harmoniously; it is through "temporal conditioning" that "the spiritual embryo is damaged" (Cleary, 1988: 55).

(2)   *Wu-wei*, the important quality of the "realized" mind, which is non-interference with the trends of nature, or recognizing that harmony and balance among human beings and nature is the microcosmic reflection of harmony and balance within the entire universe. The analog to water is often used by both Taoists and Zennists. Water can be supple and yielding as it flows downstream over and around rocks but *at the same time* it can form powerful waves and strong currents. It can fill and adapt to any form or container without losing its essence but from within exert tremendous pressure. *Wu-wei* is often defined as non-action, which is not strictly true. It is acting wisely in light of correctly determined circumstances and not wasting energy (physical, emotional, or psychic) in the manner of martial arts judo or aikido. British physical scientist Robert Powell (1961: 18) defines *wu-wei* as "alert possibility" leaving one to act based on "a maximum of understanding with a minimum of doing." It is to be as one unobstructed with the Tao of the moment.

(3)   The mental state of *wu-nien* (literally "no-mind" or "no thought"), which is to be as one with one's *ch'i* mobilized in harmony with the Tao: detached or free from mental preoccupations and thoughts of self, others, and intentions. By "being as one" is meant to eliminate the distance between subject and object and fully intuit, not intellectualize, the interrelatedness of all actions and actors in Absolute Reality (Tao). It is to transcend the duality of opposites (e.g., good and bad, dangerous and safe, tall and short) to reach Unity and break out of conventional social reality.

The above cursory sketch of ideas corresponds to *philosophical* Taoism, which occupies much of Taoist scriptures and treatises, but there is also an *alchemical* branch which, like the first branch, has both exoteric and esoteric paths and schools within paths (See Wong, 1992). Alchemical Taoism involves divination, astrology, acupuncture, geomancy, and arcane elixirs and exercises in the pursuit of greater longevity, if not immortality. The latter's ultimate goal is not merely crass magic, as Palmer (1991: 1) emphasizes: "immortality consists of transforming the whole body into an eternal vehicle for the soul."

Many of Taoism's concepts are remarkably similar to Buddhism's, such as the "emptiness" of Reality (like *sunyata*) without human-derived discrimination, or *wu-nien*'s intuitive comprehension of Tao similar to *prajna*. Fundamentally Taoism is and has been a way of liberation, like Buddhism, but less concerned with lofty Indian-style metaphysics and focused more on pragmatic temporal issues.

On the two cultural styles, historian Arthur F. Wright (1959: 330) has remarked:

> When we turn to literary modes, we find the Chinese preference is for terseness, for metaphor from familiar nature, for the concrete image, whereas Indian literature tends to be discursive, hyperbolic, in its metaphors, and full of abstractions. The imaginative range expressed in Chinese literature—even in the Taoist classics—is far more limited, more earthbound, than in the colorful writings of the Indian tradition.

Thus, when Buddhism first encountered China during the first several centuries of the Common Era, there was a "slow take" by the Chinese, a people syncretic but nevertheless open to mastery of new spiritual forces on their own terms. By the sixth century, when Ch'an Buddhism began to emerge in schools and writings, it was the result, not of a cultural collision, but of a symbiotic interface between parallel systems of liberation, as Cleary (1983) ably argues of the first five centuries' spread of Hua-Yen Buddhism in China. Snelling (1991: 13) is effusive about Ch'an in dynastic China: "Ch'an represents the finest achievement of Chinese Buddhism: an original and highly creative re-expression of the essence of the Buddha's teaching in terms that are distinctly Chinese."

Zen Origins

Zen is the Japanese pronunciation of Ch'an, which in turn is the Chinese pronunciation of *dhyana*, Sanskrit for meditation. According to Zen historiography, Zen Buddhism officially began in 520 with the arrival of the Indian monk Bodhidharma. Bodhidharma was reputedly the twenty-eighth Patriarch descended (by apostolic succession) from Gautama Shakyamuni. Linssen (1958: 40-1) presents a list of all previous twenty-seven patriarchs, though some scholars have questioned that Bodhidharma ever lived. For example, Hanh (1995: 100) raises the possibility that Hui-neng, Ch'an's Sixth Patriarch and acknowledged founder of modern Zen, commissioned his disciple, Shen-hui, in the seventh century to create a history of Zen Buddhism's lineage back to India "to assure the grandeur and prestige" of Hui-neng's school.

Bodhidharma, according to the tradition, was a blunt and irascible character who, upon arrival in China, had an immediate confrontational audience with a self-righteous Buddhist emperor. The latter thought he ought to have received enormous karmic merit for his patronage of numerous Buddhist temples and other works; Bodhidharma summarily dismissed such material support as worth nothing. Subsequently the patriarch withdrew in disgust to a Shaolin temple to mediate for nine years. Though Buddhism had been in China for several hundred years (and some Indian scriptures had already been translated into Chinese—See Snelling, 1991: 121-7; Cleary, 1983: 3-18), it is in the seventh century during the T'ang Dynasty (618-907) that the Buddhist lineage known as Ch'an emerged.

It started with a rough, home-spun illiterate Hui-neng from Southern China and more polished Shen-hsiu from the North becoming rivals for the patriarchy to follow their teacher, Fifth Patriarch Hung-jen at Mount Tung Shan monastery. In a poetry contest aimed at determining who displayed the higher inner state of enlightenment (and thus decide Hung-jen's successor), Shen-hsiu wrote:

The body is the bodhi tree.
The mind is a clear mirror stand.
Strive to polish it always.
Letting no speck of dust to cling.

And many expected him to win.
Hui-neng, however, answered with the following superior refutation:

There is no bodhi tree.
There is no clear mirror stand.
From the beginning not one thing is.
Where then can a speck of dust cling?
(Translation from Habito, 2004: 18)

Amid controversy, Hung-jen passed the patriarchy to Hui-neng. Hui-neng emphasized the doctrine of "emptiness" in *sunyata* achieved by *wu-nien* through sudden illumination as well as an anti-scholastic bent. Indeed, the traditional Zen "homage" to Bodhidharma, which is a Zen credo disdaining scholasticism's heavy weight put on *sutras* (sacred writings recounting the Buddha's discourses and related commentaries) in favor of the direct experiential approach, reflects this emphasis:

A special transmission outside the sutras;
No reliance on words and letters;
Direct pointing to the very soul;
Seeing into one's own essence.

Shen-hsiu was more scholarly and favored gradual progress toward Awakening, and his different approach to Hui-neng's was to presage an eventual major division in Japanese Zen Buddhism. In fact, much of Ch'an's influence during succeeding Chinese dynasties began to wane, but by the twelfth century a number of Japanese Buddhist monks had journeyed to China to study and then returned to Japan to proselytize the different "Houses of Zen," as they were called, to be discussed below.

Essential Zen Doctrines

Zennists hold the belief, though it is undoubtedly considered a conceit by other Buddhists, that their version of the Buddha's revelations represents the most authentic expression, or quintessence, of his Enlightenment, shorn of Hindu deities and demons, layers of heaven, and symbolism as well as *sutras* and their convoluted commentaries. For example, the premier Japanese scholar who introduced Zen to the West, Daisetz Teitaro Suzuki (1961: 60-1) comments that

> if Enlightenment is the *raison d'etre* of Buddhism—that is to say, if Buddhism is an edifice erected on the solid basis of Enlightenment, realized by the Buddha and making up his being—Zen is the central pillar which supports the entire structure, it composes the direct line of continuation drawn out from the context of the Buddha's illumined mind.... What the Buddha wished was this self-realization, a personal experience, an actual insight into truth, and not mere discoursing about methods, or playing with concepts. He detested all philosophical reasonings.... This meant that the *Dharma* [Sanskrit for Law or Truth] was to be intuited and not to be analytically reached by concepts. The reason why the Buddha so frequently refused to answer metaphysical problems was partly due to his conviction that the ultimate truth was to be realized in oneself through one's own efforts; for all that could be gained through discursive understanding was the surface of things and not things themselves.... (Brackets ours)

Gethin (1998: 36) makes the same point in writing that "in certain important respects the nature of the knowledge that the Buddha was trying to convey to his pupils is more akin to a skill, like knowing how to play a musical instrument, than a piece of information."

Thus far we have indicated what Zen has retained doctrinally from original South Asian Buddhism and Chinese philosophical Taoism, such as the seminal insight that all daily reality, including sentient beings of every phylum and genus and even the inanimate rocks, trees, streams, clouds, and stars are interwoven, interrelated, and interdependent in a totality of mutual causation. If anything, the uniqueness of Zen Buddhism is characterized less by its doctrines and more by its methods.

Recall that Zen is the Japanese pronunciation of Ch'an, which is the Chinese pronunciation of Sanskrit *dhyana*, meaning meditation. Meditation, however, is a term used by Zen (and, Zennists maintain, originally by the Buddha) in a particular way. Zen meditation (or *zazen*, seated usually in the lotus position) is intended to achieve a return to *prajna* by dissolving the dualistic difference between subject and object in perception. This then brings one closer to the intuitive immersion in *sunyata*. By certain mental exercises Zen aims to achieve a non-dualistic mindset or state of *samadhi* that transcends the categorization of ordinary social reality. *Dhyana* is not simply profound concentration in the ordinary sense. Out of *samadhi* can ultimately result *satori*, the Zen equivalent of Primitive Buddhism's Enlightenment or nirvana, Taoism's *wu-wei* Realization, or "salvation" (in no way equivalent to its Christian meaning). "Salvation" means freedom from the illusory entrapment of and attachment to self, or the ego-I; integration with *sunyata*, the Word or Plethora; and release from dualistic thought. *Satori* provides a new perception of life and the world, a non-self conscious clarity intuited and profoundly personal. Wood (1962: 115) defines *satori* as "seeing into one's own essential nature; and finding something quite new which is known with great clarity and illumines the whole of life, but cannot be expressed in any way."

Of course, *satori* can be immediate (as in the case of Hui-neng) or may take years to achieve (as with numerous famous Zen masters and their disciples). A momentary experience or "flash" of illuminating insight, called *kensho*, does occur at times. It can be experienced by non-Zennists, sometimes called in social psychology the "Aha! Phenomenon" or the Eureka Effect. Someone mulls over a problem whose solution eludes him or her at the conscious level, then in an unrelated context, prompted unexpectedly by any number of possible stimuli, the answer emerges abruptly and intuitively. A brief example illustrates. In *Psychotherapy East and West* Alan W. Watts (1961: 112) suggests a simply two-dimensional diagram (offered in figure 1 on p. 26 as an opportunity to experience even momentarily the feeling of *kensho* as altered perspective).

Figure 1 is a cube. Or is it really two cubes simultaneously? See it first as the cube with the upper and lower a corners as the front (the cube's interior veering back to the right) and then visualize it as the second cube with the upper and lower b corners as the front (the cube's interior veering back to the left). Alternate quickly the two cubes in your mind. The depth of the cube depends on which you focus, the a's or the b's. That is a brief taste of *kensho*.

Finally, Zen has ten precepts resembling in many ways the familiar Judeo-Christian Ten Commandments except that there is no first commandment about loving or honoring a deity *and* that these precepts are really not commandments but rather guidelines for a lifestyle conducive

Figure 1
Kensho as a Perspective Change: A Simple Example

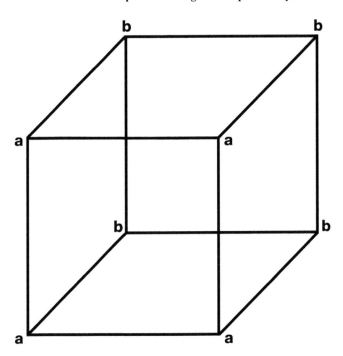

to Awakening (or as Roshi Philip Kapleau [1979: 244] terms them, "items of good character"). They are: (1) do not unnecessarily kill but cherish all life; (2) do not steal; (3) do not partake in improper sexuality (e.g., adultery or promiscuity—though Zen priests may marry) (4) do not tell falsehoods; (5) abstain from all mind-altering drugs except when medically prescribed; (6) do not gossip or speak of others' shortcomings; (7) do not promote oneself at the expense of (i.e., demeaning) others; (8) reach out to all who need spiritual, emotional, and material aid; (9) exercise anger self-management; (10) respect the Buddhist *dharma*, the person of Buddha, and Buddhist clergy (known as Buddhism's Three Treasures or Three Jewels).

Kapleau (1979: 231) observes of these:

> The precepts are like a scaffolding: necessary to erect a large structure, but who would insist on the scaffold remaining when the building is completed? Remember, the precepts are not moral commandments handed down by an omniscient or divine being. Rather, they reveal how a deeply enlightened, fully perfected person, with no sense of self-and-other, behaves.

As with the Ten Commandments and actual behavior of believers, there is ample evidence of Zennists honoring the precepts in their breach. But to violate them builds bad karmic merit that will impact doers eventually. In sum, Zen Buddhism emphasizes the experiential aspects of achieving Enlightenment, or Awakening (though as the next section shows, there is some disagreement on specific methods). Awakening is a new perspective that departs radically from whatever one's previous culturally induced social reality, whether ancient Chinese, medieval or modern Japanese, mainstream North American or European. If *kensho* is a temporary moment or experience of insight, *satori* is a transcendent transformation. This transformation, however, is not a permanent once-and-for-all experience. It can and must be cultivated, for just as a first degree black belt in any martial art would be the last to claim that he or she has mastered the system, so a Zennist regards initial *satori* breakthrough as only the beginning of liberation.

Sectarian Developments

Within Chinese Buddhism, as in India, a number of distinct schools soon developed. Some merely represented the immediate followers of local or regional charismatic leaders or of a monastery's abbot. However, between the Ninth and Eleventh centuries there coalesced Ch'an lineages known as "the Five Houses of Zen": those of Masters Lin-chi, Tsao-tung, Yun-men, Kuei-yang, and Fa-yen (Cleary, 1997). Only the first two Ch'an schools survived to become of any modern consequence. *Rinzai* for centuries after Lin-chi became the dominant school of Ch'an in China (Watson, 1993: ix-x). During Japan's medieval Kamakura Period (1185-1333) Japanese monks who trained in China brought back these dual orientations of T'ang Dynasty Zen masters Lin-chi and Tsao-tung. *Rinzai* (Lin-chi in Japanese pronunciation) and *Soto* (Tsao-tung in Japanese pronunciation) Zen schools or sects, respectively, came to contend for political patronage and influence as well as popular appeal.

Moreover, *Rinzai* and *Soto* today still somewhat reflect the old rivalry between seventh century Ch'an's Southern School of Hui-neng (abrupt *satori*) and the Northern School of Shen-hsiu (progressive, cumulative Awakening). Master Lin-chi, or Rinzai, was of the Southern School, and he is famous in his teaching style for giving loud shouts and even violent physical exhortations (i.e., blows and beatings) to hasten his pupils' breakthroughs to *satori*. (That violence is now a thing of the past.) The *Rinzai* approach has also become noted for its master presenting each pupil with an insolvable word puzzle (a *koan*, or *kung-an* in Chinese) that poses an illogical dilemma that can only be broken out of with intuitive illogic, helping the pupil transcend dualistic thinking. Pupils contemplate the meaning behind their *koans* during *zazen* and discuss them (often with frustration deliberately tailored by the master) in tutorial sessions called *dokusan* (See, e.g., Watson, 1993; Suzuki, 1961).

Soto also used *zazen*, often synonymously called *shikantaza* (in Japanese, "just sitting") wherein the pupils let their thoughts and emotions fly about until they subside, then they confront and investigate these cognitions until they gradually achieve a sense of non-attachment and mental clarity. Dogen (1200-53), who is credited with bringing this more subdued, contemplative approach to Japan, stressed the merits of *shikantaza* in his classic work *Shobogenzo Zuimonki, Soto* Zen's primer of methodology (Masunaga, 1971). *Soto* stresses the role of breathing (air slowly drawn in and expelled in the lower part of the abdomen, the *hara*) in helping regulate mind and body, and its spokespersons maintain that spiritual energy is actually produced in that region below the navel (e.g., Maezumi and Glassman, 2002; Sekida 1985). *Soto* is also famous for a monk coming up behind meditators in *zazen*, carrying a *kyosaku*—a long flat stick—with which he periodically strikes meditators around the muscles of shoulders and neck to refresh their concentration—and wake them if they are dozing.

In contemporary Zen, as Kapleau (1979) and others repeatedly have noted (and experienced), both schools use some combination of *koan* and *zazen* techniques. Both schools hold *sesshin*, which are extended seven-to-eight-day intensive meditative "workshops." But there is still evidence of sectarian criticism by some spokespersons in each camp. The eminent Zen scholar D. T. Suzuki, himself raised and trained in the *Rinzai* tradition, emphasizes that Rinzai Zen is about the action mode in seeking *satori* rather than employing quiet meditation, claiming "*prajna* is sudden and not gradual enlightenment" (Suzuki, 1970b: 98) and compares *zazen* of the *Soto* type "to a state of trance; nothing comes out of this evenness of consciousness" (Suzuki, 1970b: 97). Real *satori*, he maintains, requires a "mental upheaval." In this he is reminiscent of eighteenth-century *Rinzai* master Hakuin who resurrected and expanded use of the *koan*. (Hakuin invented the most famous *koan* known to many Westerners: "What is the sound of one hand clapping?") Hakuin denounced *Soto* adherents of "Silent Illumination" and "Do-Nothing Zen" (Stevens, 1993: 73) and believed in "moving meditation," i.e., maintaining "mindfulness" of non-self and non-dualism in all activities. "In other words," writes biographer Stevens (1993: 81), "marrying, having sex, and bearing and raising children were excellent forms of moving meditation." Zen's Sixth Patriarch from whom all Zennists trace their lineage, Hui-neng, admonished his followers about the Northern School of seventh century Ch'an: "There is also a class of foolish people who sit quietly and try to keep their minds blank" (Price and Wong, 1990: 80). Meanwhile, Lin-chi of the ninth century, himself descended from five masters after Hui-neng, is recorded as having bluntly said:

> There are a bunch of blind baldheads who, having stuffed themselves with rice, sit doing Ch'an-style meditation practice, trying to arrest the flow of thoughts and stop them from arising, hating clamor, demanding silence—but these aren't Buddhist ways! (Watson 1993: 43)

Watts and Hung (1975: 89) even conclude that virtually *all* T'ang-era Ch'an masters rejected meditation *per se* as a path or means to true insight.

At the same time, some *Soto* Zennists are equally derisive of *Rinzai* Zen. Roshi Taisen Deshimaru in *The Voice of the Valley* (1979: 54, 182) dismisses the venerable D.T. Suzuki as merely an "Oriental philosopher and psychologist," terming him a mere *sensei* (teacher) as opposed to a *roshi* (Zen master), though Suzuki in his various autobiographical accounts describes how he *did* achieve *satori* via a *koan* (the classic Mu). Deshimaru rather facilely warns that constantly sitting in *zazen* ruminating on *koans* may drive people mad (his words). Deshimaru, like Dogen and some other *Soto* spokespersons, have insisted on contemplative *shikantaza* as the only mode leading to enlightenment, sometimes equating the two:

> What is Satori? There is no need to seek Satori. Do zazen; the zazen itself is Satori. (Deshimaru 1979: 21)

Further:

> Zazen itself is Satori.... With no zazen, no Satori, Just remember Zazen is shikantaza, is Satori. (P. 54)

And again:

> Zazen is complete shikantaza.... It is nature itself, it is the cosmos itself.... During zazen you are Buddha, you are God. (P. 133)

Hyperbole aside, many modern Zen practitioners pragmatically and eclectically employ both the methods of *Rinzai* and *Soto* after an approach developed by Harada Roshi (1872-1963) and share generally the doctrines elaborated above. It would also be somewhat disingenuous to leave readers with the above vulgar image of *shikantaza* since its *Soto* rationale is a bit more sophisticated. One of us personally espouses the *Rinzai* approach, seeking periodic *kensho* with a goal of abrupt *satori* and then deepening awakening with further practice—minus the medieval beatings of Lin-chi. This is due largely to autobiographical experiences with martial arts and *Rinzai* teachers in Japan. Be that as it may, a Zen critique of social psychology can safely be made from a solid non-sectarian position.

A Primer on Social Psychology

Since most readers are likely either social scientists or at least apt to be more comfortable with concepts and research methodologies of social psychology, we offer a truncated overview of this rather unique discipline. We say unique as it is one of the few academic disciplines that has a foot in two other parent fields; namely, those of psychology and sociology. By briefly examining its purview and sketching its history, readers should gain a sufficient sense of what we mean in our comparisons of mainstream social psychology with Zen Buddhism. Further elaborations on the self, self-concept, attitudes, emotions, and empathy/compassion will be dealt with by the tandem perspectives in the next three successive chapters.

A Brief History of Social Psychology

What exactly is social psychology? Is it simply a subdiscipline within sociology, or is it just one aspect of the field of psychology? Is it merely a blending of sociological and psychological knowledge, or is there something more to social psychology? At times one may have heard these and similar questions concerning the nature and scope of social psychology from students, non-social science colleagues and even social psychologists themselves. Questions like these effectively illustrate that there are many people who consider the field of social psychology to be little more than the immature offspring of sociology and psychology. It has even been suggested that social psychology is nothing more than a marginal field of study, given that its subject material has too much overlap with its parent disciplines (Kelley, 2000). However, these characterizations of social psychology are incorrect. One of the primary strengths of social psychology is that it works within a more integrated meta-disciplinary framework that borrows liberally from both psychology and sociology when attempting to explain and understand the social world. Through the use of information derived from both fields of study, social psychology has been able to expand on previous sociological and psychological insights *specifically* by drawing from both parent disciplines. As such, social psychology has been able to grow and mature over the years from its humble beginnings into a broad and diverse field of study that offers new and unique contributions to the body of knowledge concerning the human condition.

Noted psychologist Gordon W. Allport (1968) suggested that social psychology is an academic discipline that originated from the American philosophical traditions of pragmatism, free inquiry, and the ethics of democracy. However, social psychology can trace its literal roots to 1908 when two books were published separately but simultaneously in the United States: *Introduction to Social Psychology* by William McDougall (a psychologist), and *Social Psychology: An Outline and Sourcebook* by Edward Allsworth Ross (a sociologist). Slow to establish itself as a separate area of academic endeavor, the field of social psychology began to grow between the early 1920s and the start of American involvement in World War II, mostly as a function of the rapid societal changes of the 1920s and 1930s. Evidence for the growth of the field is reflected in the number of textbooks in social psychology that were published from 1908 forward, which increased from five in 1922 to thirty-five by 1941 (Allport, 1954).

The period from World War II until the early 1960s is often referred to as the "golden age of social psychology," primarily because it was during this time that sociologists and psychologists worked hand-in-hand to pursue joint research projects and develop new theoretical insights. Much of this "golden age" work started as a result of research into military and civilian behavior that was conducted for the armed forces throughout World War II (House, 1977). During the war, the United States military assembled sociologists and psychologists (as well as others from similar social scientific backgrounds) to aid in projects that would help with the war effort. After the war ended, many of the academics that had worked for the military as members of the various interdisciplinary projects found that these joint activities were fertile grounds for the generation of new ideas. William H. Sewell, a noted social psychologist who worked with the military during the wartime period, believed that some of the most innovative and insightful ideas that he encountered in his career arose as a result of this collegial interaction. After the war ended, many of the personnel who were equally impressed with their collaborative experiences decided to continue this interdisciplinary approach to research once they returned to the academic setting (Sewell, 1989). This resulted in the creation of interdisciplinary social psychology programs at several universities across the nation by the early 1950s.

Unfortunately, the so-called golden age of social psychology was not to last. Throughout the late 1950s and into the early 1960s the number of interdisciplinary social psychology programs began to diminish in the United States. As a result, the field of social psychology itself began to fracture, if not wane. A lack of funding for interdisciplinary programs, coupled with the threat that the field of social psychology posed to the traditional separation of sociology and psychology departments in universities, were the two primary reasons for this turn of events (Sewell, 1989). By the end of the decade many of the interdisciplinary social psychology programs in the United States were dissolved. The personnel and materials from these now-defunct programs were typically reassigned to either psychology or sociology departments, with the majority of both personnel and materials finding their way to psychology departments.

As these facts suggest, the end of the so-called golden age did not bode well for the sociological side of social psychology. Throughout the 1960s and into the 1970s, sociological social psychology came to be overshadowed by psychological social psychology both in terms of scholastic representation and theoretical development. By 1968 it was estimated that roughly two thirds of the textbooks in social psychology were written by psychologists, with these texts emphasizing psychological knowledge over sociological knowledge (Allport, 1968). By the end of the 1970s, fully three out of every four social psychology texts on the market were authored by psychologists (Jones, 1985). Many of the scholarly journals that were established to help advance the body of theoretical knowledge in social psychology at this point were also psychological in their orientation. These journals included *Basic and Applied Social Psychology*, *Journal of Applied Social Psychology*, *Journal of Experimental Social Psychology*, *Journal of Personality*, *Journal of Personality and Social Psychology*, *Journal of Social Issues*, *Journal of Social Psychology*, *Personality and Social Psychology Bulletin*, *Social Cognition*, and *Social Psychology Quarterly*. Of these top ten journals devoted to publishing social psychological articles during this time, only one (the journal *Social Psychology Quarterly*) was edited and sponsored by sociologists (Jones, 1985). The increasing dominance of psychological social psychology over sociological social psychology during this time period led many in the field to conclude that social psychology was "in crisis," especially with respect to certain events occurring on the sociological side of the divide.

By the early-to-mid 1970s the formerly integrated field of social psychology had been bifurcated and recategorized by the academic community as separate (but related) subdisciplines within both psychology and sociology. To complicate matters further, by the late 1970s the field of sociological social psychology itself had fractured into two isolated and distinct camps. In an article entitled "The Three Faces of Social Psychology," James House (1977) identified these two camps as "symbolic interactionism" and "social structure and personality." Those in the symbolic interactionist camp tended to favor a more qualitative research approach in their study of face-to-face social interactions; in contrast, those in the social structure and personality camp preferred to use quantitative survey techniques to investigate the impact that macrosocial phenomena have on a person's attitudes and behaviors. House also identified a third camp in his article: psychological social psychology, which, as the name implies, refers to the more psychological side of the social psychology divide (this camp was "housed" within the separate discipline of psychology). Together these three different camps, or "faces," represented the entire discipline of social psychology at the end of the 1970s, often with much reduced inter-camp contact or correspondence. These three faces of social psychology were therefore relatively isolated, were sometimes antagonistic towards each other, and were largely dissatisfied with the state of affairs in the field of social psychology (House, 1977).

The late 1970s was arguably the low point for social psychology. Scholars from each of the "faces" of social psychology spoke often, and at great length, of the crisis within their shared field. A common complaint espoused by all sides concerned the intensifying isolation of psychological social psychology from sociological social psychology, and how this increased isolation did not bode well for the discipline (Boutilier, Roed, and Svendsen, 1980). There were even fears that the divisions would eventually diminish social psychology to such an extent that it would disappear as a distinct academic field of study altogether within a few years' time.

Fortunately this dissolution of social psychology as an academic field has not happened. From the 1980s to the present, the field of social psychology has undergone a great deal of revitalization. This change was due in large part to the tremendous diversity of new topics that were being identified as areas of possible investigation by both psychological and sociological social psychologists. As opposed to bemoaning the split between psychological and sociological social psychologists, a new generation of researchers began instead to embrace the diversity of the field and use it as a means of inspiring work in previously unconsidered areas. New collaborative investigations were undertaken as work in one area informed and inspired work in other areas (Smith-Lovin and Molm,

2000). This cross-fertilization has led to solid advancements in research and theoretical development for both camps, as well as for the field of social psychology as a whole.

So what is the state of social psychology today? On the sociological side of the divide, much of the research and work being done can be compartmentalized into three distinct areas: symbolic interactionism, social structure and personality, and the study of small group dynamics. On the psychological side, a robust amount of research continues to be developed in the areas that psychological social psychologists have excelled at for decades. These include investigation into attributions, attitude formation, cognitive development and other forms of intrapersonal processes; altruism, aggression, prosocial behavior and other types of interpersonal behaviors; and small group processes, an area of overlap between sociologists and psychologists where the cross-fertilization of ideas and knowledge continues to flourish. Another area of investigation that the two sides of social psychology have shared for close to a century centers on the development and maintenance of the self, a subject that will surface repeatedly throughout this book.

A Final Definition

The above paragraphs provide a brief summary of the current state of affairs in the arena of social psychology. Yet we have failed to directly answer our original question: what is social psychology? As Fine, House, and Cook (1995: xii) elegantly state, social psychology is the academic discipline

> that investigates questions concerning the nature of the self, identity, emotion, cognition, and perception in human life. It also examines the role [of] impression management, exchange, aggression, liking, and discourse in human interaction. Finally it is the discipline that links the individual to organizational and even societal phenomena, such as group life, justice and legal systems, organizational dynamics, and collective action.

Put succinctly, social psychology examines (using the scientific methods insofar as it can be applied to human beings) individual behavior within the group context. If we substitute "experiential" or "intuitive" for "scientific," this line of thought would also fairly fit as a working definition of Zen.

A Last Note on Zen and Social Psychology

With all its emphasis on linguistic influence in the Sapir-Whorf manner, from objects and limitations of thought to the mental constraints of social reality and the "mind game" breakthrough function served by *koans*, an inevitable question then to be finally asked is: Is Zen Buddhism merely an Asian form of social psychology? Of course, the same question has been asked in a parallel way about Zen being a religion or a philosophy, or both simultaneously.

In reverse order, these questions can be answered. Yes, Zen Buddhism can be considered a religion, if by religion one means a system of thought that deals with fundamental issues of the meaning of life and death, correct morality, faith, our duty to other creatures, and essential spirituality. Both *Rinzai* and *Soto* forms of Zen agree on this (for examples of two respective proponents, see Suzuki, 1961; Masunaga, 1971).

Is it a philosophy? Here things are slightly less clear. Masao Abe, a Zennist scholar with a strong North American theological background, contends that "philosophy" is a term originating in the West referring to a process of human self-examination that began with the Greeks millennia ago. In fact, the Japanese only coined the term *tetsugaku* (philosophy) in the late nineteenth century to have a way of referring to *Western* philosophy since their language did not have an equivalent. Abe observes "what we today call Oriental philosophy is nothing but a reinterpretation of the Oriental thought from this standpoint of Western philosophy" (Abe, 1986: 74). Not to put words into Professor Abe's mouth, but thinking of any system of ideas dealing with telic matters as a philosophy is a uniquely Western designation. In the East, as Watts' quote at the beginning of "The Zen Innovation" section earlier in this chapter made explicit, such non-Western systems as Zen Buddhism are ways of liberation. Says Suzuki (1961: 13) in his classic *Essays in Zen Buddhism*: "By making us drink right from the fountain of life, it liberates us from all the yokes under which we finite beings are visually suffering in this world." So is it a philosophy? We suggest that term is too Western, too ambiguous, and perhaps even too ethnocentric to be of use in understanding what Zen is.

Then is Zen a social psychology of sorts? Or is it really *a* social psychological orientation, one of many possible, perhaps, even if not the Western social psychology taught in Anglo-European universities? It would seem not to be if afforded no more than a superficial first glance, but on deeper reflection there are strong commonalities, enough—we suggest—to warrant a serious comparison of the two approaches. Both Zen Buddhism and Western social psychology are vitally concerned with explicating the thought processes of the individual within a group context. Furthermore, for each perspective the influences and effects of that context are critical. The two perspectives, moreover, acknowledge the specific determining forces of language, learning, and social group pressures to produce both conformity (much of it implicitly demanded and therefore "invisible" or unconscious) and uncritical acceptance of the physical, social, and political status quo.

To be sure, there are differences. Social psychology generally proceeds by way of more quantitative methodologies while Zen is entirely qualitative and subjective. Zen is rather straightforward about using the insights that it helps promote to allow individuals to see alternative courses of action and self-redefinitions. But social psychology, for its part, has always recognized its potential for practical application and betterment of individuals and society—recall the previous historical section and social scientists' involvement in wartime service as an exemplar of this point. Zen aims to undo many effects of (by Western standards) "normal" social psychological processes, but so do social psychologists whom are concerned with such important social problems as racial hatred, prejudice, and the dangers that lurk within the group dynamic. Gordon W. Allport's *The Nature of Prejudice* (1979) or the milestone Adorno and colleagues. *The Authoritarian Personality* (1950) are just two examples of works that underscore this line of reasoning. Or consider the studies on the mental strangleholds of obedience to authority, conformity, and groupthink offered by Janis, Asch, and Milgrim—these are but a few in a litany of studies that could be cited.

Social psychology, like all forms of Western thought, leans toward the linear, cause-and-effect, discursive model. Thus, for example, learning laws of conditioning or extinguishing responses according to reinforcement schedules have been well documented for half a century. Zen leans the other way, toward holistic intuition. If anything, social psychology could be faulted for artificially delimiting its subject matter into manageable small-sized topics, while Zen more ambitiously targets a radical *weltanschauung*-inverting perspective in the human psyche. But these are differences in methodology, not in the substance of what is experienced, analyzed, and reported.

With these overlaps between the interests of Zen and social psychology in mind, there have been attempts in Europe (e.g., Humphreys, 1986) and elsewhere to seek correspondences between psychotherapy and Zen Buddhism, particularly in its techniques of self-knowledge and meditation (e.g., Linssen, 1958; Rosenbaum, 1999; Fromm, 1960). Indeed, American Zen Roshi Kapleau (1997; 1989; 1979) has made extensive reports of his dialogues with psychiatrists and clinical psychologists, both in their roles of professionals and as his (*Soto*) Zen students.

While notable neo-psychoanalyst Erich Fromm conducted a friendship and had discussions with *Rinzai* Zen's D. T. Suzuki, perhaps the meeting of minds between psychoanalyst Carl G. Jung and Zen Master Shinichi Hisomatsu in 1958 best illustrates the quantum distance of Zen even from some Western psychotherapy. To their credit, Meckel and Moore (1992: 103-40), avowed Jungians, report on the Jung-Hisomatsu dialogue, which covered such ground as Jung's multi-layered concept of self and Self, the Zen rejection thereof, different concepts of suffering, Jung's evident repeated confusion of Hindu concepts with Buddhist ones, and so forth. Aside from the clear disparities in perspectives, Jung seems to have come off the worse in the conversation, frustrated because of his apparent dilettantish understanding of Eastern spirituality and terminology. He even tried to deny permission to publish the transcripts of their rather embarrassing talk. (Evidently writing forewords to D. T. Suzuki's 1964 *An Introduction to Zen Buddhism* and the classic edition of *The Tibetan Book of the Great Liberation* (Evans-Wentz, 1969) did not prepare him to seek rapprochement between his analytic system and Zen's militant rejection of the latter's conceptual underpinnings.) Suffice it to say, psychoanalysis—of any variety—with its overarching metaphysical conceptualizations of ego and self finds no ready intellectual ally in Zen Buddhism once terms are defined. In particular, the attempts by Jungian enthusiasts to find common ground with Zen seem at bottom an effort by them to validate a quasi-mystical/quasi-mythological therapy with the prestige of a venerable Asian religion locating its roots in antiquity.

Finally, as will be reiterated in the pages to follow, Zen appreciates that there is a phenomenal world, which pragmatically has to be acknowledged as we live in it. Multiplicity of form is no less real than Ultimate Unity (*sunyata*). Indeed, that is a key doctrine of all *Mahayana* Buddhism, of which Zen is a part. After all, Zennists believe like anyone else that they should watch for cars when crossing a street. But metaphysics aside, the issue is *how* we acknowledge the phenomenal world. To be sure, *maya* (illusion), or the relativity of measured reality as we conceive it, *is* here, with all its apparent shades and differences. For Zennists

> The aim of a way of liberation is not the destruction of *maya* but seeing it for what it is, or seeing through it ... ideas of the world and of oneself which are social convention and institutions are not to be confused with reality. (Watts, 1961: 21)

Alongside conventional Western social psychology, this too is an empirical stance. And so we proceed.

2

Self and Self-Concept:
The Absolute and the Relative

There exists undoubtedly no more venerable construct in social psychology, both from psychological and sociological standpoints, than that of the *self*. Indeed, it naturally flows out of the very definition of social psychology we cited in the previous chapter. It would be no exaggeration to claim that over the past century the topic of self has continued to be the primary area of investigation for social psychologists, especially given that many aspects of social psychological research intersect with the self and self-concept at some level. The self and the self-concept are the foundations for understanding how society and culture produce personal reflexive awareness and sense of identity (and correlate issues of esteem, efficacy, control, individualism, and alternately, anomia, alienation, and powerlessness) as well as interpersonal interaction (i.e., presenting one's preferred image to others and managing others' opinions of us to our advantage) and the origins of social conformity.

The term "self" can be defined as the ongoing accumulation of social experiences and social interactions that an individual has over time (Jary and Jary, 1991). What social psychologists usually mean by the "self-concept" is that an individual will possess *a sense of one's own person*, or will have an opinion of one's own image and abilities as seen by an independent audience, just as that same person can also hold an opinion, conception, or evaluation of another's attributes. In social interaction we are able through an imaginary process to take the viewpoint or stance of the other person(s) and regard ourselves as we believe those others see us. (In the symbolic interactionist approach this is called "taking the role of the other," or the reflexive act.) Consequently we react to this perceived view of us and adjust or maintain our appearance, actions, and so forth, usually as a function of whether or not the other's reactions matter to us.

No one is born possessing a self or the accompanying self-concept. It is indisputably learned from others through innumerable social contacts, beginning in earliest childhood. We internalize overall judgments of everything from our physical appearance to our behavior under many circumstances and make these perceived assessments our own. Thus: "I consider myself good-looking," or "I am not very good at math," or "I have real bankable musical ability," *ad infinitum*.

Since the turn of the late nineteenth/early twentieth centuries when the original social psychological theorists wrote on the subject, an ever-expanding field of books and articles has debated the exact nature, role, and meaning of the theoretical construct known as the self. Part of what contributes to this theorizing is the sheer number of written works in the body of literature that deals with the self. Evidence to support this assertion can be found by doing a simple keyword search in any of the sociological databases for the subject of "self." A search of this type will typically return a good 15,000 (as opposed to 15,000 good) references. Much of this extant literature focuses on the nature of the self, while many other articles and books delve instead into an exploration of self-concept. This often creates a situation where these two terms are confused as synonymous. Indeed, Greene and Reed (1992: 267) point out how distinguishing between these terms (the self and the self-concept) has become something of a "controversial topic" within social psychology. As Gecas (1982, 1989, 1991) and Rosenberg, Schooler, Schoenbach, and Rosenberg (1995) note, this confusion and controversy have risen to the level where some researchers insist that the self and self-concept are interchangeable constructs.

We maintain that this should not be the case. In fact, illuminating the distinction between the self and self-concept is critically important when building a bridge between social psychology and Zen Buddhism. As we shall see, explicating how the self and self-concept differ uncovers one of the strongest pieces of connective tissue that links Zen to social psychology.

Later in this chapter we will present a review of the classic social psychological statements on self, and then go on to outline how Zen's position on that same self as a concept shows that this notion is not solely the possession of social scientists. We will also compare the commonalities of each approach in an effort to reach a middle ground where both social psychology and Zen sort out on the issue of the self versus self-concept. At first it might appear that the two perspectives are antagonistic or irreconcilable, yet in fact there is a definite *rapprochement* possible, one which surprisingly does not nearly require the great stretch of imagination a Zennist might suspect. Often the two perspectives are talking about the same thing, for the same reasons, though not always with precision or the same vocabulary. To anticipate our later argument: Zen and social psychology do not always mean the same thing when they refer to the self, but they do agree on the significance of the self-concept for interpersonal life.

Finally, we clarify that the self is not the same as personality. Whereas the notion of self or the awareness of one's self belongs intimately to each of us, personality is a purely external attribute provided about us, and maintained, by other persons. Thus: "He has a real aggressive type-A personality," or "Isn't that just like Bobbi to do that!" Though psychology maintains numerous definitions for the concept of personality (depending on the particular theorists doing the defining), they all have in common the element of a discernable continuity of style and mannerism in how a person comports and acts across situations. Anthropologist Ralph Linton (1945: 85) years ago put it succinctly when he observed that "the only grounds for assuming the existence of personalities as operative entities persisting through time is the consistency in the overt behavior of individuals."

The Classic Statements on the Self

So as to not be accused of disciplinary favoritism, we present the two seminal statements about this vintage area of social psychology by the chronological order in which they were published.

The Definitive Psychological Statement: William James

Harvard professor William James wrote at the end of the Victorian Age. Though his descriptive language (particularly as regards the soul and the psyche) today reads as a bit quaint, his treatment of the self-concept has endured as a benchmark in social psychology. While ideas about the self, the ego, consciousness, and so forth can be traced back through the seventeenth century Age of Reason's Rene Descartes to the Greeks (e.g., Prus, 2003; Holstein and Gubrian, 2000: 18-24), James is where modern social psychology starts.

In *Psychology: The Briefer Course* (1985), originally published in 1892, James set out the essential dimensions of the self, both in its object sense as a thing to be known (the "Me") and in its active subject sense as the knower (the "I"). James was adamant that the self was a *social* psychological construct. In his book's introductory section (p. xxvii) he cautioned: "Mental facts cannot be properly studied apart from the physical environment of which they take cognizance." James wrote at length about the subject-object aspects of the self of each person, and, as we argue later in this chapter and in the next chapter, many of his dynamic ideas about the self in action, while in practice ignored by many modern scholars, correspond reasonably well with some aspects of Zennists' "take" on the so-called self or "relative" self.

For James the self had three dimensions: (1) constituents (the material Me, the social Me, and the spiritual Me), (2) feelings and emotions aroused by the acting "I" (self-appreciation), and (3) acts which both the "I" and "Me" prompt in a fluid dialectic between themselves when interacting with physical and social environments, i.e., what James called in surprisingly modern terms (See, e.g., Goffman, 1959) *self-seeking* and *self-presentation.*

The Me

The *material* Me includes our bodily, visceral demands, most importantly emotions, and natural physiological goal-seeking.

The *social* Me is more complex, attuned as it is to various types of interactions with other persons. Among other things, "A man's social Me is the recognition which he gets from his mates" (p. 46). (Obviously James intended more than today's narrow interpretation of "mates" as spouses.) For James, human beings are naturally gregarious. As a consequence, a person actually maintains many social selves simultaneously, each corresponding to different situations and groups out of which the Me arises. Says James (p. 46), "Properly speaking, a man has as many social selves as there are individuals who recognize him and carry an image of him in their minds." (In symbolic interactionist and role theory terms, respectively, we would say significant others/reference groups and audiences.) Correspondingly "He generally shows different sides of himself to each of these different groups." (We would term these role-situated identities.) Not surprisingly, multiple selves can come into "discordant splitting of selves" (role conflict and role strain) or exist in consistency and integration, *and* these selves are ordinarily ranked in a hierarchy of dominance in terms of importance to the person.

The *spiritual* Me constitutes "the entire collection of my states of consciousness, my psychic faculties and dispositions taken concretely" (p. 48). The spiritual Me has a profound capability to awaken emotions and emerges when we think of ourselves as thinkers, i.e., reflection. And spiritual aspects of the self, like its material and social constituents, can seem as if they were relatively external possessions. (*All* reflexive thoughts lend the Me an external objective sense for thinkers.) Moreover, the spiritual "awakening" of emotions prompts or motivates activity. Noted James (p. 48), "The more *active-feeling* states of consciousness are the more central portion of the spiritual Me."

James emphasized the role of emotions in a self-directed activity, as did a later colleague C. G. Lange (1922), with emotions being the primary and physiological origins of subsequent self-thoughts, self-analyses, and subjective interpretations of such feelings. In other words, physiological arousal by a stimulus is followed by a meaning-construction process that we often call attitudes. As an identified object, it becomes an awareness of "How I must feel." In modern social psychological terms this arousal-to-interpretation process is known as the James-Lange formulation or theory. (This will be reviewed again in Chapter 3 when we examine the overlap between social psychological and Zennist approaches to experiences and "tagging" cognitions onto physiological arousal as well as the organic origins of emotions.)

There are two sorts of self-appreciation, self-complacency, and self-satisfaction, and they involve dimensions of the Me such as pride, conceit, vanity, and self-esteem, or alternately, humility, confusion, modesty, and so forth. Actual successes or failures in life activities (what now would be called positive and negative reinforcements through both operant conditioning and social learning) form these self-feelings. Self-seeking and self-presentation, therefore, are the activities that produce interactions that in turn result in the Me. For example, James (p. 51) maintained:

> Our social self-seeking ... is carried on directly through our amativeness and friendliness, our desire to please and attract notice and admiration, our emulation and jealousy, our love of glory, influence, and power, and indirectly through whichever of the material self-seeking impulses prove serviceable as means to social ends.

Finally, alongside a hierarchy of selves in the Me there is a distinction made by most persons between the immediate and actual aspects versus the remote and potential outcomes of self-seeking activities:

> ... men have arranged the various selves which they may seek in an hierarchical scale according to their worth. A certain amount of bodily selfishness is required as basis for all the other selves. But too much sensuality is despised, or at least condoned on account of the other qualities of the individual. The wider material selves are regarded as higher than the material body. He is esteemed a poor creature who is unable to forego a little meat and drink and warmth and sleep for the sake of getting on in the world. The social self as a whole, again, ranks higher than the material self as a whole. We must care more for our honor, our friends, our humanities, than for a sound skin or wealth. And the spiritual self is so supremely precious that rather than

lose it, a man ought to be willing to give up friends and good fame, and property, and life itself (p. 58).

The I

The I is a fluid decision-maker, active, engaged with the social world around each person. "It is that which at any given moment *is* conscious, whereas the Me is only one of the things which it is conscious of" (p. 62). James questioned if the "I" was a primary state of consciousness or "some thing deeper and less mutable?" (p. 62). He settled (albeit with vague references to philosophy) for the euphemism "the Thinker" (an acting component somewhat akin to Freud's ego).

James spent less effort in defining the "I" than in explaining how it worked. For instance, in the stream of consciousness (an entire chapter to which is devoted immediately preceding discussion of the self) several separate ideas do not sum to form one composite idea; rather, persons have unitary thought. In his example of the thought "The pack of cards is on the table," there are not separate thoughts related to the cards and their suites, dimensions and style of the table, and so forth but rather a single cognition. "The pack of cards is on the table" is one idea (p. 64).

More importantly for issues such as the continuity of the sense of personal identity, thoughts do not "fly about" at random. *Memory* preserves the sense of continuity in the self. So "the result is a Me of yesterday, judged to be in some peculiarly subtle sense the *same* with the I who now make [*sic*] the judgment." Memory permits the generalization from the previous Me to current I. Of course, the generalization is not strictly accurate. "I" at this moment am not the same literal "I" of yesterday. "I" now am a bit older, more enlightened perhaps on certain subjects, hungry then and satiated now, and on and on. Says James

> And yet in other ways I *am* the same, and we may call these the essential ways. My name and profession and relations to the world are identical, my faculties and store of memories are practically indistinguishable, now and then. Moreover, the Me of now and the Me of then are *continuous*: the alterations were gradual and never affected the whole of me at once ... the past and present selves compared are the same just so far as they *are* the same, and no further. They are the same in *kind* ... it gives to the self the unity of mere connectedness, or unbrokenness, a perfectly definite phenomenal thing ... (pp. 68-69).

However, this continuity is true only of the Me. The active Thinker ("I") appropriates the "Me of the past" when useful, but the Thinker ("I") has to be more flexible, even selective as to which Me it might choose. The "I" exists in an ongoing flow of consciousness, bombarded as it is by constant stimuli. "Yesterday's and today's state of consciousness have no *substantial* identity, for when one is here the other is irrevocably dead and gone" (p. 69). What does remain is what James termed a *functional identity*, which passes from one moment's Thinker ("I") to that of the next moment. Says James (p. 70), "Successive thinkers, numerically distinct, but all aware of the same past in the same way, form an adequate vehicle for all the experience of personal unity and sameness which we actually have."

Thus the thinking "I" takes ownership of its predecessor "I" (now a Me with the aid of memory) with the unifying assumption of *mine*, identifying the Me with the self. As James neatly summarizes by metaphor: "Who owns the last self owns the self before the last, for what possesses the possessor possesses the possessed" (p. 71). The "I" finds continuity of identity in the Me, but only loosely because the "I" must still demonstrate flexibility and adaptation to external conditions (and of course depending on which self is being expressed).

James did integrate his concept of the self into a loose theory of not just extreme imbalance, like egotism, but also mental disturbances such as obsessions, delusions, and insanity, and allowed for more complex "subconscious selves." He also later foresaw how the self could be pathologically alienated or divided but also healed through religious conversion (1929: 163-253).

James was forced to rely on the homunculus-like Thinker and employ metaphors because he did not have the advantage of modern neurological research. Still, the composition of the self-concept (active and passive components), its origins, and its operations have not been significantly altered in modern social psychology, but rather only elaborated upon. Most importantly, James' self is an empirical organizing aspect of social interaction for each individual, not some noumenal ideal of philosophers. For James, "The social self emerges, grows, and is altered, within our daily affairs; it doesn't transcend them" (Holstein and Gubrium, 2000: 24).

The Self, Not the Freudian Ego

Almost parenthetically, one other seemingly possible entry in considering psychology's early development of the self-concept is the ego (Latin for "I") of Sigmund Freud's psychoanalytic theory, developed as it was several decades congruent with and after William James. Early Freudian incarnations of the ego included it thought of as a hunger drive (versus aggressive drives), then later something akin to a life drive (*eros*, or *libido*) opposite a drive for the organism to die or materially decompose into its component elements (*thanatos*). In its mature phase Freudian theory postulated that the ego played the role of (or functioned as) pragmatic conciliator (based on "the reality principle") between the animalistic, constantly charged id drive's cathexis (based on "the pleasure principle") and the repressive anti-cathexis qualms of the superego (Freud, 1936, 1947; Brown, 1967). "Should the ego abdicate or surrender too much of its power to the id, to the superego, or to the external world, disharmony and maladjustments will ensue" (Hall, 1954: 28).

Pals (1996: 61) refers to this as the "idea of an unavoidable competition at the center of the self," but the id/ego/superego schema is really about an external interpretation of personality (with personality writ larger as a complex psychosomatic entity constantly, even laboriously seeking at best equilibrium or homeostasis). Worse for the self-concept in both psychological and sociological conceptualizations, in Freud's internal dramaturgy of the organism "the ego is not master in its house, the mind" (LaBarre, 1968: 66).

Later neo-Freudians, like the psychoanalytic Alfred Adler, did approach in his Individual Psychology something like a reflective self, with children's self-images of low esteem and inferiority, developing compensatory needs to diminish insecurities in later life interactions, and so forth, but James' concept of self was a good deal more parsimonious minus the psychoanalytic baggage of childhood determinism (See e.g., Ansbacher and Ansbacher, 1964; Adler, 1954). Even Karen Horney (1966), originally a classic Freudian who became a detractor of Freud, rejected much of the classic Freudian ego notion in analysis (though like Adler and others she never fully developed a competing concept of self to match the Jamesian original).

In their writings some Asian Zennists refer to the Western notion of the social self as the "ego-I," perhaps thinking of Freud, but what they mean is the Western preoccupation with individuals' self-awareness and attachment to an interactive world with themselves as the prime referent. Such misunderstandings aside, in the social psychological discipline's development of the self-concept William James' original construct has been seminal; Freud's ego can be dismissed.

The Definitive Sociological Statement: Charles Horton Cooley

Charles Horton Cooley is best remembered by contemporary sociologists for two books he published at each end of the first decade of the twentieth century: *Human Nature and the Social Order* (1902) and

Social Organizations: A Study of the Larger Mind (1909). In his first book Cooley dealt most importantly with the self-concept; in the latter he introduced (among other things) the venerable distinction between primary and secondary groups.

Cooley's description of the self was to the point and inclusive:

> It is well to say at the outset that by the word "self" in this discussion is meant simply that which is designated in common speech by the pronouns of the first person singular, "I," "me," "my," "mine," and "myself".... The distinctive thing in the idea for which the pronouns of the first person are names is apparently a characteristic kind of feeling which may be called the my-feeling or sense of appropriation. (1964: 168-9)

Writing a decade after William James published seminal psychological treatment of the self-concept, Cooley several times in *Human Nature and the Social Order* acknowledged James' earlier work. Though not as systematic as James at breaking the self into constituent levels and dimensions, in many ways Cooley nevertheless paralleled James' approach. Like James, he did not want to become mired in philosophical or lofty metaphysical nuancing and went to lengths to say so. Like James, Cooley was a behavioral scientist and wanted nothing less than a pragmatic, everyday "empirical self." Like James, he relied heavily in his explanations on pedestrian anecdotes and metaphors to make his points. Like James, he stated that he meant a truly *social self* ("Self-feeling has its chief scope within the general life, not outside of it..." p. 179), not some purely psychological-level cognition apart from the sociological level. Like James, Cooley's self formulation was both a reaction and proactive concept, formed from, and continually asserting itself in, social interaction. It had, as human creatures do, an element of imagination at the same time it was engaged in actual behavior. And like James, Cooley grounded the self (and the sense of an acting "I") explicitly in emotions and feelings:

> "I" means primarily self-feeling.... Since "I" is known to our experiences primarily as a feeling, or as a feeling-ingredient in our ideas, it cannot be described or defined without suggesting that feeling.... A formal definition of self-feeling, or indeed of any sort of feeling, must be as hollow as a formal definition of the taste of salt, or the color red.... (1964: 172)

While Cooley believed that the emotion or feeling of self was undoubtedly instinctive at some level, he never developed a Jamesian notion of "material self" and distanced himself from claiming that most usages of "I" referred to a person's body *per se*. Indeed

> Ordinarily it will be found that in not more than ten cases in a hundred does "I" have reference to the body of the person speaking. It refers chiefly to opinions, purposes,

desires, claims, and the like, concerning matters that involve no thought of the body....
It should also be remembered that "my" and "mine" are as much the names of the
self as "I." (1964: 176)

Cooley was somewhat less interested in the formation of the self
(compared to James) and more in its dynamic involvement in mediat-
ing everyday social interaction, but self formation was nevertheless of
considerable importance to him. To explain the formation aspect Cooley
inductively studied his own developing children (not unlike the French
cognitive development psychologist Jean Piaget, who would do the same
years later) and described how they came to distinguish themselves from
others, mastered the social and moral meanings of possessiveness, and
appreciated similar delineations of life. To convey the dynamic mediation aspect, Cooley coined one of the most famous metaphoric terms in
sociological social psychology, "the looking-glass self," analogous to a
mirror's reflection. (We invoked the substance of Cooley's metaphor in
describing self-concept at the start of this chapter.) In Cooley's words
(p. 184):

As we see our face, figure, and dress in the glass, and are interested in them because
they are ours, and pleased or otherwise with them according as they do or do not
answer to what we should like them to be; so in imagination we perceive in another's
mind some thought of our appearance, manners, aims, deeds, character, friends, and
so on, and are variously affected by it.

Cooley broke this reflexive exercise down into three stages: (1) our
imagination of *how we appear* to others; (2) our further imagination of
their *judgment* of our appearance, and (3) our own *self-feeling* about that
presumed judgment. The exercise, Cooley emphasized, is purely mental and imaginative, though its tools, templates, and substance (not his
words) are socially provided. Most normal persons learn to perform the
reflexive act more or less well through the trial and error reinforcements
received in their early years. (A person who does not successfully learn
to take on the role of the other, hence never fully cultivates the ability
to empathize with others, is known in modern social psychology as a
sociopath, and though neither James nor Cooley developed this concept,
there are certainly hints of it in both of their writings.)

Later sociological social psychologists have often paid homage to
Cooley's foundational statement on self with citations and tip-of-the-hat
quotes from *Human Nature and the Social Order*, but one often wonders
how closely some have read him. (More on professional points-scoring
in academic careers in the following section.) Holstein and Gubrium
(2000: 27), for example, in writing effusively about George H. Mead

(who acknowledged, if sometimes critically, his intellectual debt to James and Cooley), say in *The Self We Live By*:

The self becomes less instinctive and more socially interactive when Mead takes up the narrative. With telling reference to both James and Cooley, Mead discusses the place of cognition, feeling, and interaction in the formation of the self.

An instinctive self? Cooley the cultural determinist barely made any reference to the sociologically-taboo word "instinct:" once in passing, and then only in a disclaiming footnote (1964: 170-71) where he was only referring to the feeling or emotion associated with self, and not to a self-drive or anything close to it.

As another example, Pampel (2007: 195) claims "whereas Cooley assumed an already developed self, Mead went further to show how the self emerges from communication and social interaction." A taken-for-grant already-developed self? It is difficult to account for how Pampel missed the parts of Cooley's writings regarding communication and self formation (as covered in our aforementioned review of the pains taken by Cooley to ascertain just such formative issues). In Cooley's first of two chapters on self, these points would include his brilliant analysis of how a very small youngster develops the ability to conceive of the generic label "mine" apart from the physical object *sui generis*. And if Pampel is correct, for a supremely important early social psychologist supposedly uninterested in formative processes but only interested in adult interactive involvement of a fully formed self-concept, Cooley is then curiously absent from the entire reference list of a major essay purportedly surveying "socialization through the life cycle" (Brim, 1966) written over forty years ago.

Sociologist John A. Clausen (1968: 25-6) more correctly, even-handedly, and summarily observes of Cooley's analysis of self:

... Charles Horton Cooley was concerned with the ways in which human nature was shaped by participation in the social order. Influenced by the writings of William James and James Mark Baldwin on the social self and the origins of selfhood, Cooley drew on his own observations of social life (including the development of his children) to formulate the relationship of the individual to society.... He was interested in the early sociability of children and in the origins of personal ideas in the communication process.... Further, more than any other early writer in the fields of sociology and social psychology, he recognized the crucial importance of the primary group relationship for the development of personality and for a conception of human nature.

Later Elaborations on the Construct of Self

George H. Mead, a professor of philosophy at the University of Chicago, appropriated the James/Cooley "I" and "Me" concepts along with the social self during the early years of the twentieth century. Herbert Blumer, a sociology Ph.D. graduate (1928) of the same university and one of Mead's students, actually coined the term *symbolic interaction* in 1937 and is credited not only for having made Mead's writings known generally to sociologists but also for systematizing the approach (Blumer, 1969). Thus, in the minds of most sociologists, George H. Mead is the prominent name associated with the self-concept, the fields of symbolic interactionism, social psychology, and sociology (Pampel, 2007: 168-209). (This would presumably render social psychologists William James and Charles H. Cooley "proto-symbolic interactionists.")

Our interest here is in reviewing the behavioral science constructs of self and self-concept, not symbolic interaction, but since Mead made the self the linchpin of what is arguably the dominant sociological social psychological approach (and because it has certain relevance for Zen), a few words are in order regarding what is often loosely called "S.I. Theory."

Out of all the summary statements of what symbolic interactionism offers by way of fundamental assumptions, that of Howard S. Becker (another University of Chicago sociologist) is as succinct as any. Becker (1968: 196) sees as S.I.'s core theme

> the mutual adjustment of individual lines of activity by invoking a connected set of conceptions: meanings, symbols, taking the role of the other, society, and the self. Actions come to have meaning in a human sense when the person attributes to them the quality of foreshadowing certain other actions that will follow. The meaning is the as yet uncompleted portion of the total line of activity.... The actor, in short, inspects the meaning his action will have for others, assesses its utility in the light of the actions that meaning will provoke in others, and may change the direction of his activity in such a way as to make the anticipated response more nearly what he would like. Each of the actors in a situation does this.

Becker obviously considers analysis of the self and symbolic interaction's "logic" the special innovation of Mead (with, in Becker's dismissive terms, "assists from [John] Dewey and Cooley"—p. 195. Brackets ours). For example, following James' original idea that persons have numerous selves that they display for different others and situations, Becker also argues for a crossover from Mead's symbolic interactionism to the parallel approach of role theory as pioneered by anthropologists (e.g., Linton, 1945):

> The self consists, from one point of view, all the roles we are prepared to take in formulating our own line of actions, both the roles of individuals and of generalized others. From another and complementary view, the self is best concerned as a process in which the roles of others are taken and made use of in organizing our own activities (p. 197).

This use of James' and Cooley's self, continually reflecting on others' evaluations and expectations, their reactions and sanctions, is incorporated directly into role theory. Observes role theorist Ralph Turner (1969: 218):

> Behavior is said to make sense when a series of actions is interpretable as indicating that the actor has in mind some role which guides his behavior.... It is the nature of the role that it is capable of being evoked by different actors, but remains recognizable in spite of individual idiosyncrasies. While people tend to be given stable classification according to the major roles they play, the specific referent for the term "role" is a type of actor rather than a type of person.

But to return focus strictly to the self issue: Mead was critical of both James' and Cooley's development of the self construct on three counts: (1) neither of his predecessors allegedly emphasized *process* enough in the formation of an individual's self through language, communication, and social interaction; (2) both James and Cooley overemphasized self-feelings at the expense of cognition; and (3) neither earlier theorist brought into the self-concept enough of society's normative structure, i.e., that the James/Cooley self was a far too psychological concept based solely on individuals' reactions to how others respond to them. One sample of Mead's criticisms bears out this point:

> Cooley and James, it is true, endeavor to find the basis of the self in reflexive affective experiences, i.e., experiences involving "self-feeling"; but the theory that the nature of the self is to be found in such experiences does not account for the origin of the self, or of the self-feeling which is supposed to characterize such experiences. The individual need not take the attitudes of others toward himself in these experiences, since these experiences merely in themselves do not necessitate his doing so, and unless he does so, he cannot develop a self; and he will not do so in these experiences unless his self has already originated otherwise, namely, in the way we have been describing. *The essence of the self, as we have said, is cognitive*: it lies in the internalized conversation of gestures which constitutes thinking, or in terms of which thought or reflection proceeds. And hence the origin and foundation of the self, like those of thinking, are social. (Mead, 1962: 173; Emphasis ours)

It was not until the 1970s that Cooley's emphasis on self-feelings enjoyed a "rediscovery" by S.I.-oriented social psychologists, so thoroughly had Mead succeeded in "cognitizing" the self and its formation for many. As Weigert and Gecas (2003: 278) assert in their overview of recent S.I. research on the self-concept in the extensive *Handbook of Symbolic Interaction*:

> In general, all emotions have relevance for self ... since we define ourselves in terms of our emotions; use emotions as indicators of who we "really" are ... experience emotions when our valued self-conceptions are either affirmed or challenged ... and use our reflexive process to generate, suppress, control, and express just about any emotion.

Thus, not only for a current generation of social psychologists but also for fifteen centuries of Zennists as well, Cooley's self-feelings matter. Indeed, emotion is a key element in the Zen emphasis on "awakening" to Reality. Along with the language labels and thoughts that "contaminate, corrupt, and disease our minds," emotions run rampant like pillaging Visigoths in fifth century Rome. (We will focus on emotions' contributions to attitudes from both a social psychological and Zennist perspectives in Chapter 3.)

To sum up: it seems a harsh overstatement to conclude that most of the symbolic interactionist research in sociological social psychology subsequent to James and Cooley has been simply an elaboration, with additional technological jargon and neologisms, but that contention stands. For example, Riesman (1950) expanded Cooley's primary/secondary group distinction to talk of inner-directed versus other-direct social character in modern North America; Whyte (1956) wrote of the merger of self with bureaucratic or "organizational" man's needs to depress autonomy, creativity, and self-authenticity; Goffman (1959) incorporated James' *self-presentation* idea into an explicitly dramaturgical model that employed the everyday terms of stagecraft (front-stage versus off-stage and back-stage behavior, fronts, scripts, and audiences); Shibutani (1962) and Hyman and Singer (1971) elaborated the James/Cooley importance of other social actors as *reference groups* to which the self is attuned as sources of approval or social control; and others, including anthropologists such as Wallace (1968), developed the concept of *identity* as a person's image of self.

But while Mead and his terminology (significant symbols, significant others, the generalized other, and so forth) along with more modern contributions indisputably enriched our vocabulary about the circumstances and dynamics surrounding the self, they are really only derivatives based on many earlier seminal ideas that were to that point not fully cultivated. Put another way, after James and Cooley the social psychological understanding of the social self purportedly held by human beings was firmly established. Most of the rest of the conceptualizations, as scholars in any discipline in the liberal arts tradition can attest, has been a series of elaborations of earlier ideas, the understandable purposes of which have been career enhancement and advancement, which depend on such fine-tuning of earlier concepts (usually for conference papers and publications in journals and books). Zennists, who have seen their own neologisms and bifurcation of such concepts as phenomenal versus noumenal realities and the mind itself, are familiar with the intellectualizing process.

However, before turning to what discursive (and non-discursive) sense Zen Buddhism makes out of the self-concept, there is one more issue that must be further explored: the distinction between the self and the self-concept.

The Self and the Self-Concept

Recall that the term "self" can be defined as the ongoing accumulation of social experiences and social interactions that an individual has over time (Jary and Jary, 1991). The "self-concept" refers to the perception that a person has of him or herself, i.e., the idea one has of one's self. Morris Rosenberg (1979: ix) helped to flesh out the difference between the two by noting that the self-concept is "the totality of the individual's thoughts and feelings with reference to [the] self as an object." At first glance the similarities between the self and self-concept would suggest that they are but different aspects of the same construct. However, a subtle but critical difference between the two is present: the self arises via the *process* of social interaction, whereas the self-concept is the *product* of this social interaction. In other words, the self lives in the moment, while the self-concept is the accumulated product or result of the experiences of the self, with these experiences being retained in memory. Thus, the difference between the self and self-concept is somewhat analogous to the differences between the "I" and the "Me" that were outlined by Mead (1962).

Mead maintained that there is an ongoing dialectical relationship between the "I" (the impulsive, active, spontaneous aspect of self, or the self as subject that lives in the moment) and the "Me" (the aspect of self that contemplates, evaluates, and judges interaction with others, or the object in one's own memory). The tension that is present within this dialectical relationship eventually gives rise to the self-concept, provided that the actions of the subjective self, or the "I," can be later recalled by the reflections of the objective self, or the "Me." While Mead is given credit by Blumer and other symbolic interactionists as being the first to articulate the dialectic between the "I" and "Me," a closer examination of the work done by Charles H. Cooley and William James shows how Mead liberally borrowed from these theorists to arrive at his own postulations concerning these two aspects of self. James (1993) in *The Self and Its Selves*, notes that an individual's social self is nothing more than the recognition he or she gets via interactions with others. That is to say, James maintains that an individual's self-concept develops out of the information gleaned during social interaction with others, provided a person later reflects upon the interaction.

The formulation of the social self by James is akin to Cooley's metaphor of the looking-glass self. Like James, Cooley posits that a person's sense of self develops through interactions with others and through that person's interpretations of his or her interactions with others. But whereas James sees the process of reflection as critical to the development of self-concept, Cooley conceives of the self, which he refers to as the "I," as more dynamic and somewhat less reflective in nature. In *Human Nature and the Social Order* Cooley (1964) asserts that changes in a person's self-concept arise immediately *after* the subjective self has interacted with others. That is to say, Cooley put forward that a person uses others as a "looking glass" or mirror to see if that individual's projection of self to others is consonant with the reactions gleaned from others. For Cooley, the "I," or the subjective aspect of self, needs to be nimble enough when living in the moment to adjust "on the fly," with any adjustments to one's self-concept being dependent upon the reactions of others. In a fluid manner, favorable reflections in the social looking glass will lead to a positive self-concept. Likewise, unfavorable reflections will lead to self-concept diminishment and possibly a readjustment of self-concept.

It becomes obvious that Mead stood on the shoulders of others when crafting his arguments concerning how the aspects of self give rise to the self-concept. Mead's definition of the "I" can be directly traced to Cooley's much earlier position that an individual's self-concept arises out of the subjective moment-to-moment interaction with others, just as Mead's definition of the "Me" is traceable to James's somewhat earlier work concerning the social self. For both James and Mead, the "Me" represents how the reflective, objective part of self influences the self-concept long after any interaction with others. Yet there is one thing shared in common by James, Cooley, and Mead and that is that all of their theories are posited upon the notion of reflexivity. Reflexivity is the belief that certain social accounts act to affect change upon those situations to which they refer (Jary and Jary, 1991). Thus reflexivity is the process by which something relates back to itself. As Rosenberg (1990) points out, reflexivity is rooted in the process of taking the role of the other, or seeing the self from another's perspective. As a result of this reflexivity, a person develops both an awareness of and a conception of self: in essence, his or her own self-concept. In *The Self Concept*, Gecas (1982) makes an excellent observation concerning how the process of reflexivity is further related to the self and the self-concept. He states that the self is the foundation for the process of reflexivity, which in turn stems from the dialectical relationship of the "I" and the "Me." In contrast, the self-concept is the product of any reflexive activity.

But reflexivity alone will not completely form the concept a person will hold about himself or herself. Other processes must come into play for the self-concept to successfully take shape. In the first chapter of his seminal work *Conceiving the Self,* Morris Rosenberg (1979) outlined four additional processes that have become generally accepted in sociological self-concept research as playing a major part in the development of the self-concept. These four processes are reflected appraisals (the process by which an individual's feelings about himself or herself are shaped and influenced by the evaluations of others), social comparisons (taking facets of one's own life and correlating them against similar or dissimilar aspects of other individuals or groups), self-attributions (the process by which people make causal inferences about their own actions), and psychological centrality (as each role a person has is called forth as a situation demands, it becomes more salient to a person's conception of self) (For a comprehensive review of these processes, see Gecas, 1982; Rosenberg, 1979; Stryker and Serpe, 1994). Working together with reflexivity, these four principles play a considerable role in the formation of one's self-concept.

Lastly there is one other element that plays a vital role in self-concept formation: the acquisition of language. This is also a significant factor—perhaps the most significant single factor—in Zen's formulations of where the self-concept originates.

It seems somewhat obvious to suggest that learning how to use language would be an essential element in the growth and development of a person's self-concept. After all, newborns have no conception of self, just as they have no innate language skills. Granted, the newborn does rely on various forms of verbal utterances and cries to draw attention to itself, but these cries are often without structure, syntax, or symbolic meaning (excluding, of course, the symbolic message of "Attend to Me **NOW!**"). The infant is nothing more than an instinctual organism which, as John Hewitt (2000: 79) confirms, has only the *capability* to acquire selfhood:

> the neonate does not yet have language, and so lacks the developed symbolic capacity necessary for self-designation. Hence, the infant neither acts towards itself as an object, nor is its behavior regulated by a dialogue between "I" and "me."

As Hewitt goes on to explain, it is only after the acquisition of language that an individual begins to develop the symbolic capacity that is necessary for self-reference. Hewitt further outlines how it is only after a child discovers that he or she has a name that the child's self-concept begins to take shape. A name, he writes (p. 80), "is a child's way of getting outside his or her own perspective and viewing [his or her] self from the perspective of others" (Brackets ours).

In the previous chapter we referred to the Sapir-Whorf hypothesis, an idea that argues that the language of an individual's native culture will shape and constrain the thoughts and actions of that person. As it is with the language of a culture, so it is with the impact that learning a language will have on one's self-concept, as the acquisition of language via the process of socialization will help to shape and constrain a person's self-concept. It is, as Meltzer, Petras, and Reynolds (1975) denote: learning how to use language causes humans to organize and pattern their thoughts, beliefs, and feelings within the context of the larger social world into which they are socialized. In other words, learning a language is really a process of mastering the symbolic environment of a society, an environment that is complete with rules and artifacts, which represent both social and cultural beliefs about the world at large (Moser, 2007).

Language also has the added benefits of allowing an individual to describe to other people the conceptualization one has of self that exists as an object within one's own mind's eye. Without the ability to symbolically communicate with others (regardless of the medium of this communication, be it written word, spoken language, bodily gestures, facial expressions, or manner of dress), an individual would not be able to express any aspects of self to others beyond those aspects that are observable in basic physicality. There would be no way to express the thoughts, emotions, and attitudes that all socialized humans hold within the realm of the mind. Thus the key to being human is to use language, as all of the symbols used by humans can only be interpreted by means of language (Hertzler, 1965).

This is not to say, as we noted in the previous chapter, that humans are the only animals on this planet that are capable of utilizing language and other forms of symbolic communication. But for many of the original social psychologists (such as James, Cooley, Mead, and Dewey, to name a few), the use of a spoken language was the elemental difference between human and non-human animals on the phylogenetic continuum (Meltzer et al., 1975). This was especially true for Mead. Echoing the Meadian perspective, Irvine (2004: 4) writes how Mead believed that

> spoken language constituted the social psychological barrier between humans and nonhumans because [Mead felt] it enables humans to understand and communicates the symbols for self, such as our names and the names of objects.... In making spo-

ken language the key to what distinguished humans from other animals, Mead (and, consequently, social psychology) established two states of consciousness: one for those who could converse about it and another, lesser form for those who could not. [Brackets ours]

The so-called "conversation of gestures" that Mead (1962) spoke of was, in his opinion, inadequate for self-awareness among non-human animals. The reasoning for his position rested upon his firmly held belief that the instinctual behaviors that animals use to communicate was an insufficient medium in which to successfully transfer the self as a symbolic object from one entity to another. Thus for Mead the lack of a symbolically-rich language was the principle factor that separated humans from other forms of life.

The Zen Position on Self

The Zen position on self is as basic to its doctrines and practice as it is to Gautama Buddha's Second Noble Truth, i.e., suffering arises from incessant desires, and to his fundamental tenet of impermanence, or *anitya*, i.e., that impermanence is the rule of all existence. A stable, consistent sense of personal selfhood held by a person is therefore an impossibility, an illusion of the mind, and an impediment to realizing Reality as it is (its *tathata*, or "thusness").

Zennists alternately refer to the self, the ego, the ego-soul, or the ego-I, but they mean the same purportedly phantasmal misconstruction. Again, the language (no doubt to have a dramatic effect) is harsh. "The ego is the dark spot where the rays of intellect fail to penetrate, it is the last hiding-lair of Ignorance, where the latter serenely keeps itself from the light" (Suzuki, 1961: 139). Soyen Shaku, a Zen Buddhist monastery abbot and lecturer/visitor in the United States during the early 1900s, put the matter of the self most forcefully to his American audiences: "I find it producing the most pernicious effects in our daily life, for the assertion of self-will, which is the root of all evil, is the logical, inevitable conclusion of the belief in the existence of a real ego-soul" (Shaku, 1993: 43). This illusion, he and others have suggested, spawns a myriad of non-stop associated problems in our lives, from pride and honor or status and privilege to avarice, invidiousness, possessiveness, relative deprivation, disappointment, insecurity, and so forth.

Thus Zen denies there is actually an entity anything like the construct of a stable self, despite the social convention of persons each believing he or she has one and social psychologists believing they are measuring it. Zen maintains the Buddhist view of "not-self" (*anatman*), that there is no such thing, however real and actual it seems to us. Indeed, Vietnamese Zen Buddhist monk Thich Nhat Hahn (1995: 38) states, "It can thus be said that the notion of not-self is the point of departure of Buddhism." He elaborates (p. 39),

> Nothing in itself contains an absolute identity.... Nothing remains the same for two consecutive *ksanas* (the shortest imaginable periods of time). It is because things transform themselves ceaselessly that they cannot maintain their identity, even two consecutive *ksanas*. Not being able to fix their identity they are not-self, that is to say, devoid of absolute identity.

In Zen the self as conceived by Western behavioral science is nonexistent, the misunderstood end-product of how our brains work in processing sense perceptions and memories. In the remainder of this chapter we examine this seemingly dismissive summary judgment by drawing on arguments of Zennists (old and recent) and non-Zennists (old and recent) to arrive at a different conclusion, exploring what we can learn from a rereading of the Zen position.

Why Do We Imagine the "Ghost" of Self?

It is important to observe that Zen distinguishes between the *relative self* (or William James' *empirical* self) of social psychology and everyday life, on the one hand, and the Absolute Self, on the other. The former relative self in Zen corresponds closely to what social psychologists call the self-concept. Absolute Self, on the other hand, has been coincident with an array of synonyms over the centuries in Zen, among them: the Void; "Mind;" Ordinary Mind; The Way; The Tao; The Ground of All Being; Reality; Ultimate Reality; the Plethora; or the Awakening or the Enlightenment one experiences in *nirvana* and *satori*. It is a larger Reality beyond the individual, but which includes the individual and is in the individual.

The "inside joke" or ironic meaning of the final two stanzas of the Homage to Bodhidharma (presented in chapter 1) is that the experience of

Direct pointing to the very soul;

Seeing into one's own essence

is that there *is no* permanent soul, essence, or self in the individual person at all beyond cultural conditioning. In Awakening one comes to realize abruptly, directly, and intuitively that there is only the Ultimate Reality, which all persons share and are a part of but not separately. Pure individuality in any meaningful sense (especially psychologically) is a colossal myth. When Zen masters exhort disciples to look into and examine their self-nature, they know successful practitioners will eventually discover that the essential or absolute personal self as fiction. There is no essential self-nature apart or separate from the web of life around us.

This doctrine of *anatman*, or not-self, was a radical Buddhist departure from the classic Hindu (Vedic) belief that each person has an *atman* or little soul that is part of the great *Atman* or Soul of the impersonal god-head Brahma. In fact, the original Buddhist emphasis on not-self was a reaction against the older Brahmanic doctrine of *atman* (personal soul) and *Atman* (Great or Universal Soul) which was so much a part of the sixth century B.C.E. Indian caste system. The idea that an everyday sense of personal identity with obvious utility because of its relative permanence, complete with memories of accumulating formative experiences, was a total illusion or without reality whatsoever would be as absurd to Bodhidharma or the Zen masters as it is to Westerners today. The fact that the relative self *has* a definable, palatable existence in social reality, with observable effects (both from self-reflection and person-other perceptions) on interactions was and is undeniable to everyone, social psychologists and Buddhists alike.

That social reality has every bit as real of an effect on human behavior as does physical reality (sometimes more) is why Zen writers for centuries have railed against it as spiritually misleading and even pernicious. And if it were not mutable, there would be no point in Zen practice. Like social psychologists, modern Zen masters know that social reality, while without permanence, has to become something to which persons are sensitized before they can be "inoculated" against its effects. That is, its relativity *as maya* (i.e., an illusion if taken for granted as permanent and unchangeable due to ignorance) has to be exposed and the results of its existence directly challenged. A permanent self is a chimera; a relative self has consequences and has to be contended with through meditation exercises and a radical reorientation of values and perspectives.

The mental aspects of social reality have always been fully appreciated by Zen teachers. Mind, as Japanese *Rinzai* Zen master Bassui claimed in the fourteenth century, is everything, the heart and secret of the Buddha's wisdom and message (Braverman, 1989: 62-65). There is the Mind of the Dharma and the mind of the person. The social world to which we respond exists, for social psychological and Zennist purposes, to a considerable extent in our heads, whether in our perceptions, hopes, fears, or even nighttime dreams. Thus, that is where Zen intervention must occur to remake our personal social realities. An absolute self, like an eternal soul, is more a theological matter. But the relative self is here and now, a practical matter affecting our perceptions, therefore our intentions, therefore our actions, therefore our niche in the Dharma. The permanent self to which classical Zen masters referred resembled more what Westerners in the Judeo-Christian tradition would consider a soul.

But we return to the Zen Buddhist claims for how we must learn to separate the relative self from the illusion that it is anything but impermanent.

Ignorance of the Buddha-Nature

Zen writings reflecting the sayings of venerable Zen masters when they "ascended to the platform" (i.e., gave a lecture, or *teisho*, in the *zendo*, or practice/lecture hall) are replete with admonishment to have no doubts about the not-self issue and relative self issues. For example:

- We say that the essence of mind is great because it embraces all things, since all things are within our nature. (Seventh century Chinese Sixth Patriarch Hui-neng—Price and Mou-lam, 1990: 80)
- Students of the Way should be sure that the four elements composing the body do not constitute the "self," that the "self" is not an entity; and that it can be deduced from this that the body is neither "self" nor "entity." (Ninth century Chinese Zen master Huang Po—Blofield, 1958: 38)
- If you want to be free, get to know your real self. It has no form, no appearance, no root, no basis, no abode.... (Ninth century Chinese Zen master Lin-chi—Cleary, 2000: 6)

The last cited Zen master Lin-chi (founder of the *Rinzai* sect of Zen) said: "the pure light in a moment of awareness in your mind is the Buddha ... the only concern is to clarify the mind to arrive at its source" (Cleary, 1994: 6, 27). The larger problem with the self-concept (i.e., myself, yourself, herself) as Lin-chi was indicating to his disciples, is that the relative self blinds us to interdependent, interwoven Reality that is as much a part of each of us as all of us are with Reality.

This quality of interwoven, mutually causative Reality is its *emptiness*, a term important in both Zen and Taoism. Emptiness does not mean a total existence devoid of anything—far from it—but rather the totality of existence minus our human logical discriminations and concepts of form. "By emptiness of things is meant principally that this existence, being so thoroughly mutually conditioned, nowhere obtains the false notion of distinctive individuality, and that when analysis is carried to its logical consequence there exists nothing that will separate one object from another..." (Suzuki, 1961: 91).

Zen is not pantheistic; however, Zennists refer to the all-inclusive ground of reality *as it is*, not as we label and denominate it, as the *Buddha-nature*. The Buddha-nature is within each of us, not merely some paltry self of our very own. The Buddha-nature is Ultimate Reality. The Buddha-nature is the source of our *prajna*, or original understanding of Reality, before the ratiocination of cultural conditioning took hold of our thinking. It is not to be revealed like some mysterious or occult wisdom or granted on the basis of grace or merit, but rather to be awakened through discipline and intuition (non-logical *bodhi*). Speaking in a sermon of this innate intuition (which he called the Unborn Buddha Mind) and the effects of socialization, seventeenth century Japanese Buddhist monk and Zen populizer Bankei said:

> ... What everyone has from his parents innately is the Buddha Mind alone. But since your parents themselves fail to realize this, you become deluded, too, and then display this illusion in raising your own children.... Originally, when you're born, you're without delusion. But on account of the faults of the people who raise you, someone abiding in the Buddha Mind is turned into a first-rate unenlightened being. (Haskel, 1984: 17)

Thus one of the most famous Zen *koans*, aimed at breaking out a person's thinking from the constraints of subject-object logic, is that of Joshu's dog, or *Mu*. Zen master Joshu (in Chinese: Chao-chou Chan-shih Yu-lu) was asked by a monk

> Does a dog have a Buddha-nature or not?
>
> The master said, "Not [*Mu*]!"

The dilemma for novitiate Zennists, of course, is that a dog is intellectually inferior to a human and seemingly incapable of Awakening, yet all sentient creatures are supposed to possess a Buddha-nature. Joshu answered "Not!" to a double-barreled question, providing no either-or logical resolution. Hence this *koan* is named *Mu* and can only be resolved by the person through *sanzen* or *dokusan*, a prolonged tutorial question-and-answer interview process with a master. The successful end result is to further *kensho*, an intermediate non-logical, non-dualistic state of sudden illumination pointing at least initially to one's "true self" or "original self" or Buddha-nature. Such *koans* are often arduously contemplated and frustrating, for the master will not accept a pat or facilely interpreted answer, and an interpretation correct for one person is not necessarily so for another.

Unawakened thinking is directly linked to the individual's taken-for-granted sense of self. Tibetan/Chinese scholar John Blofeld (1958: 17, 20-1) concurs that most persons confuse the relative self with the real self, which is the true nature of all things.... If All is One, then knowledge of a being's true self-nature—his original Self—is equally a knowledge of all-nature, the nature of everything in the universe ... the Enlightened man is capable of perceiving both unity and multiplicity without the least contradiction between them!

Alan W. Watts (1958b: 10) explains the irony of misplaced concreteness in the relative self versus the Absolute Self of which we are all part due to our inherent Buddha-nature by using the analogy of a complexly-interwoven knot of a single cord, where all the loops sticking out are not parts of separate entities (except for practical purposes of trying to untangle it). The knot seems at first as made up of the loops of many cords, but "in reality the loops are the knot, differences within identity like the two sides of a coin, neither of which can be removed without removing the other." The knot is real, the loops only apparently distinct entities.

Recognizing the authentic Buddha-nature in lieu of the imaginary relative self, then, is the meaning of the term "liberation." Says John C. H. Wu, a noted Christian translator and interpreter of Zen Buddhism in *The Golden Age of Zen* (1996: 87),

> Once you have found your true self, you are emancipated from your little ego with all its selfish interests, because the true self is one with reality and embraces all beings. In this state you can love and work in the world without being a worldling, and you can be contemplative and a hermit without being a self-enclosed and egocentric seeker of happiness.

Ignorance in Zen terms prevents freedom from the constraints of the ego, or relative self. Wu (1996: 75) states: "Self-discovery ... is the real meaning of all Ch'an," or Zen. Likewise, Daisetz Teitaro (D.T.) Suzuki (1961: 132), premier Japanese scholar and promulgator of Zen to the West, himself an awakened *Rinzai* Zennist, adds: "When Ignorance is understood in the deeper-sense, its dispelling unavoidably results in the negation of an ego-identity as the basis for all our activities." American Zennist Ezra Bayda suggests that the sense of a relative self creates for many what he calls "a substitute life," premised as it is on identity, self-image, and accompanying insecurity that together fabricate an ensuing "maze of constructs and strategies to avoid being with our life as it is" (2003: 48). And the late Roman Catholic writer-mystic Thomas Merton, in *Mystics and Zen Masters* (1967: 67) concluded the answer to this artificiality borne of ignorance:

> Zen insight is at once a liberation from the limitations of the individual ego, and a discovery of one's "original nature" and "true face" which is no longer restricted to the empirical self but is in all and above all.

The Dynamics of Attachment and the Formation of Self

The core notion by which Zen explains the rise and maintenance of the relative self is *attachment*. Ceaseless desires to obtain satisfaction by obtaining and/or preserving treasured aspects of reality result in frustration, even misery. Seventh-century Zen master Hui-neng made this issue the crux of his approach (according to Wu, 1996: 63) when he put the matter plainly:

> If we never let our mind attach to anything, we shall gain emancipation. For this reason, we take nonattachment as our fundamental principle. (Price and Mou-lam, 1990: 96)

And nowhere is the tenacious wish to grasp and hold onto an every-shifting reality more clear than with the self-concept. It is the final salient prize of attachment, which most persons imagine rests at the core of their humanity. Robert Powell, a twentieth-century British physical scientist, identified two factors that reinforce attachment to self. One is memory, or what he terms "psychological residues" (the Me of James, Cooley, and Mead) from previous experiences. Memory "get[s] revitalized when challenged by the present—giving rise to the illusion of the 'self' (which is the sum total of habitual thought patterns with which intelligence has identified itself)" (Powell, 1961: 36).

As a second factor, Powell believes current experiences trigger memories associated with the permanent thought of self, tying them to previous experiences, and the perceived continuity therein called the self is further reified. We tend therefore to take possession of, or identify with, experiences and conditions in our immediate environment as they do, indeed, have some relevance for us. He uses the example "The heat makes 'me' sweat." In this case there is identification with one's self: The "me" in the previous self-expression is "my body." So instead of thinking (or saying) "it is hot," we take possession in the first person. Or, instead of "there is suffering," we more typically say "I suffer" as a form of "owning" the situation. The relative self places us by its logic either as subject or object of much activity that otherwise is simply happening. But Powell warns: "There is only thought, and thought about a self, but that self has no absolute reality apart from being a concept in the mind."

This tendency to identify one's person, physically or socially, with experiences and objects and attach them to the self-concept was originally recognized by both James and Cooley at the inception of social scientific theorizing about the self. Consider: William James (1985:

43-4): "Between what a man calls *me* and what he simply calls *mine* the line is difficult to draw. We feel and act about certain things that are ours very much as we feel and act about ourselves.... We see then that we are dealing with a fluctuating material; the same object being sometimes treated as a part of me, at other times as simply mine, and then again as if I had nothing to do with it at all. *In its wider possible sense, however, a man's Me is the sum total of all that he CAN call his....*" [Emphasis in the original].

James then presents a list of the possible "mine" objects: house, wife and children, reputation, ancestors and family pets and livestock, "and yacht and bank account." In his earlier chapter "The Stream of Consciousness" James writes that we make this leap of attachment through "careless thinking" regarding both concrete and abstract realities, imagining a continuity from one to another. Or consider Charles Horton Cooley:

> One need only imagine some attack on his "me," say ridicule of his dress, or an attempt to take away his property or his child, or his good name by slander, and self-feeling immediately appears. Indeed, he need only pronounce, with strong emphasis, one of the self-words, like "I" or ""my" and self-feeling will be recalled by association. (1964: 172-3)

The concept of attachment also finds strong resonance in the writings of Enlightenment British philosopher David Hume. Interestingly Hume's *A Treatise of Human Nature*, first published in 1739-40, makes the same point as Zen regarding the psychological illusion of a permanent or inherent self, and for the same reasons. Hume details the process of similar *perceptions*, strung together so as to make them by mutual identification seem continuous, to consider all as belonging to the same self. To these discrete and discontinuous perceptions, analogous to still picture frames running rapidly through our thoughts like film in a motion picture projector, aided by memory of the preceding frames before each successive one, we imagine the attribution of self.

But self and identity, Hume claims, "are nothing but a bundle or collection of different perceptions, which succeed each other with an inconceivable rapidity, and are in a perpetual flux and movement" (1978: 252). The self or sense of self-identity, says Hume, is

> a propension to ascribe an identity to these successive perceptions, and to suppose ourselves possest of an invariable and uninterrupted existence thru' the whole courses of our lives (p. 253).

Our sense of sameness and stable identity derive from perceptions of objects, events, and persons that are attached to us and that thereby resemble one another with regard to the "me-ness" element. These similarities generalized across time and objects/conditions smooth mental transitions and set up the illusion of identity. In other words, we lose or overlook the reality of discreteness among all these clusters of perception. As a result,

> when we attribute identity, in an improper sense, to variable or interrupted objects, our mistake is not confin'd to the expression, but is commonly attended with a fiction, either of something invariable and uninterrupted, or of something mysterious and inexplicable, or at least with a propensity to such fictions. (p. 255)

Hume would concur with Zen that the self-concept and sense of unique personal identity are tricks of the undiscerning mind through perceptions attached by memory:

> Thus we often feign the confin'd existence of the perceptions of our senses, to remove the interruption; and run into the notion of a *soul*, and *self*, and *substance*, to disguise the variation.... 'Tis still true, that every distinct perception, which enters into the composition of the mind, is a distinct existence, and is different, and distinguishes, and separable from every other perception, either contemporary or successive. But as, not withstanding this distinction and separability, we suppose the whole train of perceptions to be united by identity, a question naturally arises concerning this relation of identity; whether it be something that really binds our several perceptions together, or only associates their ideas in the imagination. (pp. 254, 259)

There is scientific support for Hume's conceptualization of "not-self" or only a relative self in our thought processes. Belgian scientist Robert Linssen (more than a few scientists have been drawn to Zen) sees the logic of Zen Buddhism on thought processes in sympathy with modern physics. He argues that the "apparent continuity of consciousness" holds considerable affinity with the similar "appearance" of continuity in matter.

> Physics has shown that all distribution of apparently continuous energy on our usual scale of observation is, in fact, basically discontinuous. All energy is manifested by successive leaps and bounds like the second hand of a chronometer. Living organisms conquer space by "quantic" jumps. Everything that exists is prolonged in duration by quanta. (Linssen, 1958: 95)

Linssen uses the example of a straight staircase. At first (and not a close-up) glance, it is a smooth incline. But on approach it can be seen to really be successive levels of steps with discontinuity between each. He says, "The flight of stairs represents the apparently continuous movement of all phenomena, of all distributions of energy. The steps represent the process of the discontinuous climbing which is carried out by successive leap" (p. 95).

Linssen also illustrates real discontinuity/apparent continuity with a candle's flame (an old Zen example): the apparent solitary pillar of flame is actually recreated every instant, fed on thousands of millions of stearine molecules that enter into combustion with oxygen. He concludes: "The higher forms of Buddhism and Zen teach that the process of the consciousness of self is identical with this" (Linssen, 1958: 97).

The actual mental processes that produce perceptions and attached memories, in Buddhism, are the elements of the "I-process." They are termed (in Sanskrit) *skandas*. *Skandas* are:

1. material body or form;
2. sensations experienced by various organs and parts of the body;
3. tactile or visual perceptions;
4. impulses and reactions of our life will *vis-a-vis* 1-3;
5. consciousness of all of them.

These *skandas* are the literal "fuel" that permits the mind's "I-process," but, in Humesian/Zen fashion, Linssen (1958: 100) reminds us that "there is no 'thinker-entity'; but a succession of thoughts."

In sum, the conclusion about self that most persons draw, i.e., from their self-concepts and the sense that they possess essentially stable identities, which they intimately feel to be themselves, originates not just from the reinforcement others provide to them but also from the way consciousness normally works. At best the self is a part of social reality and a useful social convention. At worst it ultimately has the effect of attaching our needs, desires, anxieties, and biases to the world around us, obscuring our perception of reality as it is. In the final analysis of what the sense of self really is, however, Coomaraswamy (1943: 59) observes that it

> *is nothing but a process*; its context changes from day to day and is just as much causally determined as is the context of the body. Our personality is constantly being destroyed and renewed; there is neither self nor anything of the nature of self in the world; and all this applies to all being, or rather *becomings*.... [Emphasis mine]

A related point is that given that the self is an artifice of cognitive assembly by those mental elements such as the *skandas*, it then ought to be amenable, with diligent effort, to being *disassembled*, whether by analogy or meditation. For example, in Chapter 1 we provided Coomaraswamy's classic comparison of the chariot with *anatman* (not-self): the chariot is only considered such a vehicle or entity when its separate parts, none of which individually resembles a chariot in form or function, are put together in a specific manner. Japanese Zen Buddhist clergyman Soyen Shaku offered a similar analogy to a house: take away the component roof, beams, walls, and so forth, and there is no house except in memory and imagination. "The house did not have any independent existence outside the material whose combination only in a certain form made it possible" (Shaku, 1993: 43).

Tibetan Buddhist Sakong Mipham (2008: 19) suggests one traditional but useful mental exercise: to contemplate the term "ourself" by, through imagination, breaking the body into its separate parts and searching for the essence of "me" in each:

> Am I my hand? Am I my head? Am I my breath? Am I my blood? With this contemplation, we discover that there is no body called "me." Rather, the body is a form made up of elements.

Counselors and therapists who deal regularly with persons who have experienced organ transplants, amputations, mastectomies, and major joint replacement can appreciate the psychological readjustment of persons to such an altered "self."

Such examples are grist for mediation, and as such represent a form of "mind control." The term "mind control" received an unfortunate negative connotation during the 1970s and 1980s from the North American Anti-Cult Movement (ACM), largely due to fears that allegedly nefarious "cult" leaders were using powerful, exploitive tactics of "brainwashing" to steal literally the free will of converts to their groups. (For a comprehensive overview, see Shupe and Darnell, 2006.) It is ironic that some today would interpret the term in that negative light since classic Chinese Zen masters, such as the ninth century's Huang Po, used the same term (in Sanskrit, *sammasamadhi*) to mean mental discipline. Zennists deliberately seek to focus and develop their minds so as to free themselves from emotion-laden and untethered cascades of thought. It requires work and constant application. Mind control is a virtue and an achievement in Zen, to be cultivated for spiritual growth and the heightened awareness or liberated awakening to the reality around us (Blofield, 1958: 22-3). Moreover, mind control is a mainstay of all Buddhist (not just Zen) training, as E. H. Shattock (1958: 16), a post-world War II U.S. Navy Rear Admiral, wrote about after his experiences at a Burmese spiritual retreat. Its primary purpose, he noted, was to net and control "the butterfly mind," otherwise often referred to (unflatteringly) by Zennists as "the monkey mind."

What Self Is Really Being Measured?

The goal of Zen, in symbolic interactionist terms, is to transcend the limitations of the social reality of every culture and cognition system while not denying that social reality is expedient for daily behavior by human interactors. In this it is simply more radical in its goals than social psychology. For social psychology, understanding is an end. For Zen it is merely a means. Zen wants to cut through the cultural fabrication of it all in order to appreciate reality as it is, not interpreted, filtered, or intellectualized. And this includes interpersonal interaction as well as physical reality. That is why the Buddha, when asked what he had learned from Enlightenment, replied, "I know nothing." One cannot *know* Enlightenment, or *satori* (Awakening) through logical, analytical processes. Awakening is not a product of ratiocination. One intuits it and experiences it, without labels that could not begin to describe (much less explain) it. As Hahn (1995: 2) notes: "For in Zen, intellectual learning is nothing but the studying of the menu, while actually practice is the eating of the meal."

Yet the foregoing argument does not mean that social psychologists should or could dispense with the self-concept. The "social self" of James and "the looking-glass self" of Cooley are too ingrained and valuable a part of the discipline's professional social reality.

In sum: the relative self is ultimately the product of extremely small, discrete, chemically-produced electrical charges or nerve impulses fired via connecting synapses across neurons in the brain. Through memory these separate stimulations are associated and give rise to the appearance of continuity and an *inward* sense of self. These discontinuous changes are similar to the constant decay and renewal of cells in hair, skin, blood, tissues and so forth that lend each of us an *outward* appearance of continuity and identity. To paraphrase William James, biologically I know I am not literally, in all components, the same person today that I was yesterday, but for all practical purposes, I feel and am treated as if I am.

So, then, aside from what individuals subjectively feel to be "themselves," what are social psychologists measuring?

Consider the Twenty Statements Test (TST) found in (among other sources), *Measures of Social Psychological Attitudes* (Robinson and Shaver, 1970). The TST was developed by Kuhn and Mcpertland (1954), sociologists who were part of "the Iowa School" of symbolic interactionism (Katovich, Miller, and Stewart, 2003). The TST was designed to further George H. Mead's social behaviorist intention "to establish a theory of self that was both testable and usable," that would enhance S.I. as "a bonafide scientific enterprise" (Katovich, Miller, and Stewart, 2003: 120).

The measure is simple: at the top of a single sheet of paper is the question, "Who Am I?" and below are twenty numbered lines. Open-ended responses are supposed to be as if the person is spontaneously giving them to one's self rather than to another, and there are no instructions to prioritize identities. Answers are to be coded into one of four categories or "modes": (1) the *physical* self (looks and other such characteristics); (2) the *social* self (roles and statuses, such as student, sophomore in school, ROTC member, young woman, and so forth); (3) the *reflective* self (immediate moods, feelings, and so forth); and (4) the *oceanic* self (a broad grab-bag category for descriptions not falling into 1–3).

The TST has proven a popular measure for social psychologists because it is easy to administer and complete, has "face validity" since it allows respondents to choose their own words, and is fairly easy to code. One sociological social psychology text describes the TST with a sample form that is encouraging to students:

> One of the ways you can assess your own identity is by taking the Twenty Statements Test or TST.... Go try it now! (Rohall, Milkie, and Lucas, 2007: 131)

One double-bias of the TST is that it makes no pretense of discriminating between the "I" and the "Me," among self-presentations, or among any other of the myriad later referents to the James-Cooley self (beyond roles/non-roles and self-feelings) and that answers received are influenced by the context within which the answers are filled out. Thus, Rohall, Milkie, and Lucas (2007: 133) advise readers:

> TST results can be influenced by context. If you took it in the classroom, for example, the "student" identity might be highly salient and listed among the first few responses.

The single orienting question, "Who Am I?" is really asking respondents to provide twenty descriptions of the self component "Me" as if it were stable and attached to each respondent. Yet it is the active "I" component that does the describing. While the "I" incorporates awareness of the "Me" as past residues of "I" actions, nevertheless any reflective action called for in a measurement is performed by the "I". And the "I," whether of the variety posited by James, Cooley, or Mead, is spontaneous, dynamic, fluid, even volatile. It may be thought of as a "Me"-in-becoming, but as an "I" it is in flux. Moreover, the "I" has to act under the influences of the moment: the "Me's" past internalized judgments from significant others (past, present, or even imagined) as well as contextual pressures, situational symbolic cues, even somatic considerations of mood, emotions, discomfort, fatigue, or body temperature. No considered response to the TST about the "Me," in other words, can be found that is not hopelessly conflated or contaminated by the factors that constrain and influence the "I". What the TST is really measuring is an incredibly shifting sampling within a short period of time of feelings and perceptions held by memory. Thus the measure of self is somewhat compromised analytically.

What Zen Buddhism calls for is an examination and transcendence of the "Me" and a total embracing of the "I," which for Zennists is the Buddha-nature. Any "I" that clings to the "Me" is unawakened, soiled by dualistic thinking, and yields only a measurement of the latter elements. As a measure of the self-concept, or sense of the relative self, however, with all the James-Cooley-Mead nuancing of I's and Me's ignored, the TST does measure what social psychology and Zen should expect it generally to measure.

Conclusion

Our analysis thus far finds considerable overlap between social psychology's emphasis on the self-concept and the symbolic interactionist Me, on one hand, and Zen's relative self, on the other. (For Zen the only permanent self is a more spiritual supra-human concept of Self.) Both the social science self-concept and Zen's relative self are part of social reality, the latter a concept well-established (though not necessarily with the same terminology) in each perspective. That social psychologists have invested so much effort in studying the dynamics of how the self and self-concept are formed and influence each other reflects the subdiscipline's preponderant interest in understanding for its own scientific value, not intervention. Zen, although a descendent of heavily scholastic Mahayana Buddhism, eschews pedantic learning and is more interventionist. Zen has sought to understand the role of the self and self-concept in human lives only insofar as necessary to liberate the human mind from such cultural influences. That this is a daunting challenge Zen is well aware.

3

Attitudes and Emotions ... From Where?

If there is one concept that permeates the social psychological litera-ture more than the notion of self, it is the idea that is known as *attitude*. Indeed, of the two, attitude is the more salient of the pair since, after all, the self is considered to be made up of others' reactions or attitudes to each of us, which are then internalized and personalized to become our own attitudes toward our own persons. The study of attitudes is at least as old as the field of social psychology itself. Ajzen and Fishbein (2005: 174) point out how early sociologists (such as W. I. Thomas) and psychologists (most notably John B. Watson) originally defined the field of social psychology as "the scientific study of attitudes" because they believed that understanding attitudes was the key to discerning why a person would behave in a certain manner. In 1935 the preeminent social psychologist Gordon W. Allport (1967: 3) wrote:

> The concept of attitude is probably the most distinctive and indispensable concept in contemporary American social psychology. No other term appears more frequently in experimental and theoretical literature.

Thirty-five years later three social psychologists (Kiesler, Collins, and Miller, 1969: 1) still agreed with Allport: "The concept of attitude has played a central role in the development of American social psychology." The importance of the construct *attitude* continues for social psycholo-gists, of course, due to the key assumption of what attitudes "do." In other words, attitudes are worth studying, measuring, dissecting, and refining because they are presumed by social psychologists to be the central predictor for much of a person's behavior in the social world.

But will a particular attitude give rise to a specific behavior? Although the preponderance of the empirical evidence to date does suggest that attitudes will influence behavioral outcomes, the answer to this ques-tion often hinges on several factors, not the least of which is the point in history in which the research was conducted, the specific behavior that is being evaluated, and how a particular attitude is both conceptualized and operationalized. While each of these points will have some bearing on whether or not attitudes cause behaviors, it can be stated with a great deal of confidence that the attitude-behavior link has been solidly established within the extant research. A quick scan of the sociological and psychological literature on the relationship between behaviors and attitudes yields tens of thousands of articles, books, and other materials that, over the course of time, have come to confirm a consistent and definitive relationship between the two.

Social psychology understands the construct of attitude according to what has sometimes been called the ABC model: A for affect (emotion); B for behavior; and C for cognition. The affective dimension has experienced ebb and flow in emphasis throughout the history of social psychology (Allport, 1967: 3-6; McGuire, 1969: 136-41), but the current emphasis for the past several decades has swung to the cognitive dimension, or "cognitizing" aspects of the construct. There are signs as well, as we will indicate, that the emotional factor is once again on the ascendency in current social psychological understanding.

Much of the theoretical cultivation of the attitude construct—its fine-tuning into factor analytic dimensions, sub-varieties specified, and so forth—are, as McGuire (1969: 137) has noted, "top-heavy with conceptual elaboration, including contentious questions of definition, analyses into components, and distinctions between attitudes and related constructs." Indeed, there are a myriad of definitions of just what attitudes are. (See, e.g., McGuire, 1969: 142, for a partial but illustrative review *of* reviews of the large number of definitions even forty years ago.) Rather than engage in conceptual hair-splitting, we offer a pragmatic, generic definition that will allow this discussion to proceed: an attitude is a predisposition (rather than behavior) toward a person, object, and/or category of either, or a reasoned interpretation of self-events provided by situational cues. While generally stated, this definition, particularly the second half, may seem a bit arcane. But many social psychologists emphasize largely the first half, i.e., "incipient and preparatory" aspects of attitudes toward behavior (Mead, 1962: 5-6; Allport 1967: 8) and de-emphasize attitudes as attributions or explanations of mental views *following* feelings and subsequent behavior. Fewer adopt the latter focus (Kemper, 1981).

But regarding attitudes as something other than as preexisting states of mind, or predispositions, as we will show, forms much of the Zen emphasis and is in fact compatible with some social psychological approaches. Zen Buddhism has never tried to elaborate all the dimensions and constructs associated with attitudes as has social psychology. Rather, Zen's approach has sought to analyze *where* attitudes primarily originate, and on that basis, block them out entirely or at least short-circuit their effects on our minds. Attitudes, to Zennists, perform the same dysfunctions as relative self-concepts in distorting Reality, even contaminating the relative reality of daily social life, through presuppositions and expectations, presentiments and prejudices, fears and insecurities, ambitions and self-interests, and incomplete and lazy categorizations.

In this chapter we review the social psychological study of attitudes and narrow the focus on Zen Buddhism's approach to attitudes (which Zen does acknowledge are real phenomena in individuals' and groups' social realities). We will not address a number of issues that have consumed efforts of attitudinal social psychologists, such as how attitudes relate to one another in a person's mind (i.e., the psychological need to avoid the stress presumably caused by discrepant, inconsistent, or "imbalanced" cognitions so that they do not "collide" or create dissonance), or the defensive, expressive, and orienting functions that attitudes may serve for personalities and egos. We also bypass (for brevity's sake) considerations of how persons are persuaded to alter attitudes by messages aimed at us by mass media and other sources, attitudes associated either with pro-social interventions or aggression, group dynamics and ideologies, and so forth. Zen cuts to the mental core in starkly analyzing attitudes' sources: human emotions, where they come from, and how they distort our thinking and perception. And that will entail consideration of what social psychologists now refer to as emotion work and where the seat of emotions resides in the brain.

Attitudes versus Behavior: The Apparent False Divide and Reconciliation

In 1934 sociologist Richard LaPiere published a profoundly disturbing article in the respected journal *Social Forces* simply entitled "Attitudes versus Actions." We say that the article was "profoundly disturbing" because it challenged very directly a notion that had up to that time been routinely accepted as an article of faith by most social psychologists: that attitudes cause and predict behavior. LaPiere did not employ an elaborate sampling procedure or sophisticated statistics. He simply recounted his experiences from a car trip across the United States taken with a young Chinese couple in 1930.

During the 10,000-mile motor trip, in an era when racial segregation was legal and prejudice against Asians existed in many Western states,

LaPiere reported that the couple (with or without LaPiere present) stayed overnight in a total of 66 hotels, tourist homes, and auto-camps and were served in over 184 restaurants. Only once were they refused service (the owner declaring, "I don't take Japs!"). Six months later LaPiere contacted each of the 250-plus establishments, asking if they would provide services to a variety of types of customers (including French, Germans, Japanese, Chinese, and so forth). His results showed a major divide between what had actually transpired and what the owner-managers *said* they would do. Of the 81 restaurant-cafes and 47 overnight residences replying to LaPiere's questionnaire, 92 percent of the eateries and 91 percent of the residences said they *definitely would not serve or service* the type (Chinese) of persons they *had in fact* served or serviced.

The harsh lesson drawn from LaPiere's study (which is why it is still worth an essential mention even in undergraduate social psychology texts) is that social attitudes

> must be derived from a study of human behavior in actual social situations. They must not be imputed on the basis of questionnaire data. (LaPiere, 1934: 237)

Thereafter the attempt to bridge the apparent gap between measured attitudes and "real behavior" became a sort of "Holy Grail" quest for attitudinal social psychologists. Part of this quest became how to more accurately measure attitudes in order to bring them into line with observed behaviors. And this quest continued long after LaPiere. Over thirty years later, after thousands of attitude studies by sociologists and psychologists, noted social psychologist Martin Fishbein (1967: 477) lamented,

> It is my contention that we psychologists have been rather naive in our attempts to understand and to investigate the relationships between attitude and behavior. More often than not, we have attempted to predict some behavior from some measure of attitude and found little or no relationship between these variables.

Most significantly, Fishbein questioned the very attitude-behavior causation model: "What one should be questioning ... is the critical assumption that the behavior being considered is a function of the attitude being measured" (Fishbein, 1967: 483).

Using LaPiere's work as a starting point, other researchers from his era attempted to address what was being referred to in social psychological circles as the "attitude-behavior inconsistency problem" (Azjen and Fishbein, 2005; Schuman, 1995). In alignment with the findings of LaPiere, most of the research on the relationship between attitudes and behavior that was generated from the early 1930s through the late 1960s found that attitudes were generally poor predictors of behavioral outcomes (Deutscher, 1966; for a review of the literature during this time period, see Wicker, 1969). This led many social psychologists of the period to worry and fret about the utility of the attitude construct (Azjen and Fishbein, 2005).

In stark contrast to this earlier body of work are the overwhelming majority of studies on the connections between attitudes and behaviors that have been conducted from the 1970s to the present day. Investigations undertaken during this later period have consistently found that attitudes guide, influence, and predict a variety of behavioral outcomes. For example, a review conducted by Canary and Seibold (1984) of over 600 articles that were written between 1969 and 1984 led them to conclude that attitudes do influence an entire host of behavioral outcomes, including altruism, consumer behavior, deviance, drug and alcohol use, family planning activities, job performance outcomes, voting patterns, interpersonal relationship dynamics, and religious activities. A meta-analysis of 88 attitude-behavior studies done by Kraus (1995) demonstrated that attitudes are substantial and highly statistically-significant predictors of future behaviors, a result that dovetails with the earlier literature review compiled by Canary and Seibold. In 2005, Albarracin, Johnson, and Zanna compiled an edited volume entitled *The Handbook of Attitudes*, a volume that is replete with citations and examples of how a person's attitudes will guide, influence, and produce certain behaviors. Their volume builds on the earlier works conducted from the 1970s forward and rounds out our understanding of the attitude-behavior relationship to the present time. In the field of social psychology today, suffice it to say, there is little doubt that attitudes do in fact guide behavior.

One of the reasons why social psychologists can claim that a particular attitude will lead to a certain behavioral outcome is because researchers have become adept in defining and conceptualizing what they mean when they invoke the term attitude. Granted, the definition for the concept of attitude varies from one researcher to another (for several examples, see Jaccard and Blanton, 2005), but these differences are often small and nuanced, thus allowing for an easily aggregated definition. At its essence, an attitude is typically defined as the positive or negative evaluations an individual will express towards a particular entity or object (Eagly and Chaiken, 1993; Rohall, Milkie, and Lucas, 2007; Schuman, 1995), a definition that is similar in scope to the one we presented at the beginning of this chapter. In other words, an attitude is a cognitively-based behavioral predisposition, one that causes an individual to act in a certain way (Charon, 2004). Although the exact definition will shift as a function of which particular attitude is being examined, in general it can be said that most (if not all) of the attitudes investigated in the field of social psychology will fall under the definitional framework provided above.

Another factor that has enhanced our understanding of how attitudes influence behaviors is through the ability of modern researchers to clearly articulate what an attitude is *not*. Past theorists often confused or conflated their definitions of attitude with other concepts, such as sentiments, emotions, beliefs, opinions, and values, to name just a few. Although attitudes are, from time to time, interrelated at some level with each of the previously mentioned terms, attitude nevertheless remains an idea that is distinct from each of the other concepts. That is why Mueller (1986: 2) is correct in stating that the failure to have a precise and unambiguous definition for a concept (such as attitude) will render any scientific enterprise involving that concept fruitless. He is also correct in noting that when a person defines a concept, "its distinctiveness from, as well as its similarity to, related constructs must be articulated." Only once a particular attitude has been meticulously defined and differentiated from other concepts can one go about the business of trying to capture that concept through the process of measurement. Thus by providing a careful and explicit definition of what an attitude is (and is not), social psychologists are able to sufficiently discriminate between attitudes and other social psychological phenomena, which, as Fishbein and Azjen (1975: 5) note, is a "minimal prerequisite for the development of valid measurement procedures."

Defining what we mean when we invoke the term attitude is only one part of the job. Operationalization of this concept is another matter entirely, and when it comes to measuring something as abstract as an attitude, it is a task often easier said than done. Since the time of Louis Thurstone (1928) and Renis Likert (1932), researchers have grappled with how one goes about measuring attitudes. This is a considerably complicated issue because, by its very nature as a cognitive entity, attitudes cannot be *directly* observed or estimated, but can only be *inferred* through the process of measurement. As Henerson, Morris, and Fitz-Gibbon (1987: 11-12) eloquently state, measuring an attitude is not a straightforward proposition:

> To begin with, the concept of attitude, like many abstract concepts, is a creation [or] a construct.... An attitude is not something we can examine and measure in the same way we examine the cells of a person's skin or measure the rate of her heartbeat. *We can only infer that a person has attitudes by her words and actions.* [Italics theirs]

Attempting to estimate something that cannot be directly observed would seem, at first blush, to be a non-starter when conducting any scientific activity. After all, without the ability to accurately produce sound measurements, "empirical science is a vacuous endeavor" (Maxim, 1999: 201). Yet it is equally foolish to abandon all attempts to measure attitudes simply because researchers (at this time) cannot directly observe a cognition. Unless (or until) we can peer inside a human skull and precisely identify where a particular cognition is lurking with a specific neural fiber of the brain, we must use cruder methods to estimate what a person is thinking. Hence social psychologists often rely on scales, indices, and questionnaires when attempting to measure the so-called "latent concept" known as attitude.

This is not to say that the use of an approximating (rather than precise) method for attitude estimation is completely unsatisfactory. Quite the opposite is true, especially in light of the fact that there have been multiple and significant advances in the measurement of latent concepts since the times of Thurstone and Likert. One advancement is the recognition that attitudes are often multidimensional in nature; therefore, to successfully capture an attitude, respondents must often fill out a multiple indicator scale (Maxim, 1999). Progress in the field of reliability assessment for the scales that are used to measure attitudes has also strengthened the ability of a researcher to ensure that an attitude scale is relatively free of systematic bias (Zeller and Carmines, 1980). But it is the advances in statistical modeling procedures, most especially in the field of structural equation modeling, that have produced the greatest gains in estimating latent concepts such as attitudes. This last point can be best explained by considering the following equation:

$$Y = T + e$$

In this formula, Y equals the observed score of a variable, T equals the true score of a variable and e represents any form of error present in the measurement model. Since Spearman (1910) first discussed the logic behind this equation, it has appeared in numerous sources (Alwin, 1995; Gulliksen, 1950; Krosnick, Judd, and Wittenbrink, 2005; Maxim, 1991; Zeller and Carmines, 1980) and is most often used today to represent the measurement of a latent concept. As Maxim (1999) outlines, we can alter the above formula in the following manner without significantly changing the basic principle of the equation:

$$Y = F + e$$

In this second equation, F represents the true score of a latent concept, such as an attitude. Continuing with the logic of Maxim, let us further modify this equation by including the parameter λ, and let us set λ to equal a value of 1. Given these modifications, we can rewrite the equation (without significantly changing the nature of the equation[1]) as follows:

$$Y = \lambda F + e$$

Because most (if not all) attitudes are captured through the use of multiple indicator scales, it is advantageous to disaggregate this equation into its constituent parts. In agreement with Bollen (1989) and Maxim (1999), we find that the above equation can be restated as:

$$Y_1 = \lambda_1 F + e_1$$

$$Y_2 = \lambda_2 F + e_2$$

$$Y_k = \lambda_k F + e_k$$

In this series of equations, each subscript represents a different indicator used to estimate the latent concept under scrutiny, with the kth parameter being the final indicator in the series of items on the scale questionnaire. Graphically we see in Figure 2 that our disaggregated equations can be expressed as a single structural equation model[2].

There is one other factor that must be considered in Figure 2. It is possible that the error terms may be correlated, with any correlation among the error terms being produced either as an artifact of the manner in which the attitude questionnaire was designed (Maxim, 1999; Tourangeau, Rips, and Tasinki, 2000) or as a result of collinearity among scale indicators (McClendon, 1994). As a result of this new understanding, the graphic in Figure 2 can be modified accordingly, as in Figure 3.

The articulation of this type of measurement model strengthens the ability of a researcher to capture the latent concept of attitude he or she wishes to measure for three distinct reasons. First, the ability to more precisely estimate the amount of error associated with each individual indicator of an attitude, as well as the ability to account for any potential

Figure 2

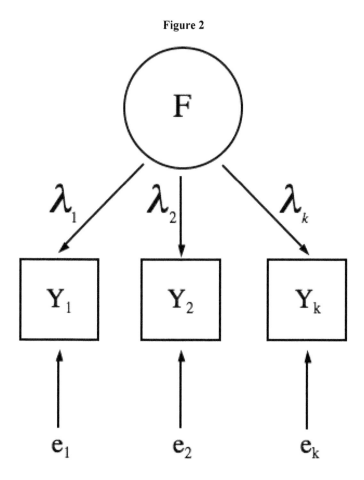

covariation among the error terms, allows for a fuller approximation of the total amount of error variance present within a measurement model. It is, as Bollen (1989) insists: without a better estimate of error, a researcher will have a poorer assessment of the latent concept in question.

The second reason is related to the first insofar as both reasons stem from ongoing advances in statistical modeling. From the late 1960s forward, social psychologists have been creating increasingly complex measurement models to represent a given attitude. One reason why researchers have been able to do this is because of the expanding utilization of advanced mathematical techniques (such as regression, factor analysis, and structural equation modeling) in the field of social psychology. This ever-increasing use of elaborate mathematical techniques by social psy-

Figure 3

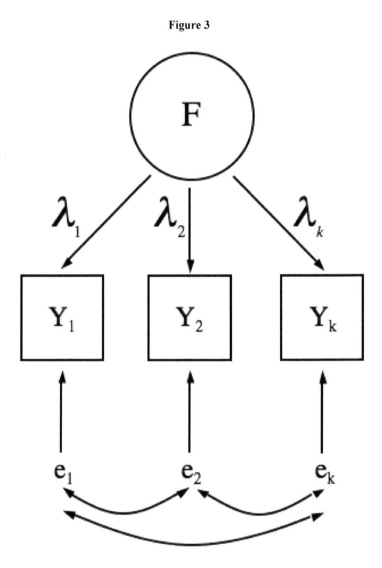

chologists is in turn due to the widespread availability of easy-to-use yet sophisticated statistical software packages, such as SAS, LISREL, EQS, and STATA, to name a few. Many of these software packages first became widely accessible to academics in the late 1960s and early 1970s, which is about the same time that social psychologists began to consistently find significant relationships between attitudes and behavior.

An example of how statistical software packages and advanced mathematical modeling combine to assist the modern process of attitude measurement can be seen in Figure 4 below. This figure is a graphical representation of a confirmatory factor analysis undertaken by Dorman (2001) to validate a 30-item questionnaire that assesses six different

Figure 4

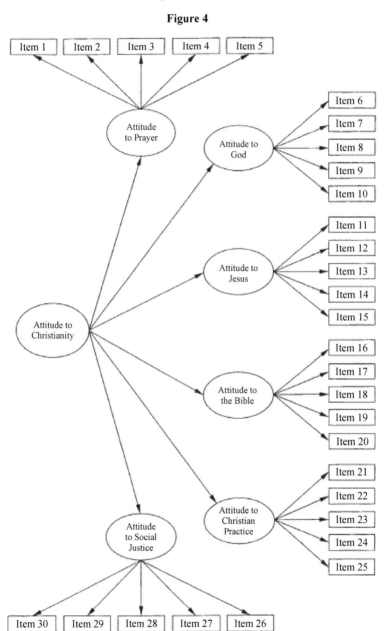

dimensions of attitude toward Christianity.[3] As Figure 4 demonstrates, attitude toward Christianity is not a monolithic concept; rather, it is a multidimensional attitude, one that cannot be effectively (or anywhere near accurately) captured through the use of a simple summated scale. Most of the instrumentation used today to measure attitudes is similar in scope to Figure 4, as most current measurement questionnaires often include indicators that can be factor analyzed into several subcomponents, with each subcomponent being reflective on a different dimension of the overarching attitude being measured. Thus it is the ability of advanced statistical modeling procedures, like factor analysis, that provides the means by which social psychologists are better able to measure attitudes.

This last line of thought brings us to the final reason why a measurement model of the type being currently discussed is effective in articulating the latent concept known as attitude: the recognition that attitudes are often multidimensional in nature. Granted, this recognition has existed since Spearman (1904) first developed factor analysis as a method to estimate latent concepts such as attitudes. However, early social psychologists were somewhat hampered in their ability to statistically identify the exact nature of a multidimensional attitude in any meaningful way, mostly because of the time and effort it took to hand-calculate a factor analysis. As such, the early tradition within social psychology for measuring attitudes became one of either using a unidimensional summated scale comprised of a limited number of questions to represent a specific attitude, or worse, involved the researcher's guesstimating which items of a scale represented a given dimension of a given attitude. This tradition (which was relatively widespread in the field of social psychology prior to the 1970s) of forgoing the use of complicated statistical procedures to articulate the multidimensional structure of an attitude was, in all likelihood, the key factor that contributed to the inability of early attitude researchers to find a consistent relationship between attitudes and behaviors. Conversely, the abundance of investigations that have taken place from the 1970s on have time and again found relationships between attitudes and behaviors specifically because of the use of advanced modeling techniques.

The Zen Perspective on Attitudes and Behavior

Something on which all Zen Buddhists and social psychologists would seem to agree, at least at first glance, is the notion that attitudes belong to the mind, i.e., are mental phenomena. Zennists, like most Buddhists, however, can mean several things by the word "mind." Some classical

Chinese Zen masters like Ma-Tsu employed the term "True Mind" or "Original Mind" or "Ordinary Mind" to mean the pure Awakened state of *prajna* in which culturally based discriminations and labels do not enter into perception (Bhikshu, 1992: 14-29); whereas one of his disciples, Huang Po, used Mind somewhat similarly to refer to the "inexpressible Reality beyond the reach of conceptual thought" (Blofeld, 1958: 18).

Indeed, the upper and lower-case words Mind and mind appear throughout the Buddha's discourses, meaning either the relative thinking mind that each of us uses to operate in daily life or the Eternal Mind, i.e., the Tao of Lao-Tzu. The relative mind reference is the way in which the term is used in the *Lankavatara-sutra*, compiled in the late fourth century and one of the two Indian Buddhist scriptures (the other *The Diamond Sutra*) most influential in the history of Zen (Sutton, 1991: 202-04). That is, the world that our relative minds apprehend is just that: a limited, culturally-relative as-apprehended world, not Reality beyond ratiocination centuries ago. In other words, Zennists appreciated an understanding similar to the formula $Y = T + e$ presented earlier. The seventh century's Hui-neng, Sixth (and last) Zen Patriarch, used the term *mushin* (in Chinese, *wu-hsin*) to mean "no-mind," i.e., the lack of conceptual dualism needed to transcend ordinary subject-object limitations when perceiving the social and physical realities around us. In *The Zen Doctrine of No-Mind*, D.T. Suzuki (1972: 122) summarizes: "To attain *mushin* means to recover, objectively speaking, the *prajna* of non-discrimination."

Most importantly, Zen vigorously eschews dualism in all our thinking. With *prajna*, or in the meditative state of *samadhi*, a distinction is not drawn between the worlds outside or inside of us, or between our perceptions (as mental activities) and our grosser bodily actions. All mental events, or thoughts, or consciousness of affect are therefore behaviors as real in their phenomenal existence as chopping wood, driving a car, or pounding a nail with a hammer. They are the results of real electrochemical behavior cellular brain processes. For Zen, to have and experience a thought is as much a behavior as one actually writing about it at this moment. To see our actions as set apart from our thoughts, as if the latter exist on some rarified separate level, is dualistic and un-Realistic. As American Zennist Steve Hagen (2003: 147) observes,

Mind is basic, Mind is primary. Mind is ever-present in each situation. For anything to be happening in *this moment*, Mind is necessarily present. Mind is the basis for *this*, for what's going on *now*.

For Zen, mental events must be treated the same as actions, or physical events. Indeed, Japanese Zennist Katsuki Sekida (1985: 123) claims, based on the law of karma, that "Thoughts are a kind of behavior." If so, then the *apparent* Zen position is that all mental phenomena are behaviors, thus rendering the entire social psychological attitude-behavior issue moot. But it is not that simple. Social psychologists can agree to split the difference and concur (or concede) that, yes, thoughts can be seen as "a kind" of behavior, but thoughts are also a qualitatively *different form* of behavior that needs to be gauged with uniquely appropriate techniques, especially when juxtaposed against other behaviors that can be observed or measured through grosser motor actions. Zen never embraced nor even envisioned Western scientific methods and analytic techniques for observing/estimating such mental activities (nor has it ever tried). Neuroscientist and medical doctor James H. Austin, author of the remarkable voluminous collection of findings on Zen meditation and its effect on brain functions entitled *Zen and the Brain* (1999) has commented that "Zen enters not through words but through experience (p. xx) and (written tongue in cheek) reminds us "Zen doesn't get preoccupied with such scientific flappings of the mind" (p. 6). Saying that mental events (thoughts and so forth) are ultimately behaviors every much as overt physical actions may be generically correct, but it dodges their qualitative differences of type and motor level.

For example, in social psychology's attempts to operationalize attitudes it was once popular to use such measures as pupil dilation and skin temperature as reactions (or dependent variables) in studies of racial tension (ex., Mueller, 1970; Porier and Lott, 1970; Woodmanseee, 1970). One could consider such responses of the autonomic nervous system as behaviors, indeed subtle ones, but physiologically and psychologically they cannot meaningfully be considered in the same way as cognitive, kinetic, verbal, written, or some other more deliberate responses.

But there is an important dimension of an attitude—its emotional valence, or simply emotion—that we have not introduced thus far. Social psychology now has an appreciation of the origins and dynamics of emotions that Zen Buddhism, lacking physiological and brain autonomy knowledge, has never had. Put another way, readers will see that Zen, with its interventionist interests to simply stifle and control the influence of attitudes on the mind, has always worked more at the "street level" of cognition while social psychology can now benefit from neurological research to delve into more "subterranean" strata behind the ABC attitude formulation.

One possible way to resolve much of the issue of an apparent divide between attitudes and behaviors is to view the issue in situational social exchange, or cost/benefit terms. To anticipate this alternative interpretation: different situations present varying costs to an actor if an attitude is to be displayed. Consider the following vignette:

A young bachelor, engaged to be married, lives alone in his apartment. He does not particularly care for the taste of asparagus. Given the choice of side-vegetables with his entrees at restaurants, he does not order it. He never buys asparagus fresh or canned at the supermarket. Yet when he visits his fiancee's home for the first time, and his future mother-in-law serves asparagus (according to a special family recipe, she announces), he takes some, eats it, and tells her it is delicious. Is he a hypocrite? A liar? Why is his behavior at the dinner so inconsistent with what one presumes is his real attitude toward asparagus?

The answer is obvious: the social cost of not buying or ordering asparagus when he is out is very low. There are many other options for him. But in his fiancee's parents' home, where he does not want to embarrass the hostess or himself, the social cost to refuse to take or eat the asparagus (or even to express his indifference to it) is much higher. His sentiments regarding asparagus are not strong enough to cause a mild scene. Put another way, the social cost to express his mild anti-asparagus affect in a restaurant or store has a low threshold; as a guest in a special someone's home the cost-threshold is higher.

But imagine a second scenario. From past experience the young man knows he has a severe allergic reaction to asparagus in the same way some people are deathly allergic to peanuts. After eating it his throat will constrict until he has difficulty breathing, his lips will swell and turn purple, and red blotchy hives will break out across his face and body. The social cost of saying nothing and eating the asparagus could result in a trip to a hospital emergency room! Now the cost threshold for *not* refusing the asparagus is higher than the cost to create a brief awkward moment for the hostess and quick apologies all around. The costs of revealing his true sentiments regarding asparagus are not uniform with the first scenario.

Thus the social costs to engage in the same behavior (refusing the asparagus) differ by the social circumstances. We would not expect the two behaviors (refuse/not refuse) to be uniform unless both the sentiments and social circumstances were similar. LaPiere was getting at this point in his study. The cost of a server-manager providing negative answers in the abstract on a pencil-and-paper questionnaire about various minorities is much less than when confronting a minority couple in the flesh with money in hand. The inconsistencies in the Chinese couple/asparagus examples could be seen as not of attitudes versus behaviors but of behaviors under very different social circumstances, with different pressures and consequences. There is a divide among the various circumstances within which a behavior will or will not occur, not a divide between attitudes and behaviors.

Considered another way, this cost/benefit model is really just an example of what was discussed earlier in the previous section regarding latent concepts and multidimensional defining of attitudes, i.e., refinements about the way social psychologists conceptualize attitudes. Earlier methods of measuring attitudes with only a relatively few items now seems imprecise or downright crude. To deduce an attitude from (in hindsight) rather superficial observations made by a witness to the above dinner scenario without more information about the young man's dining (and health) predispositions would either cause confusion at the so-called attitude-behavior discrepancy or perhaps lead one to abandon the value of attitude study altogether.

Zen, Emotions, and Attitudes

Attitudes historically have been somewhat slippery (i.e., imprecise) constructs; emotions which make up (according to the ABC model) important parts of attitudes have seemed slipperier still. The late nineteenth century's William James (1985: 240) put the matter succinctly:

> As inner mental conditions, emotions are quite indescribable. Description, moreover, would be superfluous, for the reader knows already how they feel. Their relations to the objects which prompt them and to the reactions which they provoke are all that one can put down in a book.

Worse, adds James, "Their internal shadings merge endlessly into one another ..." (p. 241).

This is undoubtedly why, in opinion polling and attitude measurement, despite the plethora of scales and statistical formats for gauging attitudes (from the classic Guttman, Bogardus, and Thurstone varieties to the more sophisticated factor analytic technique used in the development of Semantic Differential scaling), the most common, efficient, and durable type of scale used is that created by industrial psychologist Renis Likert (1967, 1970). A Likert-format scale calls for a simple range of agreement/disagreement responses to an attitude statement: strongly agree, agree, neutral, disagree, strongly disagree, with respective points 5, 4, 3, 2, 1 awarded to each response. (Or the order of approval/disapproval can be reversed, and researchers who want to force respondents to take positive or negative positions can delete the "neutral" option.) In this way a fairly large number of attitude statements can be presented and answered in a reasonably short period of time.

The Likert scale, statistically speaking, is an ordinal scale, measuring rough indications of the reactive emotional valence, or strength, to any statement, such as "Belief in Jesus Christ as personal savior is the only way a person may have eternal life." As James reiterated, emotions are, after all, difficult to pin down. The advantage of the Likert scale is that it does not try to over-quantify or over-specify amounts of feeling. It gauges feeling/reactions at only a "more-or-less" extent, which corresponds to thinking in everyday life. (If you say you are "mad as hell," is that 1.5 or 2.5 times more emphatic than just "mad?" Of course, to apply decimals to rough emotional amounts would be pseudo-precision.)

Likewise, in expressing emotions human beings often employ deliberately unspecified, immeasurable metaphors and similes to suggest intensity of feeling. Thus we might hear the following dialogue:

She: Harry, do you love me?

Harry: Oh, yes! I love you!

She: How much do you love me?

Harry: My love for you is higher than the highest mountain (or alternately: deeper than the deepest ocean).

It would cheapen (even ruin) the expressed sentiment if Harry were to try to be more precise than these ordinal amounts (say, if he replied, "My love for you is at least 12.5 meters below the deepest point in Lake Erie," or "My love for you is 1.5 kilometers higher than the peak of Mt. McKinley."). Such sentiments are not supposed to have quantifiable limits. As an early attempt, the Likert scale respects the "slipperiness" of the emotional component of attitudes by settling for rough estimates of attitude intensity.

The James-Lange Hypothesis

The word *emotion* derives from the root of the Latin verb "to move out or away, to expel" (*emoveo, emovere, emovi, emotum*), and in fact, emotions *are* vital, action-oriented. Most persons correctly think of emotions as stimulating many of their thoughts, actions, and even other emotions in a chain reaction effect.

During the early years of the twentieth century William James and another psychologist, C. G. Lange, independently proposed the origins and influence of emotions on attitudes in a unique form that has come to be called the *James-Lange hypothesis*. Simply put, a three-step process in the awareness of emotions is involved:

1. some stimulus (an injury, sensation, or a perceptual cue in the environment) acting on a person
2. is immediately followed by a physiological or somatic reaction
3. which is then cognitively processed and interpreted by the person as an emotion.

In this short process emotions are the *interpreted outcomes* of physiological stimuli. As two modern social psychologists (DeLamater and Myers, 2007: 253) have elaborated: "The physiological component of the emotional experience (for example, increased blood pressure) helps us to identify the emotion (anger) rather than anger causing the physiological change." What influences *which* possible self-constructed interpretation occurs are other elements, often interpersonal ones, in the immediate social situation. Thus the James-Lange hypothesis stands the role that emotions are usually thought to play in attitudes on its head.

The James-Lange formulation is worth examining here for several reasons. First, it corresponds closely with the Zen interpretation of attitudes and emotions (and portends how to "tag" and defuse their influence on our thinking). Second, it has some roots in Western philosophy. Third, there is a body of evidence in modern social psychology that corroborates somewhat the James-Lange and Zen approaches.

Zen, the Thought Impulse, and Thought Labeling

Emotions, particularly destructive and harmful (to one's inner person and to others) ones, constitute a major issue in Zen as well as in all Buddhism. Daniel Goleman (2003: xxviii), a Harvard science doctorate and journalist, writes: "The Buddhist tradition has long pointed out that recognizing and transforming destructive emotions lies at the heart of spiritual practice – indeed, some hold that whatever lessens destructive emotions *is* spiritual practice." [Emphasis in original.] Matthieu Ricard, a French genetic biologist who earned his doctorate at the Pasteur Institute in Paris during the late 1960s and went on to become a Tibetan monk, says that often destructive, or what he terms "obscuring," emotions are pernicious because such emotional states impair one's judgement, the ability to make a correct assessment of the nature of things ... obscuring emotions impair one's freedom by chaining thoughts in a way that compels us to think, speak, and act in a biased way. (Cited in Goleman, 2003: 75-6)

Much of the obscuring is the result, according to Zen, of attachment to the illusion of a permanent self, and what is imagined to be in the best narrow interest of the relative self becomes the implicit personal standard for the attitudes we adopt. As Ricard concludes, "So attachment means clinging to one's way of perceiving things" (Cited in Goleman, 2003: 75-76).

Katsuki Sekida, a twentieth-century Japanese Soto Zen master who pragmatically integrated *Rinzai's koan* study with *Soto's* breathing-meditation exercises, wrote a classic modern manual on the methods and philosophy of meditation entitled *Zen Training* (1985). The central theme running throughout the book is that Zen practitioners, trying to cope with the constant stream of emotions and related thoughts that arise unbidden during meditation, will better find success if they can reflectively and immediately dissect these thoughts to see their origins and functions. Sekida writes (1985: 108):

Man thinks and acts without noticing. When he thinks "It is fine today," he is aware of the weather but not of his own thought. It is the reflecting action of consciousness that comes immediately after the thought that makes him aware of his own thinking. The act of thinking of the weather is an outward-looking one and is absorbed in the object of its thought. On the other hand, the reflecting action of consciousness looks inward and notes the preceding action that has just gone by, wrapped up in thinking of the weather—still leaving its trace behind as the direct past. By this reflecting action of consciousness, man comes to know what is going on in his mind...

What is implied in this quote is a reflective process, remarkably like that of the James-Lange hypothesis, employing the Japanese concept of *nen* which Sekida translates as "thought impulse." In Japanese *nen* has several related meanings, among them a thought as well as a sense, notion, or feeling. Thus Sekida's *nen* as thought impulse is synonymous in its "slipperiness" with what social psychologists regard as emotion or affect.

Sekida's *nen* model (elaborated specially in pp. 108-27 in his book) is a non-cursive or one-way progression of reflective self-awareness of emotions:

The first *nen* is the visceral sensation itself, the pure physical-mental reaction from a stimulus.

The second *nen* is the awareness that *something* has been felt.

The third *nen* is becoming further observant of one's initial awareness of that initial sensation (first and second *nens*).

In other words, there is the raw or pure experience of an emotion, then an awareness of it, and lastly a cognitizing or interpretation in one's mind as to what the first two levels *mean*. In Sekida's words: "Thus any given third nen presents in itself all the previous nen" (p. 112). Sekida provides an impressively worked out set of diagrams to illustrate what he (and social psychologists) term a unified, integrated stream of consciousness, third *nen* interpretations constantly encountering and subsuming other third *nen* interpretations (as well as the first and second *nen* levels of each third *nen*), like the spreading branches of a tree. Says Sekida (1985: 122-31),

> Every moment you are creating yourself; your thought is of your own making, and it affects all your succeeding thoughts ...

It is also possible to conceive of further abstracting the *nen*-levels of reflection at fourth, fifth, and further levels, as when one has to make a more public professing or historical accounting of how one recalls the first few *nen*-levels, say from a courtroom's witness chair, in a face-to-face interview concerning attitudes, or under the glare of an angry boss or spouse after some transgression. (In social psychology this is usually termed constructing a narrative of events.)

Sekida's three-step reflective *nen*-interpretation process is an independent schema parallel to the James-Lange formulation. However, Zennists, as we have observed, have an additional, distinctly-applied interest: how to understand the origins and mental processing of emotions so as to anticipate and vitiate their influence on perception and intuition. American Zen writer Ezra Bayda, for example, advocates accomplishing this end by the process he terms "thought labeling" as described in his book *Being Zen* (2002). Rather than enduring the frustration of trying to block emotions during meditation (particularly hurtful ones), Bayda's thought labeling basically works backward down the *nen*-levels of Sekida's model by asking the question of the intruding affective thought, "What *is* this?" By probing through the appearance in consciousness of thoughts back to their first raw, unfiltered level, by examining the first sensation of each emotion and re-experiencing its awareness *at this moment* in all its fullness of feeling, such emotions may not disappear but it is possible that "we hold them much more lightly" (p. 28). Says Bayda (p. 42):

> Learning to stay with—to reside in—our emotions in this way allows us to see how most of our emotional distress is based on our conditioning, and particularly on the decisions and beliefs that arose out of that conditioning. We come to see that these emotional reactions—which we often fear and prefer to avoid—amount to little more than believed thoughts and strong or unpleasant physical sensations. We can see that

when we are willing to experience them with precision and curiosity, we no longer have to fear them or push them away.

Bayda compares asking the "What *is* this?" question to pondering a Zen *koan* because there is no way the answer can come from thinking about your experience. "It can only come from actually experiencing it" (p. 36). Which is another way of saying the "answer" must be a product of intuitive insight, or *bodhi*. There is also a liberating effect of such probing in that thought labeling helps one to "break out" of the relative self tendency to identify with one's thoughts, no matter how negative, and literally hold onto them like possessions.

Other Buddhists (not just Zennists) concur independently with the James-Lange/Sekida sensation-awareness-emotion definition process. His Holiness Tenzin Gyatso, the fourteenth Dalai Lama of Tibet, has said in lecture:

> Sensory cognitions are considered to be nonconceptual; their engagement with the object is unmediated by language or concepts. They are also said to be more direct and nondiscriminating.... In comparison to the feeling or sensation in the realm of the senses, the feeling in the realm of the mental is thought to be of greater significance from the Buddhist point of view. Evaluative judgements ... take place at the mental, conceptual level as opposed to the sensory ... we are talking about activity in the realm Buddhists call discursive thought. (Cited in Goleman, 2003: 89)

Paul Ekman, a psychologist and recognized expert on emotions at the University of California at San Francisco Medical School, observes how subtle the James-Lange/Sekida three-step type of process of emotion construction/labeling can be:

> ... one of the things we say that distinguishes emotion from other mental phenomena is that an emotion can occur very quickly. It can begin in a fraction of a second.... A second distinguishing aspect is automatic appraising. The evaluation that turns on an emotion happens so quickly that we are not aware it is occurring.... We typically become aware that we are afraid, or angry, or sad, after the emotion begins, not before ... people feel as if emotion happens *to* us. (Cited in Goleman, 2003: 132)

And other Western Buddhists advocate the Bayda approach of confronting, even re-experiencing an intense emotion analytically to militate its corrosive and perhaps debilitating effect on our thinking. For example, Tibetan monk Ricard, cited above, stresses introspectively questioning the source of one's anger:

> One classical approach in Buddhist practice is for the meditator to look straight into the anger ... the more you look at anger, the more it disappears beneath one's very eyes, like the frost melting under the morning sun. When one genuinely looks at it, it suddenly loses its strength.... It is a collection of events.... It is the [self] grasping associated with one's tendencies that leads to a chain reaction in which the initial

thought develops into anger, hatred, and malevolence. (Cited in Goleman, 2003: 139) [Brackets ours]

Interestingly, modern Zennists' methods for analyzing and dealing with emotions, particularly the unpleasant varieties, are somewhat reformulations of earlier eras. For example, the popular but iconoclastic Zen monk Bankei, who lived in seventeenth century Japan during a reform-minded resurgence of Zen Buddhism, preached that persons should not struggle to shut out emotion-laden thoughts that plague them. Rather, he advised confronting and "dwelling" in them to defuse their affect intensity. Bankei once said in a lecture to both monks and lay persons:

> [If] ... you people try to stop your thoughts of anger and rage, clinging and craving from arising, then by stopping them you divide one mind into two. It's as if you were pursuing something that's running away. As long as you deliberately try to stop your rising thoughts, the thought of trying to stop them wars against the continually arising thoughts themselves, and there's never an end to it. Even if suddenly, despite yourself and wholly unawares, rage or anger should appear, or thoughts of clinging and craving arise, just let them come—don't develop them any farther, don't attach to them. (Haskel, 1984: 50)

There is a continuity in Zen teachings, not out of some theological dogma but because of experiential practicality.

David Hume, Impressions, and Ideas

Certainly others have tried to understand the role played by emotions in the dynamics of conscious thought and perception besides Zennists (who admittedly have their own practical reasons). One interesting parallel to the *nen*-level model of Zen Roshi Katsuki Sekida can be found in *A Treatise of Human Nature* by the mid-eighteenth-century British philosopher David Hume. We cited this book liberally in the previous chapter on the self-concept and turn to it again on the subject of attitudes. Hume was unquestionably a proto-social psychologist, and his marvelous book spans a vast number of subjects concerned with the scientific method and human behavior. That his insights, formed over a century before anything resembling modern psychology had begun to coalesce, have proven so prophetic is testimony to his powers of observation and deduction.

Hume's language reads a bit archaic but at the same time lays out his arguments in a straightforward manner. Briefly, Hume saw the relation of emotional arousal and stimulation (what he termed "impressions") to interpretations of the latter (becoming his "ideas" or our "attitudes") as follows:

Since it appears, that our simple impressions are prior to their correspondent ideas, and that the exceptions are very rare, method seems to require we should examine our impressions, before we consider our ideas.... An impression first strikes upon the senses, and makes us perceive heat or cold, thirst or hunger, pleasure or pain of some kind or other. Of this impression there is a copy taken by the mind, which remains after the impression ceases; and this we call an idea. This idea of pleasure or pain ... produces the new impressions of desire and aversion, hope and fear, which may properly be called impressions of *reflexion*, because derived from it ... the impressions of *reflexion* are only antecedent to the correspondent ideas. (Hume, 1978: 7-8) [Emphasis ours]

Hume goes on to discuss at length the scientific method, reliably ascertaining cause and effect, and this continuity of ideas with each other. Then he introduces the transition that "... when any impression becomes present to us, it not only transports the mind to such ideas as are related to it, but likewise communicates to them a share of its force and vivacity" (p. 98). Most importantly, Hume describes Sekida's third *nen*, i.e., when an emotional mood, or "disposition," is now sensed and an interpretation of the original sensation must be reflected upon, made sense of, or cognitized. This is done *via* objects and relevant stimuli in the immediate social situation that provide or suggest explanations:

Now 'tis evident the continuance of the disposition depends entirely on the objects, about which the mind is employ'd; and that any new object naturally gives a new direction to the spirits, and change the disposition; or on the contrary, when the mind fixes constantly on the same object, the disposition has a much longer duration. *Hence it happens, that when the mind is once inliven'd by a present impression, it proceeds to form a more lively idea of the related objects, by a natural transition of the disposition from the one to to the other.* (1978: 98-99) [Emphasis ours]

In other words, impressions or emotional arousal lead to reflective interpretations of it, which in turn can be influenced by relevant (or seemingly relevant) cues in the immediate social environment of the person. All three Zen *nen*-levels are there in Hume's three-step model: pure experience of the physiological arousal, conscious awareness of it, and cognitive attribution of the source of the feeling.

All this represents more than just a curious parallel of the emotions-attitudes relationship drawn independently by two very different students of the human mind. It is also very relevant to one aspect of attitude formation in modern social psychology.

Modern Social Psychology, Cognitive Labeling Theory, and Emotion Work

As William James observed in the 1890s, emotions are imprecise. Yet they are knowable (or realizable) even if we cannot realistically quantify their intensities any better than at the ordinal ("more than" or "less than") level. Something in our mental makeup allows us to recognize emotions in ourselves and, through empathy (which in large part is an interpersonal ability learned through socialization and practiced in primary and secondary groups) experience them vicariously in actors. It might seem surprising that some persons (such as violent male partners in heterosexual intimate relationships) are sometimes inept at recognizing such primal emotions as building rage and anger, but even that lack of inner awareness is primarily a skills deficit amenable to remedy (See Shupe, Stacey, and Hazlewood, 1987; Stacey, Hazlewood, and Shupe, 1994).

In most cases, personal emotions are considered as fundamentally "ours" or a part of "us" physically as they are of our social "selves." We assume we ought to be able to read the inner signs for "how we feel" every bit as much as we know "who we are."

The social psychology of emotions has been advanced since the era of the pioneer William James. At its core, an emotion starts off as a biological reaction in the brain to some form of stimuli received from the external world (Massey, 2002). The exact stimulus is immaterial. What is important to elucidate is in which of the various structures of the brain an emotion originates. It has been suggested (Cytowic, 1996; MacLean, 1990; Massey, 2002; Panksepp, 1998) that the human brain can be divided into three overarching general structures: the basal ganglia (or reptilian brain), the limbic system (or mammalian brain), and the neocortex (or neomammalian brain). Figure 5 on page 95 illustrates these three different components areas.[4]

As Massey (2002) eloquently states, nature is conservative: it does not create from scratch what is needed, but rather adds what is necessary onto what already exists. So it is with the human brain, which over the course of millions of years of evolution has developed these three distinct layers of neural anatomy. The basal ganglia developed first, followed by the limbic system and then the neocortex. When expressed another way, we find that the instinctual areas of the brain developed first, followed by the emotive regions, and then the rational cognition centers.

In Figure 5 the amygdala is highlighted. Current advances in the field of social cognitive neuroscience suggest that this structure is the seat of emotional awareness and emotional memory (Cardinal, Parkinson, Hall, and Everitt, 2002; Davis, 1992; Ochsner and Lieberman, 2001; Phelps, 2004). Research in neuroscience also shows how an external stimulus is perceived, assessed, and acted upon by the amygdala up to one-fourth of a second faster than any of the structures contained in the neocortex

Figure 5

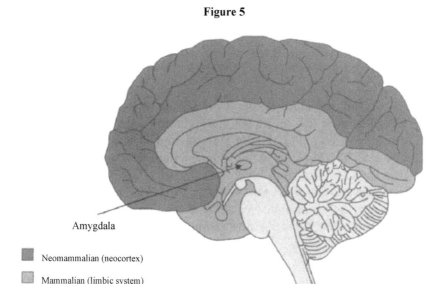

Amygdala

Neomammalian (neocortex)

Mammalian (limbic system)

Reptilian (basal ganglia)

(LeDoux, 1996; Massey, 2002). Thus, when the emotional center of the brain is made aware of a stimulus, the amygdala will rapidly send out signals to engage other areas of the brain contained within the limbic system (such as hypothalamus, hippocampus, pituitary glands, and so forth) prior to a person even being consciously aware of the external stimuli. The practical upshot is that before an individual can even form an attitude towards an object, the emotive areas of the brain have already been activated by their awareness of that object. In turn, the emotional centers will have sent neurochemical transmissions out to other areas of the brain (Cunningham and Zelazo, 2007; Cunningham, Zelazo, Packer, and Bauel, 2007; LeDoux, 1996), including those structures in the prefrontal cortex that play a role in attitude formation and decision-making (such as the orbitofrontal cortex, ventrolateral cortex, and dorsolateral cortex—Cunningham and Zelazo 2007; Massey 2002). Thus it can be argued that at a biological level, emotions both precede and subsequently guide attitude formation, a point that lends credence to the idea that emotions and attitudes can be considered distinctive entities. LeDoux provides further evidence in support of the separation of emotions and attitudes in his book, *The Emotional Brain*. Referring to attitudes as cognitions, LeDoux (1996: 40) describes how in emotions, unlike in cognitions, the brain does not usually function independently of the body. Many if not most emotions involve bodily responses. But no such relation exists between cognitions and actions. In the case of cognitively driven responses, the response is arbitrarily linked to cognition. This is partly why cognition is so powerful—cognitions allow us to be flexible, to choose how we will respond in a certain situation.

As a result, the attitude can occur separately from the biological features that are often indicative of an emotive state, such as a rapid heartbeat, sweating, a tingling of the skin, and so forth. Not so for the emotion, as "the response of the body is an integral part of the overall emotion process" (LeDoux, 1996: 40).

But the discussion above raises another question: is an emotion simply a neurochemically transmitted reaction to a stimulus, or can emotions also be social in nature? This question, in one form or another, has plagued academics, intellectuals, and philosophers alike since at least the time of Plato (Cleve, 1969). An answer to this conundrum can be found in part by examining the definition of emotion used in social psychology today. Admittedly, there are several different definitions for the term emotion that are bandied about in the existing literature on the subject, but within the field of sociological social psychology consensus definitions have been reached in recent years. Von Scheve and Von Luede (2005: 303) provide a succinct definition by suggesting that emotions can be defined as "regular, stable and ... predictable phenomena that have their origins in the (equally stable) fabrics of society." Thoits (1989) provides a more expansive definition by articulating that emotions possess the following four elements: appraisals of the situation, which provoked the emotion; changes in bodily or physiological sensations; a display of expressive gestures; and the cultural label or meaning attached to the specific constellations of one or more of the prior elements (Ridgeway, 1994; Smith-Lovin, 1995; Thoits, 1989). Although Thoits' definition recognizes that emotions are rooted in the biological, it also dovetails with Von Scheve and Von Luede's definition by showing that emotions are inherently social, insofar as three of the four defining elements of an emotion are *social in nature* (Ridgeway, 1994).

Even though emotions are both biologically and socially determined, demonstrating how the social aspects of an emotion can influence a person's interpretation of any biological facets of that emotional state is critical, as the following study demonstrates.

One approach to understanding the stimulation of emotions and how they interface with the emergence of attitudes developed during the 1960s along the lines suggested by the James-Lange hypothesis. *Cognitive labeling theory*, in large part developed by social psychologist Stanley Schachter and elaborated by many others, closely parallels both philosopher David Hume and the Zen approach. Cognitive labeling theory answers the question *"How* should I feel?" when one is aroused, but needs a "lead" or cue from one's surroundings to interpret that sensation as a specific emotion. We can see it in the following prosaic example: A father hides from an approaching toddler and abruptly jumps out to startle him or her. The child momentarily registers shock, mouth and eyes wide open; for a nanosecond there is in his or her young mind the question of what the shock means. Then there emerges a clear expression of relief and pleasure with the recognition of the parent's face. Now try startling the toddler while wearing a hideous, leering Halloween mask....

Schachter started with the premise that physiological arousal is a general phenomenon not directly linked to any particular emotions. True, there could exist some unique connection between a specific type of bodily arousal and some distinct emotion(s), but such "differences are at best rather subtle and the variety of emotional states are by no means matched by an equal variety of visceral patterns" (Schachter and Singer, 1962: 380). A single visceral state can thus be the source of many emotions.

What Schachter and his colleague Singer (1962) did in one seminal experiment was to demonstrate that *how* a physical stimulation becomes accounted for, or an emotional interpretation constructed after arousal, depends on cues in the social context. The experimenters administered epinephrine, a sympathomimetic (physiologically arousing) drug, to a group of college students. Some students (the control group) were told straightforwardly about the likely effects, or sympathetic activation, of the drug on their bodies, such as racing heartbeats, flushing in the face, and feelings of tremors in their limbs. The remainder of the students (the experimental group) were *not* told beforehand to expect any of these drug-related effects.

Then *all* the student subjects were individually placed in a room where a single confederate (a student actor who, unknown to the subjects, was part of the experiment) appeared to be just another subject. While they both filled out questionnaires, the confederate began acting in one of two ways: giddily ecstatic as acted out by making paper airplanes out of the questionnaire, crumpling its pages into balls and "shooting baskets," and so forth; *or* becoming verbally hostile, angrily destroying the questionnaire, and so forth.

The cognitive labeling approach would predict that students who had been prepared for the drug's stimulating effects would attribute their physical excitement in the presence of the confederates to the drug and not to either the actions of the buffoonish or angry confederates. And this was so. Conversely, the experimental group of (drug-effect-not-informed) student subjects attributed their feelings to what they witnessed, or took a "lead" from in the situation: growing irritated and angry along with the hostile confederate or sharing in the merriment with the euphoric confederate. Students informed beforehand about epinephrine's effects had a ready explanation for any arousal they felt and did not take a "cue" from either type of confederate. Uninformed students, on the other hand, took their "meaning" of their arousal from the confederates' behaviors. Schachter and Wheeler (1962) performed a similar experiment on students, again after the latter were given an arousing drug, who viewed a movie comedy. Manipulating the levels of induced arousal found essentially the same pattern: those more artificially aroused considered the movie more amusing.

A large body of research has accompanied cognitive labeling theory. It all points to the conclusion that cognition plays an important part in determining or explaining a person's emotional state (i.e. where the feeling has come from and what it should mean) to him or herself.

As Schachter and Singer (1962: 381) concluded: "An emotional state may be considered a function of physiological arousal and of a cognition appropriate to this state of arousal." These inputs of situational information "provide the framework within which one understands and labels his feelings."

Yet while still relevant in the arena of emotion research, the work of Schachter and Singer should not be taken to a logical extreme. That is to say, a person will not always express a particular emotion in a consistent manner. Depending on the circumstances, the situation, and the environment, individuals may choose to express, repress, or manage a given emotion (Charon, 2004; Hoschschild, 1983), even though they may be experiencing a physiological state of arousal association with a specific emotion. This line of thought supports the contention that in addition to being a biological reaction, emotions are also social objects that can be defined, manipulated, and used as a situation demands (Charon, 2004), a contention quite compatible with Zen Buddhism's understanding of emotions. Therefore it can be said that when a person experiences an emotion, he or she recognizes that something is happening internally, defines what it is (anger, depression, frustration, happiness), judges it as positive or negative, expresses it, represses it, or manages it; the actor [*sic*] may store it and in the future recall it. In all of these ways—and undoubtedly others—emotions become social objects. (Charon, 2004: 135)

That single quotation contains all three *nen* levels that Zen master Sekida described earlier. An example of Charon's point can also be found in the research of Arlie Russel Hochschild (1979; 1983). Her work on "emotional labor," which can be defined as "the management of feelings to create a publicly observable facial and bodily display (Hochschild, 1983: 7), explains nicely what many people in America have to endure on a daily basis as part of their labor activities. In almost every employment setting, the management of personal feelings and emotions has become a standard (and often required) feature of work, especially when a worker is called upon to have contact with the general public (Hochschild, 1983; Leidner, 1993). In essence, workers today are not only tasked with performing their jobs correctly, but must also learn to do so in a manner, which will convince the public that they actually *enjoy* their job task (Hill and Bradley, 2010; Italics theirs).

As most will agree, repressing certain emotions while managing others is part of the daily grind of work. But the workplace is not the only arena in which we consciously choose to express certain emotions while also managing and repressing other emotions. Indeed, humans are socialized from an early age to recognize that specific emotional reactions are required in certain situational contexts and prohibited in others (Leach and Tiedens, 2004; Pollak and Thoits, 1989). This fact of social life demonstrates that emotions cannot be totally disentangled from the social world, a pointed echoed by Leach and Tiedens (2004: 2):

A social approach to emotion requires that we ... stop seeing [emotion] as an individual response, and start considering it as a bridge between the individual and the world that blurs the boundaries between individuals and their context. From this perspective, emotions are one channel through which the individual knows the social world, and the social world is what allows people to know emotion.

A parting social psychological thought: the notion that emotions are tied to the social world is, admittedly, somewhat restrictive, especially in terms of what emotion a person can choose to display at any given moment. However, without a shared social understanding of which emotions are acceptable to display (and not display) as a situation warrants, life in the social world would be a lot less predictable ... and probably just a little bit more interesting.

The Zen Perspective on Emotion Work and Attitudes

The bulk of this chapter has not meant to provide just the interesting convergence of theories on emotions and attitudes by an ancient Eastern religion, a Western philosopher who penned his thoughts two and a half centuries ago, and social psychologists from one hundred years ago proposing a radical reinterpretation of how we feel and think. Nor has it meant to be anything more than a cursory look at the biological and social roots of emotions. Rather, our purpose has been to indicate the particular overlapping emphasis Zen Buddhism and contemporary social psychology place on emotions as significant formulators of attitudes. Like the earlier statements by well-known social psychologists on the salience of attitude study for their discipline, attitudes have received a central focus for Zen techniques to recognize their origins and how they be dealt with.

Social psychologists have for decades ascertained the pernicious consequences of attitudes that foster stereotypes of racism, sexism, nativism, religious hate, and the "we-they" dichotomous sentiments that engender conflict among groups. They have explored the nature of attitudes that prejudge whole categories of human beings because of their ascribed characteristics and then use these prejudgments to justify harmful discrimination. The classic example, of course, is *The Authoritarian Personality* (Adorno, *et al.*, 1950), a large volume of staggering scientific detail commissioned by various American Jewish groups in the aftermath of World War II and knowledge of the extent of Nazi genocide against Jews as well as homosexuals, intellectuals, the mentally and physically challenged, and others deemed somehow inferior to a "pure Aryan race." Alarmed that a country such as Germany, for centuries considered one of the cultural pinnacles of Western high art, scholarship, philosophy, science, and medicine, could descend under authoritarian despotism into such grotesque depths of mass murder and other abuses, the many studies reported in *The Authoritarian Personality* initially sought only to uncover the roots of anti-Semitism. What the social scientists (predominantly psychoanalytically-inclined psychiatrists and clinical psychologists) found, however, was that prejudice against Jews tended to cluster with a number of other anti-foreign, anti-religious, anti-dissenting attitudes (at times laced with Freudian sexual overtones). This "cluster" of attitudes the authors termed generically an authoritarian personality "syndrome" (syndrome as used in the medical sense).

The Zen preoccupation with attitudes is not aimed at a single cognitive-emotional entity with such malevolence but is more diffuse. If social psychology has concerned itself with the most strikingly harmful forms of prejudice that lead to discrimination as well as the dynamics of cognitive laziness or "least effort" that allow otherwise ordinary persons to dehumanize and objectify others (Allport, 1979), Zen in its own way goes further. Zen's more radical diagnosis, an obvious overstatement to dramatically strike home its points, is that *all* culturally-conditioned attitudes about interpersonal social reality, and our artificial dividing up of physical reality into our convenient units and discrete entities, distort the world in subtle as well as dramatic ways. If perceiving reality in all its undifferentiated fullness and interwoven richness (its *tathata*, or "suchness") is of any value, and for Zennists it *is* the supreme value, then emotions are the major stumbling blocks to that realization. Militating the effects of emotions *via* attitudes is what Zen teachings and mental discipline strive to accomplish, but of course, we must remind ourselves that Zen's interests are interventionist, not purely analytic.

Social psychologists use the term *emotion work* to refer to the fact that *feeling rules* for various social roles dictate which emotional displays are condoned and encouraged, or alternately, discouraged and proscribed, in specific situations. This would include when it is appropriate to giggle, frown, or roll one's eyes in exasperated disapproval. As one example: facial displays of nervousness, discomfort or pain, and uncertainty are inappropriate in the competitive matches for almost every martial art, for they convey emotions that an opponent may interpret as weakness and exploit to his or her advantage. Other instances would be stifling expressions of irritation while being berated by a boss (or other person in authority) or a parent not showing impatience at a very small child's yet-again inept attempt at performing a routine task.

But these are examples of ordinary emotional work. Again, Zen goes further. Zen encourages more complete emotional work at a greater depth in the subtle "dialogue" between emotional impulses and mental images. This does not mean, however, than Zennists are supposed to be dour; Zen does not discourage displays of humor, grief, elation, or satisfaction in achieving a skill. Nor could it ever completely insulate practitioners from fear, uncertainty, embarrassment, or other emotions. Zen simply aims to help identify the origins of emotions and their resulting self-interested attitudes, providing techniques (of which we have barely sampled) to detach them from our minds, to transcend them rather than ignore or try to crush them.

Emotions will continue to emerge and exist since in human beings they have physiological bases that at times naturally trigger them. Zen maintains that emotions just ought not have the power to shape our perceptions of what is real around us or inflate our relative selves into leading us to think these have permanent importance. It provides a systematic practice for controlling emotions. Social psychology would maintain, if we may speak for the subdiscipline, that without such decisive intervention by disciplined, reflexive exercises there is probably little alternative.

Notes

1.   Whether or not λ will equal a value of 1 is, as Maxim (1999) points out, an empirical question. For didactic purposes, it is acceptable here to set λ as equal to 1. Many useful things in life can be accomplished by algebraically adding zero or multiplying by 1, an understanding that was first brought to Christopher's attention by his graduate statistics teacher, Dr. Al DeMaris. As you can see, it does come in quite handy—many thanks to Al for this insight.

2.   This structural equation model is adapted from Chapter 11 of Paul Maxim's (1999) book, *Quantitative Research Methods in the Social Sciences.*

3.   Figure 4 is adapted from Dorman (2001), "Associations between Religious Behavior and Attitude to Christianity Among Australian Catholic Adolescents: Scale Validation," *The Journal of Social Psychology,* 141(5): 629-639.

4.   Figure 5 is adapted from Massey (2002), "A Brief History of Human Society: The Origin and Role of Emotion in Social Life," *American Sociological Review,* 67(1): 1-29.

4

Social Psychology and Zen Ethical Issues in Social Movements: Zen Meets Motivation

Late-nineteenth/early-twentieth century German sociologist Max Weber provided an image of Buddhist clergy, which unfortunately has long held currency in the social science. His stereotype of a monk or seriously devoted Buddhist practitioner was a person reclusive, intensely introspective, and detached from secular issues and events. In *The Sociology of Religion* (1964: 169) Weber characterized the overall lifestyle of Buddhist clergy as "a contemplative flight from the world, characteristic of ancient Buddhism," in all respects ascetic, otherworldly, and the last category of religionists one would expect to be social movement activists.

As argued in this chapter, Weber had it critically wrong about Buddhist clerical (and lay) disengagement from economic, political, and social-ethical issues, both in historical and modern eras. Zennist priests (and at times we will co-mingle them with Tibetan, Burmese, and other Buddhists) are not inherently any more reclusive or otherworldly than any other clergy. Certainly the monastic stereotype has been exaggerated. (For instance, Zen Buddhist priests, among other sectarian types, may marry.) In fact, Zen Buddhism's primary claim is that it offers a path to understanding *this* world, *this* Reality, not to prepare one for some hypothetical afterlife or an existence apart from experience here and now. Before exploring the Zen rationale—even imperative—for involvement in secular social concerns, however, we need to review what Western social psychology has had to say about participation in social movements and in its close kin, collective behavior.

Some Distinctions: Collective Behavior, Social Movements, and Group Movements

In a somewhat misleading way, most sociology and sociological social psychology textbooks lump collective behavior and social movements together as a subdiscipline, as if they bear some close resemblance. This is no doubt because early social psychologists saw participants in both types of group phenomena as allegedly dissatisfied, even malcontented individuals who, in concert with one another, acted out personal strains, grievances, and fears through uninhibited, if not occasionally irrational, ways. There *have* been a good many riots, panics, massacres, and bizarre and quixotic movements to lend credence to that superficial impression. This continuing bias toward participants in both collective behavior and social movements, as we illustrate below, has had the effect of reducing participants' motives (and individual social psychologies) to a conno- tatively "lower" level than those of allegedly "normal" persons who do not engage in either type of behavior.

But beyond this slanted assumption concerning participants, collec- tive behavior and social movements as phenomena are not even in the same sociological arena except as the former might possibly lead into the latter. Specifically, *collective behavior* defined is a type of *very* loose multiple-person behavior involving individuals, most of whom usually do not know each other much beyond their common purpose for coming together, whether it is a small cluster of commuters waiting at a bus stop or traffic light or is of slightly longer duration, say a theater audience or sports spectators in a stadium. Such collectivities are quickly formed and dissolved. Members (if participants may be called such) are minimally connected to one another. Such groups have minimal if any identifiable leadership; likewise, their collective goals are at most short-term.

Alternately, *social movements* display opposite characteristics on these dimensions. Social movements have definable, even well-developed organizational structures, with clear-cut decision-making/coordinating leadership cadres. They possess identifiable goals (with clear benchmarks for having reached them), many of these goals being long range in nature. Social movements endure over time and for much longer periods than instances of collective behavior.

While many actual groups may fall somewhere along a continuum between these two model types, the defining difference is one of organi- zational complexity: forms of collective behavior, which may be difficult to anticipate/research/theorize about, are minimally structured, while social movements *are* themselves organizations with all the ranks, roles, and goals we would expect. To put it colloquially, social movements, not forms of collective behavior, have *addresses*, whether on streets or the Internet. The differences between the two are, practically speaking, effectively illustrated by comparing the 1967 Detroit race riot or the 1992

Los Angeles Rodney King riots, on the one hand, to the black civil rights movement with its various wings, such as the National Association for the Advancement of Colored People, the Southern Christian Leadership Conference, or the Black Panthers, on the other.

Here we will use the term *group movements* to refer to both collective behavior and social movements for two reasons. First, both of the latter types of phenomena do involve groups of persons, but neither is as established and accepted as those bureaucratic institutions, which sociologists call *formal organizations*. To put it another way, both collective behavior and social movements are possibly institutions-in-becoming, more-or-less likely candidates to become permanent parts of the social fabric.

Second, grounded as they have been in historical/economic/sociological/psychological preconditions, social movements often require some *precipitating event* along the lines of the old clichéd analogy of a spark that ignites a powder keg. And these precipitating events often take place as acts of collective behavior. For example, Ms. Rosa Parks, an African-American woman who in 1955 in Montgomery, Alabama refused to give up her bus seat to a white man and who was subsequently arrested, did not singlehandedly create the modern civil rights movement. But conditions of widespread black resentment at second-class citizenship provided her act of resistance to segregation with the ensuing support to inspire angry demonstrations, 50,000 black citizens boycotting the Montgomery public bus system for a year, and subsequently mobilization for the larger civil rights movement. Occasional acts of collective behavior may flow (in retrospect) seamlessly into social movements. Therefore, collective behavior can serve as a *proto*-social movement, and for this reason we use the concept of engagement in group movements to include both what traditionally are called collective behavior activities and formal social movement organizations, differentiating them if need be. The usefulness of the group movements concept will become clearer when we refer later to the roles played by Buddhist monks and leaders in social activism.

Before examining Zen (and other) Buddhist involvement in secular group movements, we want to consider briefly how mainstream social psychology initially regarded, and later more rigorously conceptualized, individual participation in group movements of various kinds. Zen, it will be shown, is more interested in the sacred or moral/ethical logic of obligation, rather than the unique motives that predispose some individuals, and not others, to become engaged in group movements.

Social Psychology and Group Movements

Because the earliest speculations—and they cannot be considered much better than that—as to why persons participate in unconventional group movements has had such an important influence on later theorizing, it is important to start this brief review in the nineteenth century.

Group Hysteria, Crowd Psychology, and Early Social Psychology Theories on These Phenomena

The earliest nineteenth-century writers concerned with the behavior of persons in group movements assumed a literal disease, or *contagion*, model in which normally rational, clear-thinking individuals lost their independent faculties in the sheer presence of others, thereby displaying asocial, frenzied, berserk, and violent traits. In an age when biological Darwinian evolution was in vogue and what we now call social or cultural evolution was an accepted interpretation of history, at least by elites, this meant that crowd participants, by mentally "infecting" their fellow members, were believed to strip away the vestiges of civilization and reduce those members to earlier barbaric, primitive states. This was also the century when the emerging behavioral sciences were breaking out of natural science and forging such distinct disciplines as anthropology, psychology, sociology, and so forth but before there was a formal thing called social psychology.

The classic example of a scholar who adopted the contagion model for his own use can be found in the English academic Charles MacKay's 1841 work entitled *Extraordinary Popular Delusion and the Madness of Crowds* (1980). The explicit reference in the title to insanity, or at least a pause in otherwise normal morality and rationality, was followed through in MacKay's case studies and maintained in later derivative books. A half-century later in 1895, the French philosopher-historian Gustave LeBon published *The Crowd: A Study of the Popular Mind* (1982), or more pejoratively in the original French *Psychologie des foules*. LeBon continued the "contagion of madness" motif with particularly horrific and violent examples taken from French history. LeBon is responsible for the popular concept of a "mob mentality" or "crowd psychology" in which ordinary, responsible individuals fell victim to a somewhat mysterious, hypnotic transformation that lowered them "to the level of the least intelligent, roughest, and the most violent member of the group" (Locher, 2002: 13). LeBon's influence can be seen in the first credible textbook in social psychology written by sociologist Edward Alsworth Ross, published as *Social Psychology: An Outline and Sourcebook* in

1908. Chapters 2 through 5 of the twenty-three total chapters in the volume have as their respective titles "Suggestibility," "The Crowd," "Mob Mind," and "Prophylactics Against Mob Mind" (Ross, 1915).

Variants of this "crazed mob psychology" assumption about individuals "caught up unawares" in unconventional mass group movements lingered in writings far into the twentieth century, well after social psychology had become an established subdiscipline of both sociology and psychology. "All of them emphasized this irrationality and abnormality of the crowd" (Turner and Killian, 1993: 6). One of the neo-psychoanalytic, or what became known generically as the "pathological," twists on MacKay/Lebon was that of Everett Dean Martin's 1920 *The Behavior of Crowds*. Martin essentially redefined the crowd as itself a "mental condition" resulting in a simultaneous release of repressed libidos among persons. (Martin is the writer responsible for the popular crowd description of "people going crazy together" (Turner and Killian, 1993: 9)).

Two further variants on the MacKay/LeBon "mob mentality/crowd psychology" theme were published in the mid-twentieth century. The first was J. P. Chaplin's *Rumor, Fear, and the Madness of Crowds* (1959), which trumpeted "hysteria" as the typical mindset of persons caught up in group movements. It was a mindset that the author did not approve of or completely comprehend, but for which he was at a loss to provide other operating causes. For example:

> To delve into mass hysteria is to encounter the strange, the bizarre, the incredible.... characters as different as one could hope to find, yet all drawn together by the madness that surrounded them by hysteria. (1959: 7)

Somewhat less tabloid was Eric Hoffer's often cited and reprinted pop-social psychology tome *The True Believer* (1963). Hoffer reduced the mindset of the protean convert-follower to social movements—*any* social movement, in fact—as a suggestible person yearning to lose his or her insignificant self, even at the sacrifice of one's life, in service to a larger cause. Hoffer basically claimed the true believer type is a fanatic, with the Cold War implication that authoritarian regimes relied for their bases on turning out conditioned replicants in this mold. Hoffer wrote the following in the introduction to *The True Believer*'s first printing in 1951:

> All movements, however different in doctrine and aspiration, draw their early adherents from the same type of humanity; they all appeal to the same type of mind.... Though there are obvious differences between the fanatical Christian, the fanatical Mohammedan, the fanatical Nationalist, the fanatical Communist, and the fanatical Nazi, it is yet true that the fanaticism which animates them may be viewed and treated as one. (p. xxvii)

Hoffer was a part-time writer who worked as a longshoreman while he cultivated the persona of a homespun political philosopher. With a smattering of historical examples he would issue sweeping statements, such as

> When people are ripe for a mass movement, they are usually ripe for any effective movement, and not solely for one with a particular doctrine or program. (p. 7)

This sort of generalization, uninhibited by empirical case specifics, could still be found another half century later in the writings of select partisan intellectuals during the "cult scare" involving new religious movements during the last quarter of the twentieth century. (See for numerous examples, Shupe and Darnell, 2006: 39-53.) For one illustrative case, Dr. Margaret T. Singer, a clinical psychologist and sympathizer with the "anti-cult" or deprogramming countermovement, clearly echoed Hoffer's broad assertions about true believers when she described (albeit in colorful terms) the protean nature of "cult" adherents:

> Despite the myth that normal people don't get sucked into cults, it has become clear over the years that everyone is susceptible to the lure of these master manipulators. (Singer, 1995: xxiii)

People involved in group movements, in other words, by the judgment of MacKay, LeBon, Hoffer, Chaplin, or Singer, either are (paradoxically) *not* like you or could be *exactly* like you, or any one of us for that matter.

Modern Social Psychological Theories

In more recent theories of group movements, the emphasis on personal motives of participants shifted in two ways: first, such persons are no longer presumed to be irrational or devoid of ordinary cognitive awareness about what they are doing due to some hypnotic crowd contagion; and second, other more social psychological and purely sociological factors have supplanted the motive issue in importance.

On the first point, Schweingruber and Wolstein (2005), for example, lambasted sociology textbooks for perpetuating the nineteenth-century stereotype that crowd behavior is anti-rational, excessively emotional, highly suggestible, reliably destructive, or always rapidly formed. Far from it. Clark McPhail in *The Myth of the Madding Crowd* (1991) not only has laid to rest these earlier ideas, but has also soundly debunked the myth of primitive "crowd minds." Evidences of such "madness" are only superficial impressions in the eyes of outside observers not privy to what immediate participants know or experience.

A large number of case studies with accounts taken from movement participants, not simply outsider viewpoints, demonstrate that persons motivated to engage in change-oriented group behavior obviously *do* hold some discontent with the current arrangement of things. But their motives make rational sense in their context. For example, in a survey of persons who had joined in the July, 1967 Detroit race riot (which included three days of fighting, looting, and the progressively upgraded presence of state troopers, national guard troops, and the federal army), many black participants expressed long-standing grievances against the police, city government, and particularly white merchants who had been charging higher than average prices or excessive credit rates to their inner-city customers. Many of the rioters regarded the extended conflict as a political "uprising," not some exuberant antisocial orgy of mindless destruction. More to the point: the selected targets of snipers were deliberate, not random (Darrow and Lowinger, 1970).

Another excellent revealing analysis concerned "The Who Concert Stampede" in December, 1979 at Cincinnati, Ohio's Riverfront Coliseum. (The media termed the collective behavior a "stampede," using the imagery of panicked bovine sub-intelligence.) There a number of persons were killed or injured when some doors to the building were mistakenly locked and the waiting throng pressed forward (although not uniformly). Few victims were the products of callous, asocial competition to enter the building. A lack of communication by guards and organizers, which included the police, misinterpreted legitimate patrons as gatecrashers, with some patrons simply trying to escape the confusion, not attempting to sneak in and acquire free seating. Importantly there were numerous accounts of pro-social (helping) behavior. Sexual norms of men assisting women (sometimes strangers) persisted; 40 percent of those later interviewed reported giving, receiving, or observing helping behavior of persons amid the tight circumstances. A good amount of rational interpretation, not mindless reaction, was apparent (Johnson, 1987).

Noted theories of the processes that produce dramatic instances of the collective behavior end of the group movements continuum (most of which are stepwise descriptions rather than technically theories) would include Smelser's (1962) six-stage "value-added" model that posits preexisting grievances and generalized antipathy toward some social actors in a "we/they" dichotomy, or Turner and Killian's (1987) emergent norm theory that claims persons in groups take their cues from others in uncertain situations as to what is the best social reality to adopt (and may include all types of actors, from the concerned and aggrieved to idle spectators and self-serving exploiters). Such approaches factor in participant discontent near the beginning of the process, but only as a preliminary "conduciveness" element, which is necessary but not sufficient to account for possible unfolding developments. They assume that people motivated to engage in change-oriented groups, no matter how short-lived, obviously hold some dissatisfaction, but that these are not pathological or abnormal motives. Locher (2002: 71), in reviewing another approach known as convergence theory, summarizes its assumption about initial predispositions and motives in crowds of individuals:

> people only engage in behavior that they (as individuals) already possess some inner drives or tendencies toward. Crowds do not drive people mad and crowd members do not lose their ability to think.

A brief look at attraction and participation in just one type of group movement—unconventional religions—will illustrate the second point of a shift of emphasis away from predisposing group movement participant mindsets. There was one last major attempt at reducing the salient questions about group movements down to the motives of participants, called the *deprivational model*, or as its critics termed it, "the hearts and minds" approach. The model's logic argued that to understand a group movement sufficiently we need to focus on the ways in which possible/ actual participants are aforehand deprived, presumably explaining their motives to join up, which in turn will permit us to infer what public images movements seem to provide or promise to adherents. One leading example of this approach can be found in Charles E. Glock's (1964) article, "The Role of Deprivation and Evolution of Religious Groups." Glock explored, with scattered hypothetical examples, five types of possible deprivation (economic, social, organismic, ethical, and psychic) and suggested in particular that "Religious resolutions ... are likely to compensate for feelings of deprivation rather than eliminate its causes" (p. 29). Faith and belief, in other words, are epiphenomenal; the bedrock motive is found in the specific deprivation.

The major problem with the deprivation model, which simply asks the limiting "Why?" question (i.e., "Why do they join?"), is that it doesn't tell us very much and is frequently useless. The motives for religious conversion and adherence in real life are often far more complicated, or overdetermined, than any single deprivation even if one is found (and often one is not). Consider this brief sampler:

Garrison (1974: 327) did not uncover pathologies or simplistic deprivation in her study of Puerto Rican Pentecostals:

If it is deviant to be sectarian and to "speak in tongues," then they are deviants. But, if we demand some other criteria, such as inadequate functioning or social roles, or emotional disturbance, we have found no evidence of it.

Similar conclusions, based on research across diverse group movements, are legion. Bromley and Shupe (1979) did not find noticeable deprivations in Unification church members' own introspective accounts of their conversions—despite obvious temptations for converts to exaggerate what was wrong with their sinful lives before conversion. Most felt they had simply left an adequate or good lifestyle and found something better and with more purpose (i.e., idealism, not deprivation). Seggar and Kuntz (1972) did not uncover exceptional social, economic, health, or psychological deprivations in their study of adult Mormon (Latter-day Saint) converts. With medical (organismic) problems, most sought medical help; with money problems or marital problems, most sought financial advisors or marriage counselors. The only consistent pattern was that most converts joined the LDS Church through networks of relatives and friends who took advantage of these preexisting relationships to interest them gradually in Mormonism. Likewise, Hine (1974: 655), in her study of Pentecostal converts, found that to speak in terms of predispositional deprivations is to be inaccurate:

> Many of our informants reported the fact that they were perfectly satisfied with the dominant standards of society and with their own and others' behavior until a committed recruiter in a position to influence his thinking sensitized him to Biblical standards. In these instances perceived behavioral deprivation is an effect of movement dynamics, not a precondition ...

In fact, the distinguished sociologist of religion J. Milton Yinger (1946: 88) presciently dismissed the entire reductionist deprivational model over a half century ago:

> Scholars generally assume that sects and cults produce more emotionally unstable and mentally ill persons than denominations and churches. Many mentally ill persons indeed are found in sects, but there may be proportionately as many in churches. What appears to be a causal relationship may result only from variations in the self-selection that operates in religious bodies with voluntary membership.

The modern study of group movements has all but abandoned social psychology's old "hearts and minds" approach and no longer bothers to ask the "Why?" question because people realistically become involved in any group movement for a wide variety of reasons. Instead researchers ask the more sociological (non-social psychological) "How?" question.

Noting the decline in concern generally about the "Why?" motive question, Shupe and Darnell (2006: 11) continue:

such questions focused on the *why* dimension. *Why* do they join? *Why* do they remain involved? These are questions about motivation and not in themselves inappropriate, but they are [purely] psychological, not sociological, and quite limited. Moreover, why someone joins a social movement or countermovement may be very different from why that person continues in it. Worse, much of the writing on the *why* question has been anecdotal or speculative (that is, "armchair psychology," which is not good psychology, in any event). [Brackets ours]

With the advent of resource mobilization theory (a *real* scientific theory, with axiomatic statements and testable deductive propositions) during the 1970s, most sociologists abandoned anything resembling the older "why" questions of group movement participation (see particularly Snow, Rochford, Warden, and Benford, 1986; McCarthy and Zald, 1977). Motivation to seek some degree of change is an obvious given. (Who among us has enough of everything he or she wants, anyway?) But knowing such motivations provides rapidly diminishing returns for understanding development of a group movement as a social rather than a psychological phenomenon. Resource mobilization theory focuses instead of such matters as how vital resources (among them members, finances, and public legitimacy) are identified; how strategies for obtaining resources are decided upon and implemented; how recruitment of participants is a managed social psychological policy issue; and how resource mobilization strategies, within the context of the group movement's socio-political environment, shift to accommodate to external events and challenges. Issues of rising and falling expectations in the face of differing opportunities to realize the former may indeed be relevant to questions of why persons act together to rebel or revolt, i.e., the conditions of experiencing relative deprivation (e.g., Gurr, 1970; Davies, 1962), but by the twenty-first century they are largely theoretically passé.

In sum, much of social psychology's fascination with the allegedly exotic motives and mindsets of persons participating in group movements has been transformed or fallen off at best. Zen Buddhism's focus on group movement participation, alternately, has never been concerned with the logic of why this person becomes an activist and that one doesn't, but instead with the ethics of obligation that all persons share, how these obligations are obscured by notions of relative self-interest and person perceptions, and how these ethics become transformed into ameliorative action. That is the subject of the remainder of this chapter.

Zen Social Ethics and Group Movements

Readers by this point will have discerned that we hold an affinity at times for several of the earliest writers in the formative stages of social psychology. It is remarkable, therefore, that one of them—Charles Horton Cooley—made a seminal statement that approaches the Zen view of Reality, albeit one limited to the study of everyday social interaction. Cooley, in his 1902 classic *Human Nature and the Social Order*, argued that both the "individual" and "society" are artificial designations. The real stuff for social scientists to comprehend, he maintained, is Human Life (deliberately in capitals). There can be realistically no such thing as an individual considered apart from his or her group culture, identities, references, and affiliations; such an individual, he said, is "unknown to experience."

Likewise, no society can be understood divorced from the individual persons who make up its collective membership. Psychologists and sociologists may focus primarily on one or the other aspect of Human Life, but the choice or lens is arbitrary, pragmatic, and always limited. Human Life is a realistic unity of which "the individual" and "society" are simply abstractions of different dimensions of interaction. In other words, Human Life transcends the artificial dualism of disciplinary boundaries. As Cooley determined: "A well-developed individual can exist only in and through a well-developed whole, and vice versa" (1964: 36).

Cooley's warning against the disciplinary dividing up of Human Life offers an analogy to the Zen understanding of the human presence on this planet and the former's interpretation of the latter. If there is ultimately anything that Zen Buddhism steadfastly rejects, it is the artificial conceptualization, hence compartmentalization, of human beings and the physical world around them (including all other sentient life forms) into self and others or perceiver-subjects and object-things. This non-dualism is the key to the social ethics underlying Zen involvement in group movements.

The Dharmakaya and Emptiness

Mindful that any attempt to employ words to explain Reality or what is experienced in Zen Awakening (*satori*) is incomplete, it is still necessary to fall back on language to draw the connection between Zen doctrines and group movement activism. (The inadequacy of language is why in so many Zen aphorisms, the Master, who is unable to meet a pupil's straightforward question with a logical answer, must play word games and rely on obscure or seemingly irrelevant metaphors. Language *per se* cannot do the job.)

Zen social ethics (i.e., the moral direction an action ought to take) begin with the concept of the *Dharma* (literally in Sanskrit, carrying or holding). In fact, most Buddhists of every variety would doubtlessly say that single word encompasses every other aspect of their faith. *Dharma* to most pre and post-Buddhist Indians refers to the legalism of Brahmanism; it is one's social duty or prescribed ritualistic caste role, sometimes translated as The Law. It understandably retained something of this Hindu meaning when Buddhists referred to the teaching (oral and later written down) of Siddhartha Gautama, the historical Buddha. It is also used in Zen Buddhism as an adjective, as in a Master's *"Dharma* successor" who has received the former's *"Dharma* transmission." In Zen, *Dharma* connotes authority.

But in a more important sense the *Dharma* is equivalent to the universal or cosmic law of karmic cause and effect. It is Truth inherent in Reality, unfettered and unconditioned by any logical or limited descriptive attempts. It is not handed down or revealed by any deity or personified Supreme Intelligence. It simply exists without any past, present, or future frame. Actually it does not "exist" since that word implies not only finitude as we humans understand existence, but also in Zen's abhorrence of dualism "existence" presupposes its opposite "nonexistence." Thus one is incorrect to say the *Dharma* exists. It simply *is*, though there is no "It" in the first place. The *Dharma* defies the use of any pronoun, unlike phenomenal identities. One can see the delicate linguistic conundrum: we need a word to refer to something that is not a thing but the very completeness of all, a word to refer to a concept beyond discursive expression. So Buddhists refer to the *Dharma* much the same way Taoists refer to the Way (which, as we noted in Chapter 1, is not the real Way if it can be described or even named). The *Dharma* is purposeless and coeval to all phenomena imaginable, but other than such rough approximations it is indescribable.

For this discussion we find it more useful to refer to the (Sanskrit) *Dhramakaya*, or *Dharma* body, which also can have several subtle meanings. (The term is employed roughly to correspond to them all.) One of Mahayana Buddhism's theological developments was to reconceptualize the man Buddha, apotheosizing him as a godhead principle (as in the orthodox Christian Trinity of Father, Son, and Holy Ghost) with three aspects:

(1)   the *Nirmanakaya*, or the Buddha's physical body and brain that historically participated in Enlightenment;

(2)   the *Sambhogakaya*, or body that is the aspect of the Buddha's realization to *nirvana* and *prajna* that looks both transcendentally to the
Dharma and compassionately (with *karuna*) to the physical world
around him;

(3)   and the *Dharmakaya*, the aspect of the Buddha best referred to as his
true self-nature, which is to say his absolute unity with the *Dharma*:
"the essence of the universe [that is] timeless, permanent, devoid of
characteristics." (Kohn, 1991: 229)

Thus the *Dharmakaya* essence, for practical expository purposes, is
synonymous with *sunyata*, a concept discussed earlier, as well as with
terms such as Reality, One Mind, The Void, The Plethora, The One
Vehicle, and *nirvana*. It is truth not learned, taught, or achieved. It fundamentally *is* and has to be discovered intuitively. The *Dharmakaya* is
not all around us; it *is* us and we are all the *Dharmakaya*. The Buddha-
nature inherent in each person is what Zen calls the true self-nature or
Dharmakaya. As Bassui, the fourteenth-century Japanese Zen master,
emphasized, the "mind-nature" in each of us was originally pure, came to
be spoiled by our cultural environment of human desires and ignorance,
and can be rediscovered through Awakening. Bassui preached that the
relative mind can reclaim this One Mind:

> The One Vehicle is the One Mind. Those who seek the Buddha and dharma outside
> of mind are all children of rich men who have forgotten where their homes are. When
> you awaken to the unique and wonderful dharma of your true nature, it is as if the
> lost child had come home.... This mind-nature is the original source of all Buddhas
> ... there is no Buddha or dharma outside of the One Mind inherent in all people....
> (Braverman, 1989: 63-64)

Though beyond all finite description, *emptiness* is the one characteristic
or essence of the *Dharmakaya* on which all Zennists agree. The *Dharmakaya* is free (or empty, or void) of the form distinctions imposed by our
acculturated human minds. Since everything of our conceived reality as
well as the noumenal (transcending dualism) reality is inherent in *sunyata*
or *Dharmakaya*, Zennists maintain that the multiplicity of phenomenal
life is harmonious with the interrelated, interdependent Ultimate Reality.
Hence the hoary aphorism "Form is emptiness, and emptiness is form."
Without wishing to belabor any further Buddhist theology, this is why
the Hinayana Buddhists seek *nirvana* to escape *samsara* or the wheel
of life/death/reincarnation while the Mahayanist Buddhists claim that
nirvana and *samsara* are the same. To think otherwise, Zennists (who
are Mahayanists) say, would be to commit the error of dualism.

Social Ethics and the Dharmakaya

In his excellent comprehensive review of Zen's alleged underdevelopment of a systematic ethical perspective, *Zen Awakening and Society* (1992), *Soto* Zen Buddhist Christopher Ives examines the criticisms of Zennists and non-Zennists alike. He reminds us that philosophy is a Western (originally Greek) invention imported during the late nineteenth century into Meiji-era Japan following that country's "opening" by Commodore Perry's American gunships. Indeed, the Japanese had to coin a new word, *tetsugaku*, to express the concept. In pursuit of the "fundamental" or moral background ethic underlying Zen, Ives adopts the role of devil's advocate to lay out the inadequacies (by Western standards) of Zen for doing little more than providing a body of situational ethical guidelines. Ives unflinchingly acknowledges how Zennists, allegedly minus such an ethical system, have been caught up in group movements of nationalism and nativism and courted the corridors of secular power as much as any other religionists:

> Historically, monastic Zen has not studied, analysed, or responded self-critically to the full range of suffering in the social world. This lack of a critical spirit has contributed to problematic support of the status quo, whether the aristocracy, samurai dictators, militarists, or certain large corporations. (1992: ix)

(One personal favorite in the Zen ethical "Hall of Shame" is the unabashedly xenophobic glorification of Japan's entry into and victory in the bloody Russo-Japanese War promulgated during his American tour in 1905-1906 by The Reverend Soyen Shaku, Lord Abbot of Zen temples Engaku-ji, and Kencho-ji of Kamakura, Japan—See Shaku, 1993.)

Ives observes that critics charge that Zen ethics are said to be found wanting insofar as (to paraphrase):

> Without an acknowledged God or divine personage to reveal what is objectively good or bad, Zen's *sunyata* (*Dharmakaya*) concept leaves a practitioner with only relativist standards.
>
> Zen so thoroughly discredits the ordinary or relative "self" that there is no locus of ethical agency, that without divine moral commandments or a self accountable for obeying/disobeying them, there is no moral anchor for a conscience.
>
> Worse, classical and modern Zen masters (along with their Taoist counterparts) have consistently claimed that an Awakened person, realizing "suchness" in the emptiness of Reality, transcends all dichotomies, including "good" and "evil" or "sin" and "virtue."
>
> Zen's emphasis on Awakening basically implies that only those who have intuited/experience *satori*, always a minority of human beings anywhere at any time, possess an elite transcendent morality, which cannot be directly inculcated or taught to

any larger group. Liberation and its new ethical perspective will always belong to a relative few, and Zen's radically anti-creedal, anti-"words and letters" stance only compounds the elitism, hardly a basis for an ethical system.

Of course, Western criticisms such as these come laden with many of their own frequently unstated presuppositions. In response to the above, let us offer just a few:

that of course the world and the cosmos had to have a beginning (thus a deliberate and purposive creator);

that the creator must be a deity who can be personified;

that if our physical lives, like linear time, had conclusive beginnings,

then they must also have conclusive endings (often with some assumed accountability for a life's efforts);

that guilt rather than shame is the understood mechanism of private control and moral direction;

that the individual has to be the primary locus of spiritual worth,

and so forth.

These are ethnocentric, if subtly taken-for-granted, undercurrents in Western (primarily historic and monotheistic) religions. But if serious students of comparative religion have to learn to comprehend numerous other forms of the supernatural in terms other than of one faith, so can ethicists. For example, beyond the many straightjacket categorizations of Western religions one can see that other spiritualities—Hindu, Buddhist, Taoist—see no need to posit an absolute moment and agent of cosmic creation or a supra-human law-giver for morality to emerge as a sociological constant in every major society. When Hindus express the idea of worldly or cosmic creation, as in Brahmanism's Dance of Shiva, creation is conceived of as merely part of an endless rhythmic cycle of creation/destruction/renewal expressed in metaphorical terms (Coomaraswamy, 1957: 66-78). Chinese Taoists do not see things in nature as once-upon-a-time created but as simply accepted and naturally *growing* and expanding. The concept of *tsu-jen*, which according to Alan Watts (1958b: 10) can be translated as "of itself so," means that life proceeds in a spontaneous organismic manner from inside-out and needs no master clock-maker who operates from the outside-in. Watts (1958a: 16-17) explains:

The important difference between the Tao and the usual idea of God is that whereas God produces the world by making (*wei*), the Tao produces it by "not-making" (*wu-wei*)—"growing." For things made are separate parts put together, like machines, or things fashioned from without inwards, like sculptures. Whereas things grown divide themselves into parts, from within outwards. Because the natural universe works nearly according to the principles of growth, it would seem quite odd to the Chinese mind to ask how it was made.

The point is that a personified Divine Creator who works in linear time, with inception and conclusion in his or her plans, contradicts a spontaneous organismic development perspective, and a significant portion of Earth's religious folk think more in terms of the latter rather than the former paradigm. Nor should ethics be the special preserve of any single cosmology.

However, since most Zen (and other) Buddhists would maintain that the *Dharmakaya* is the source of their social ethics, particularly for their participation in group movements, it is the motivational aspects of this concept that need to be more carefully examined. As mentioned previously, the irony in a Zen master exhorting a pupil to examine or discover the latter's "true self" or "true nature" is that the pupil will hopefully come to realize that he or she ultimately possesses no separate, permanent self. The "true self" is the True Self, or *Dharmakaya*. (The joke is on non-Buddhists when they hear that the goal of meditation is to learn about one's own true self, as if there is one to be uncovered and perhaps improved.)

Likewise, in the West (and increasingly elsewhere) we have often institutionalized this internalized sense of self-identity through a host of required unique personal identifications: social security numbers, computer passwords, credit card pin numbers, and so forth. Each of us is treated as a discrete legal, social, and psychological entity. Medically each of us is considered an integrated biological system made up of respiratory, circulatory, neurological, skeletal, muscular, and glandular subsystems all bounded by our skin. Rarely is the skin thought of as a mediator that connects us to others and nature itself. Early social psychologist Charles Horton Cooley warned that concepts like the "individual" and "society" were abstractions used for analytic convenience but that they inevitably ignored other important aspects of larger Human Life. In parallel fashion Zen maintains that to fail to appreciate the interdependent, seamless Reality of our interpersonal lives is to become lost in sociological and psychological abstractions. *From this last point emerges the Zen social ethic.*

As Christopher Ives (1992: 40) succinctly summarizes:

In existential terms, one cannot exist apart from this world and one's experience of it. In more metaphysical terms, one is constituted by and also influences myriad things other than what one takes oneself to be. On the basis of *sunyata* one discerns society most fundamentally as a network of interdependent events, not as a collection of independent selves. This promotes the recognition that ultimately one's own well-being is inseparable from that of others. This aspect of *sunyata* is a crucial stance in the foundation of the *bodhisattva* ideal set forth in Mahayana texts.

Note that Ives uses the term *bodhisattva*, and it is well to consider briefly what one is in the Mahayana Buddhist tradition. For Zennists a *bodhisattva* (male or female) has delayed final entrance into *nirvana* for the sake of spreading Enlightenment to all sentient creatures. In the *Manual of Zen Buddhism* (1960: 114) D. T. Suzuki reproduces the common Fourfold Great Vow of a *bodhisattva* customarily repeated *en masse* by worshipers in many Zen temples after services, at study centers, while at retreats, and in private meditations:

However innumerable beings are, I vow to save them;

However inexhaustible the passions are, I vow to extinguish them;

However immeasurable the Dharmas are, I vow to master them;

However incomparable the Buddha-truth is, I vow to attain it.

A *bodhisattva* is said to exhibit (among other things) the six "perfections" (in Sanskrit, *paramitas*, often translated as bridges) of charity, moral behavior based on the Precepts, patience, vigorous endeavor, concentration, and wisdom. A *bodhisattva* is the archetype of self-sacrifice, wisdom (*prajna*) and compassion (*karuna*). In Christianity the *bodhisattva* would be the equivalent of a saint, exhibiting (at least in Roman Catholic terms) evidence of miraculous and redemptive powers and works.

But one additional function of reciting the Fourfold Great Vow is for the sake of unAwakened practitioners, and the term *bodhisattva* is often used to refer to them as well since everyone possesses the Buddha-nature and the potential to break through to this more developed spiritual level. The vow is a motivational as well as declarative one.

In fact, two important points flow from the first stanza of the Fourfold Great Vow.

First, as Ives observed in his citation above, the "interdependent network" of all sentient creatures within the entire cosmos embraced in *sunyata* forms the seminal rationale for ethical compassion. The egoist who believes in looking out primarily for himself or herself as "Number One" is not merely narcissistic in Western terms but is ultimately in

Zen destructive of his/her long-range interests when the divide between unique I and unique Thou is discovered to be a delusion. This notion was never better expressed than by German philosopher Arthur Schopenhauer (1788-1860), whom Schirmacher (1996: ix) termed a pessimist rather than a cynic. Schopenhauer became enamored with both Hindu and Buddhist thought and wove it explicitly into his philosophical writings. Consider this statement below from his essay "The World as Will: Second Aspect." It is as fine an interpretation of the basic calculus of Buddhist ethical compassionate behavior as any Zennist could present:

> ...our true self exists not only in our own person ... but in everything that lives. In this way, the heart feels itself enlarged, just as by egoism it feels contracted. For just as egoism concentrates our interest on the particular phenomenon of our own individuality ... so the knowledge that every living thing is just as much our own inner being-in-itself as is our own person, extends our interest to all that lives; and in this way the heart is enlarged. (Schirmacher, 1996: 157-58)

Schopenhauer goes on to claim that when *maya* (illusion) and *avidya* (ignorance) are lifted from a person's eyes,

> ... to such an extent that he no longer makes the egoistical distinction between himself and the person of others, but takes as much interest in the sufferings of other individuals as in his own ... then it follows automatically that such a man, recognizing in all beings his own true and innermost self, must also regard the endless sufferings of all that lives as his own, and thus take upon himself the pain of the whole world. (Schirmacher, 1996: 162)

Ancient and modern Zennists have made the same ethical inference from the *Dharmakaya*. An example can be found in one of Zen's earliest documents (translated from the early Chinese Tun Huang texts by D. T. Suzuki (1960: 75-76), "Bodhidharma and the Twofold Entrance to the Tao." It may or may not actually have been written by Zen's founder in the sixth century but certainly represents Zen thought no later than the late seventh or early eighth century T'ang Dynasty. The following statement is found:

> As there is in the essence of the Dharma no desire to possess, the wise are ever ready to practice charity with their body, life, and property. And they never begrudge, they never know what an ill grace means. As they have a perfect understanding of the threefold nature of emptiness, they are above partiality and attachments ... they, however, know also how to benefit others ... yet there is no specific consciousness on their part that they are engaged in any meritorious deeds. This is called "Being in accord with the Dharma."

Likewise, D. T. Suzuki, in his *Essays in Zen Buddhism* (1961: 194), translates part of a letter allegedly written during the early T'ang Dynasty by a Zen layperson named Hsiang to Hui-k'e, by tradition the first Chinese disciple of Bodhidharma. Again, the letter's provenience is not the more important issue but rather its sentiment as an early but common statement of Zen's "foundational ethic" grounded in the *Dharmakaya*:

> ... he who aspires to Buddhahood thinking it to be independent of the nature of sentient beings is to be likened to one who tries to listen to an echo by deadening its original sound.

Contrast the import of the previous two old quotations with the follow-ing excerpt from a transcribed lecture given during *sesshin* (an extended Soto Zen meditation retreat) in 1986 by Dennis Genpo Merzel, Dharma Successor to Hakuyu Taizen Maezumi (himself a lineage-holder in both *Rinzai* and *Soto* schools), and one can readily see the continuity of the Dharmakaya's ethical implications obligating Zennists to show compas-sion for others, akin to Schopenhauer's argument:

> When we drop our dualistic, discriminating mind, when we drop boundaries and labels, then everything is as it is: changing constantly, moving, intermingling, inseparable!... The functioning of the nondual life is compassion. When you really live in nonduality, then why would you try to hurt someone else? It would be like cutting off your own arms or legs. If you really have to amputate, you amputate, but you do not go around intentionally hurting parts of your body unnecessarily. (Merzel, 1991: 122, 126)

Citing one more modern authority: in precisely the same vein, the remarkable personage of Ruben Habito. Habito, former Jesuit priest, practicing Catholic, theology professor at Southern Methodist University, *and* Zen master, says of the *bodhisattva's* Fourfold Great Vow in his book *Living Zen, Loving God*, "Expressing this great resolve, the seekers after wisdom profess that they pursue enlightenment not only for their own narrow satisfaction or individual salvation, but seek wisdom for, on be-half of, and together with all living beings" (2004: 82). Commenting on the question of how one can be presumptuous enough to vow to liberate others before that one is even liberated, Habito returns to Zen's refutation of the false dualistic notion of separation between persons. This false no-tion "can only be genuinely and effectively overcome in the experience of enlightenment itself, whereby I realize that I am in all living beings and all living beings are in me." Seeking parallelisms with the Christian ethics of St. Ignatius Loyola and others, even a *rapprochement* between Zen concepts and key elements of Roman Catholic Christianity, Habito concludes of non-dualism in the *Dharmakaya*: "With this understanding, one is opened to an entirely new perspective in looking at this world of suffering and how to save beings in the midst of it" (p. 85).

Thus, Awakening to *sunyata*, or the *Dharmakaya*, as well as to the futility of believing in the existence of the self, brings wisdom and simultaneously awareness of compassion in which one's own interests and well-being are intuited/felt/realized to be coeval and merged with others' interests and well-being. Compassion for these others is "natural," "logical" (if one insists on rendering it into linear Western terms), and morally imperative. Zen Roshi Philip Kapleau (1997: 74) has pointed out how Zen's non-dualism reinforces the awareness of no-self (*anatman*) and compassion, writing

> In classical Buddhism, actions are not termed "good" or "bad," but rather "skillful" or "unskilled." Skillful actions are those that arise from our awareness of unity, or nonseparation. Such actions not overly bound by attachment to thoughts of self and others, are spontaneous, wise, and compassionate.

The awareness of nonseparation, in other words, could be termed a supreme form of a person's self-interest, if there was indeed such a thing as an ultimate, permanent self. In Zen Buddhist terminology, mindful of the all-inclusive essence of the *Dhramakaya*, compassion from any one to any other is thus *Self-interested*.

Second, contrary to accusations that any ethical frame of mind attained by experiencing Awakening (*satori*) must, statistically speaking, belong only to a spiritual elite, the benefits of following the Precepts (described in Chapter 1) and the rest of Zen practice are not all-or-nothing. *Rinzai* Zennists insist that *satori* must be sudden and dramatic, a "general mental upheaval" as Suzuki (1961: 262) describes what he experienced, but they also acknowledge that this Awareness deepens with further experience and meditation. *Soto* Zennists do not use the term *satori* as much as they do *kensho*, or a series of *kensho* "mini-awakenings" progressing eventually into a mental state equivalent to *Rinzai's satori*. Both "paths" recognize also the evolving benefits to practitioners who have not Awakened but still follow the Precepts and work to clear their minds of cultural discriminations.

For example, Kapleau (1997: 72) sees an overall spiritual benefit from Precept observance: "A correct attitude when accepting the precepts is to believe that they are a natural expression of harmonious conduct issued from the Buddha-nature that all possess." Zen ethicist Christopher Ives (1992: 35) addresses the matter of Zen practice benefits to the un-Awakened as well as those having experienced *satori*, in our view, most clearly and succinctly:

> ... wisdom, compassion, and ethical change do not totally elude "unawakened" practitioners. Practice has a transformative effect from the start, gradually bearing religiously and ethically important fruits, even though the fundamental religious problem may remain unresolved. By clarifying this effect, Zen may begin to shed its appearance of being a tradition for the few, a type of spiritual elitism with a "trickle-down" ethic.

He adds:

Wisdom, compassion, and other ethically significant fruits emerge throughout the process of Zen practice, not simply upon a *satori* experience, and hence *to varying degrees* play a role in the action of all Zen Buddhists, not just the fully awakened. Though a vivid and full acquisition of *prajna* and *karuna* may have to await *satori*, this does not mean that they are not realized at all before then, or that they are the exclusive possession of the awakened few. (P. 38) [Emphasis in original]

In fact, one of Buddhism's most important (Indian) scriptures, *The Vimalakirti Nirdesa Sutra* (first or second century), often cited by Ch'an and Zen masters, emphasizes the Buddha-nature of all beings and made its wise protagonist a layperson (Sutton, 1991).

A final word about the Precepts: they are moral guides, or conversely, the habits of an Awakened person to emulate. For most Zennists they are a means to an end, at least in the beginning of practice, in the same way the Ten Commandments probably are for the average Jew or Christian. Gethin (1998: 171) refers to the Precepts as "principles of training seen as helpful in the cultivation of the path, rather than prohibitions against intrinsically unwholesome ways of conduct." In popular Buddhism, where many adherents believe in reincarnation, observing such prescriptions and proscriptions builds good karma for this and future lives. But in Zen, as Gethin (1998: 173) warns, blind obedience to the letter of these moral principles

for their own sake may be an expression of rigid views and attachment—clinging to precepts and vows ... rather than those of true compassion.... Ethical precepts are a necessary part of the training that constitutes that path, but attachment to those precepts, like all attachments, must itself be given up.

Perhaps that is why ethical critics of Zen see no consistent, highly developed ethical system similar to those with which Western philosophers and theologians preoccupy themselves. Perhaps Zen's reliance on the intuitive *bodhi* experience instead of formalizing in "words and letters" more than monastic rules and general precepts will always doom it in the eyes of critics for not having a more rigorously analyzable ethical formulation. What is important, however, is not why people act ethically in spite of Zen's alleged ethical incompleteness, but why they use their understandings of Zen (and other) Buddhism to act ethically. The remainder of this chapter illustrates this ethical connection in two selected contemporary group movements.

Empathy and Compassion

To this point we have loosely used the word "compassion" as do many writers on Buddhism. According to *The Shambhala Dictionary of Bud-*

dhism and Zen (Kohn, 1991: 43), compassion is the better translation for the Sanskrit word *karuna* than pity or sympathy since the former entails the element of "active help." Thus, before examining two examples of Buddhist compassion performed in group movements for ethical reasons, compassion needs to be distinguished from several similar terms.

Empathy is the experientially learned ability of one person or persons to feel or intuit the pain or happiness of another person or persons. More than *sympathy*, which is simply an intellectual appreciation of another person's perceived feelings, in empathy individuals can literally feel themselves in the "shoes" or predicament of another. In other words, sympathy merely perceives while empathy directly experiences. In empathy one's emotions are intuitively inseparable from the emotions of another. (This sort of intuition is the goal of Zen's *samadhi* meditative state, i.e., to eliminate the dualism of subject and object in thought and perception.) *Compassion* is empathy in action. One not only intimately comprehends another's pain and suffering, but *addresses* the cause with an intervention or remedy. Empathy is a subjective reaction; compassion is doing something about it.

Social psychologists generally term compassionate intervention "prosocial" behavior, i.e., helping another whether by an ordinary favor or heroic rescue and assistance. Another frequently used term for prosocial behavior is altruism. For some prosocial acts, no matter how self-sacrificial they appear at the moment, there is some form of reciprocity, or repayment, anticipated: simple thanks, public recognition, a tangible reward, or an eventual tit-for-tat return favor. Zen Buddhism, however, holds a stricter standard for defining compassionate behavior. In Zen, unless an act of kindness is performed strictly out of selfless morality, it is not compassionate but ultimately egoistic. A truly altruistic act earns absolutely no karmic merit during the doer's lifetime or at any other time if the actor is motivated by even the remotest hint of recognition, gratitude, or reciprocity. In terms of the *Dharma* ethic, compassion is unconditionally the "right" thing to do in a situation.

Dharma Ethics, Compassion, and Group Movements

In the remainder of this chapter we discuss two case studies of Buddhist compassion in group movements in the secular arena. Both illustrate national and larger international concerns. At the very least they belie the stereotype that Buddhism is an inherently otherworldly or passive faith.

Socio-Political Activism

Traditional: China and Japan

Ch'an in ancient China, along with other Buddhist sects, was not slow to make conversion of, and/or win influence with, important luminaries in society and government. Nor was it immune to anti-Buddhist actions taken by nativist Chinese regimes. During the ninth century there was a number of widespread persecutions of Buddhists (Green, 1998: xxi), in particular a major effort undertaken by Emperor Wu (814-847) who was determined to eliminate entirely what he considered pernicious "foreign religions." Wu's Edict of 845 accused Buddhist orders of being overly wealthy, parasitic in fact, and becoming small states-within-states. Buddhist temples, his edict declared, "are all lofty and beautifully decorated, daring to rival palaces in their grandeur." During his Buddhist pogrom more than 46,000 monasteries and 40,000 temples and shrines were sacked or destroyed, and over 260,500 monks and nuns were forcibly retired to lay life, along with 150,000 Buddhists made slaves by the government (Wu, 1996: 84).

Ch'an's experiences in the midst of such periods of hostility were mixed. Overall Ch'an fared better than other sects during the Wu purges because it had earlier instituted a work ethic for monks. They were not to be mendicants (depending on seeking alms for a living) but rather expected to work productively in growing their own food and performing physical labor to make their monasteries as self-sufficient as possible. Ch'an master Pai-chang (720-814) wrote the rules for such a Spartan lifestyle in his manual of monastic life, which became known in various versions as *The Holy Rule of Pai-chang*, emphasizing application of Ch'an Buddhist doctrines in everyday life. He literally organized what Cleary (1978: 34) has termed "making the transition of the Ch'an teaching from principle to fact" and influenced Ch'an monks to become "a service elite instead of a cloistered and privileged elite, with the process of the teaching being carried out through the fabric of the community." Thus Ch'an clergy were encouraged to perform educational and charitable works outside their monasteries. Ch'an temples were also typically less ornate and expensive than those of older Buddhist sects. For such reasons Ch'an was not automatically regarded in the same light by the hostile government.

On the other hand, Burton Watson (1993: xi) in *The Zen Teachings of Master Lin-chi* recounts that during the major An Lu-shan Rebellion during the T'ang Dynasty a century earlier, the Northern Ch'an School suffered the greater repercussions of political turmoil compared to the Southern School (which was closer to the teachings of Sixth Patriarch Hui-neng) because of the former's greater patronage ties to government centers there. The Rebellion

> inflicted a severe blow on the schools of Buddhism that were centered in the capitals and had depended on the support of the ruler and the aristocracy, which included the Northern School of Ch'an.... The Southern School of Ch'an, however, with its centers all located in outlying regions, escaped the worst effect of the rebellion and was able to continue the development and propagation of its teachings.

When Ch'an arrived in medieval Japan (there pronounced Zen) via Japanese monks who had trained in China, Eisai (1141-1215) who brought the teachings of Lin-chi (Jp: *Rinzai*), and Dogen (1200-1253) who brought the teachings of Ts'ao-t'ung (Jp: *Soto*), it faced both older Buddhist sects entrenched in imperial patronage for centuries and a country (or archipelago) undergoing conflict among rival warlords. Besides the *Kegon, Tendai*, and *Shingon* Buddhist sects, there were also the emerging Pure Land (salvationist, or *tariki*) sects of *Jodo, Shin* and *Jodo Shin-shu* as well as the fiercely nationalistic millenarian sect of *Nichiren Sho-shu* Buddhism. To complicate things, the era also underwent the threat and failed invasion of a Chinese armada dispatched by the Yuan Dynasty Mongol emperor Kublai Khan.

Therefore it was understandable that Zen (initially *Rinzai* and for the most part urban) sought favor with aristocratic as well as military powers if only to gain some support against its older religionist rivals. For brevity's sake we cite Christopher Ives (1992: 57-58) on this point.

Through the efforts of Eisai and Dogen, Zen received patronage from the Kyoto aristocracy, members of the imperial family, and, most importantly, the newly emergent warrior-rulers in Kamakura.

> ... the Minamoto and Hojo warrior families offered patronage to Eisai and Dogen, and this established a pattern that lasted through the Kamakura period (1185-1333) and into the subsequent Muromachi period (1333-1573).

Indeed, Zen fostered an overall argument of its positive contribution to a Japanese "civil religion" in which devotion to its brand of Buddhism could be equated with good "citizenship" (if most Japanese had been citizens instead of subjects). Eisai (1958) even wrote a famous essay, "Propagation of Zen for the Protection of the Country," to curry sympathy for his "upstart" sect and propagandize rulers about its national security/overall social welfare value. Later, as is well known, the Tokugawa Shogunate (1600-1867) found it useful to compel every Japanese family to register with a local Buddhist temple for taxation and social control purposes, a practice which generally enriched ecclesiastical Buddhism of whatever sect, including Zen.

Thus, in Japan, where Ch'an teachings were preserved and elaborated, and where an enormous number of ordinary laypersons became Zennists, Zen Buddhism was anything but cloistered. Hoover (1978: 71-83), for example, chronicles the worldly activities of certain Zen monasteries and temples with their imperial court maneuvers, political-economic influence, and even bands of Knights Templar-like warrior-monks during the twelfth and thirteenth centuries. Far from remaining ascetic and removed from civil affairs, Ives (1992: 56) notes that "With military prowess, major monasteries had been ready and willing to defend their interests in land holdings, money lending, trade guilds, pawnshops, and other commercial interests." It should not be surprising that Zen leaders also had more than an occasional influence in cheerleading for Japanese industrialists and militarists during the 1920s and 1930s (the *zaibatsu*), merging State Shinto (emperor-worship) with what was termed "Imperial Way Zen" (Ives, 1992: 64-67).

The foregoing examples should not leave the impression, however, that Chinese Ch'an or Japanese Zen leaders were solely engaged in *un-Dharmic* political intrigues worthy of Renaissance Italy or Byzantium or strictly occupied themselves seeking official recognition to aggrandize their sects. Even during the "franchised" Buddhist parish system of the Tokugawa period and earlier, a number of exemplary *Rinzai* monks, such as Bassui in the fourteenth century and Bankei in the seventeenth, reached out to farmers and the common people in their ministries (Braverman, 1989; Haskel, 1984). To cite another example: the fourteenth century *Rinzai* monk Ikkyu, who also made such important contributions to Japanese culture in poetry, calligraphy, painting, and drama (among other areas), was a kind familiar with children, merchants as well as the poor, and even animals. (Ikkyu was known to perform funerals for believers' pets—See Stevens, 1993: 32.)

Meanwhile, *Soto* Japanese Zennists, perhaps more than their *Rinzai* cousins, reached out in compassion to rural inhabitants as teachers, also helping to build dams, irrigate rice fields, drain swamps, and manage hospitals. Ives (1992: 63) reports that Soto monasteries produced monks who responded to the daily this-worldly needs of the peasants. On more spiritual grounds they prayed with the common people for their famililes' safety, fertility, and other blessings, also officiating at funerals.

While there always were the otherworldly reclusive monastic Zennists in their mountaintop hermitages, historical Ch'an/Zen (thought of as a

Buddhist group movement) was acutely cognizant of the Mahayanist tenet that the this-world of phenomena and the noumenal Reality were one and the same.

Contemporary: The September/October 2007 Myanmar Political Protests

Dharmakaya ethical insight has inspired Buddhists of every school or sect to engage in a host of socially ameliorative group movements. Members of Japanese *Nichiren Sho-shu*, for example, have conspicuously organized to promote international peace (Green, 2000; Brown-Simmer, 2000; Metraux, 1996; Shupe, 1986, 1991, 1993) just as *Vajrayana* Buddhists have worked for an end to heavy-handed Chinese control of Tibet (Powers, 2000; Cabezon, 1996) as have Zennists for political justice in Vietnam (King, 1996a; Hanh, 1967). Zen (and other) Buddhists have addressed issues of gender inequality (Moon, 2000; Barnes, 1996), sexual orientation (Corless, 2000), the homeless and inner-city poverty (Queen, 2000; Glassman, 1998), the terminally ill (Halifax, 1998; Kapleau, 1989), the incarcerated (Loori-sensei, 1998; Malone, 1998), urban Asian refugees in North America (McClellan, 2000), and the environment (See this chapter's next section) in countries as diverse as the United States, Japan, South Africa, India, various European nations, and Australia.

Queen and King (1966: ix) observe:

Like Christian "Liberation Theology," these movements are characterized by a fundamental commitment to making Buddhism responsive to the suffering of ordinary Buddhists. They are concerned to mobilize the Buddhist laity to address their own economic, social, political, and spiritual needs; to contribute to the amelioration of conditions that produce suffering for all living beings; and, finally, to reform, in light of the demands of modernity, Buddhist doctrines and institutions.

Such a recognition is indeed exactly what happened during the 1960s and 1970s with the original "liberation theology" movement in Central and South America within the Roman Catholic Church. It also occurred, to the surprise of many political scientists and news pundits in the United States, as previously culturally alienated, premillennialist, other-worldly fundamentalist/charismatic Protestants during the mid-1970s became mobilized by the Christian Right and engaged in national politics, particularly within the Republican Party (Hadden and Shupe, 1988). In fact, the coalescing of social, economic, and political grievances against a host of developments subsumed under the rubric *secularization*, across a variety of faith traditions, is precisely what Shupe (2009) and Shupe and Hadden (1989) termed a direction toward "global fundamentalism."

Modern conditions lead to a refashioning of religious beliefs to create a new ethos of change, even of radical transformation, in spiritual (if not always some sectarian) terms.

A prime example of political activism by monastic Buddhists on behalf of a larger population, according to *Dharmakaya* values, has been the *Theravada* (*Hinayanist*) Buddhist monks in Myanmar (formerly Burma). In Myanmar, before and since British colonization, Buddhist monks have been an important part of the popular and institutional culture just as their counterparts were in China and Japan. Writes 1991 Nobel Peace Prize winner and human rights activist Aung San Suu Kyi (1995: 97):

> Traditionally, the Buddhist monasteries had been the schools of the Burmese people—the word for "school" is *kyaung*, which originally meant simply "monastery," and to this day the same name continues to be applied to both institutions—so that the link between religion and education was very strong.

Speaking of the many children who received such education, she adds: "The brighter ones would stay on to acquire further learning, and it was not unusual for some of the brightest to become monks themselves. All Burmese boys would join the religious order at least once in their lives, usually as a novice in their early teens." No stigma was attached, she notes, to those who eventually returned to lay life; indeed, they were honored further as laypersons for their scriptural knowledge.

Moreover, Buddhist clergy have had a life-long influence on the lay public in Myanmar through ongoing retreats called *satipatthana*. Former U. S. Navy Rear Admiral E. H. Shattock underwent one of these retreats in Burma for spiritual reasons not long after World War II and wrote of his experience in *An Experiment in Mindfulness*. On the institution of *satipatthana* he observed:

> In Burma it is quite common for laymen to attend for this particular course, and once or twice during their business life, and certainly on retiring, many Burmese men, some of them prominent in the affairs of their country, go to one of the meditation centres for a period of strict meditation practice of usually not less than six weeks. (1958: 8)

Most importantly, Burmese/Myanmar Buddhism has been largely monolithic (i.e., not split by sects) and closely intertwined with popular, civil, and political dimensions of national culture. As in Tibet, Buddhism in Myanmar has also been an inseparable part of national identity as well as offering a "majoritarian" moral standard. Understandably, monks literally became warriors in fighting against the Japanese with the Allied Forces and then in the effort to oust the British.

Thus, says Kyi (1995: 103):

It has often been remarked that, while Indian nationalism was essentially a product of British rule, there had always existed a traditional Burmese nationalism arising from Burma's cultural homogeneity. Buddhism obviously played a large part in creating this homogeneity, but it could not be said to have supplied ideas to support nationalism; rather it provided an essential component of the self-concept which enabled the Burmese to see themselves as different from foreigners.

Aung San Suu Kyi, either imprisoned or under house arrest by Myanmar's military dictatorship since 1989, and the icon around whom much of Myanmar's 2007 protests came to crystallize, actually entered the picture as an activist considerably before 2007. Her father, Aung San, had been a leader of the post-Second World War nationalist movement. During that war he had become Minister of Defense after Japan "gave" Burma independence from Great Britain. Disillusioned at the puppet government under Japanese rule, he organized a revolt within the Burmese army and came to join the Allies in again "liberating" Burma. After the war he headed up a nationalist coalition that was to win through peaceful means independence from Britain. However, he was assassinated while head of the Constituent Assembly as the latter was drawing up a constitution.

Aung San Suu Kyi, educated as a girl in Buddhist Burma and studying later in India and Britain (taking degrees in politics, economics, and philosophy from, among other places, St. Hugh's College, Oxford), on her return to Burma quickly assumed the leadership recognition and heroic legacy of her father, particularly when it became apparent that the military was of no mind to cede ultimate authority to a civilian government after its coup. The military tried unsuccessfully in various ways to discredit Suu Kyi, a devout lay Buddhist, in the eyes of the Burmese people and finally had to imprison her after she, too, almost faced assassination. Finally, in 1989 the government managed to machinate severe limits on her activism, though not her voice or symbolic value, for the incipient democratic movement by indefinite house arrest. Her titular martyrdom only insured her "overwhelming silent presence" opposing the military junta which, despite repeated assurances of imminent "free" elections, clearly was unwilling to give up its power. A relentless champion of civil authority within an independent Burma and leader of Burma's National League for Democracy, in 1991 she was awarded the Nobel Peace Prize, but by the time of the 2007 popular protests she was still detained under house arrest.

The September/October Myanmar protests of 2007 (the brief description of which here is based on daily non-by-lined *Associated Press* reports) reminds one of the comment of Thich Nhat Hanh (1995: 50), himself a Zennist monk veteran of engaged Buddhism in South Vietnam's earlier popular democratic movement: "It is through the close interaction of the laity and the monks that the issue of Zen penetrates social life."

In mid-September Buddhist monks reportedly vandalized shops of owners supporting the Myanmar regime, briefly took local officials hostage, and threatened a general boycott of the junta and its core families to begin September 19, the nineteenth anniversary of similar bloody demonstrations in 1988 against the government. One of the immediate grievances in 2007 was the fact that fuel prices had leaped 500 percent in recent times. These actions of the monks were preceded by demonstrations throughout the month of August. The monks had already threatened to march out of their monasteries, and, in a decidedly humiliating gesture toward the regime in this very Buddhist of cultures, to refuse alms (thereby depriving potential donors of opportunities for spiritual merit). The very word "boycott" in Burmese also means literally "to hold the bowl upside down."

Soon about 5,000 monks marched in the streets of Yangon and temporarily occupied a landmark pagoda; government troops arrived to fire tear gas canisters and warning shots. Tactics escalated on both sides. About 20,000 protesters led by 10,000 Buddhist monks marched; about 400 persons, half of them monks, tried to approach Suu Kyi's home but were turned back by troops. The monks shouted her name as they carried a large yellow banner that read: "Love and Kindness Must Win Over Everything." By the following weekend, more than 500 monks and sympathizers were able to march to her home and obtain Suu Kyi's encouragement for non-violent protest but were thereafter blocked. Protesters reportedly later swelled in number to 100,000 persons. Authorities downplayed the numbers, but there is little doubt that tens of thousands joined the protest that marched for five and one-half hours over a distance of more than twelve miles. Meanwhile, General Thura Myint Maung met with senior monks to try to defuse the situation.

Soon the military imposed a curfew after one demonstration of 35,000 protesters and seized all cameras of foreign journalists. In further response the government flooded Yangon with 20,000 troops. On September 26 Myanmar security forces opened fire on a mixed crowd of monks and civilians, killing at least one man and wounding others. The violence escalated. According to one *Associated Press* report,

> Clouds of tear gas and smoke from fires hung over streets, and defiant protesters and even bystanders pelted police with bottles and rocks in some places. Others helped monks escape arrest by bundling them into taxis and other vehicles and shouting "Go, go, go run!"

Witnesses saw soldiers beating and dragging monks away from demonstrations. The soldiers raided half a dozen Buddhist monasteries and announced elsewhere nine protesters had been killed. (One killed was a Japanese journalist—seen shot by troops at close range on a video camera smuggled out—prompting in Tokyo the Chief Cabinet Secretary Nobutaka Machimura to cancel a $4.7 million grant for a business education center at a Yangon University campus. In 2006 Japan had provided $26.1 million for technical assistance to Myanmar.) Meanwhile, the United States and some European governments issued a joint statement decrying the security forces' assaults, particularly on religious centers.

The Myanmar junta claimed the demonstrations were the product of "foreign" agitators and shut down the Internet in an attempt to black out the protests' visibility from the outside world. Public gatherings of more than five persons were banned. After, United Nations envoy Irahim Gambari was not allowed to meet with Suu Kyi, and the Tibetan Dalai Lama and South Africa's Archbishop Desmond Tutu (both previous Nobel peace Prize recipients) joined with Pope Benedict XVI to condemn the government response to the protesters. (Ten percent of Burma's 54 million citizens are Roman Catholics.) While an opposition leader died during police interrogation, the junta appointed a "liaison" official "to coordinate contacts" between the outside world and Suu Kyi. Finally U. N. Envoy Gambari was permitted to meet with Suu Kyi for one "heavily orchestrated" hour (but no more).

By the end of September fifteen Buddhist monasteries had reportedly been ransacked and emptied, monks forcibly put on trains to return to their families of origin. A total of eight monks were known to have been killed while hundreds were in custody, and a security forces sweep was conducted to arrest the "ringleader" clergy. By the first week in October, 6,000 persons were reportedly detained and over 200 persons known to have been killed. Eventually the government claimed 109 monks held in custody along with 25 of 29 monks suspected of organizing the protests.

Finally, though the Internet black out was partially lifted along with a reduced curfew, the junta leaders stood steadfast that the protests were purely "an internal matter" and nobody else's business. Only China, though worrying about its international image for the forthcoming 2008 Olympics, supported the Myanmar government's position. By mid-October two officials in the U.S. State Department cautioned members on the House Foreign Affairs Committee subcommittee that concentrated international pressure (through economic sanctions and general isolation) was the best strategy of containment and hope for democracy, though some members of Congress wanted more forceful actions. By late October, junta officials were establishing irregular meetings with Suu Kyi, though under extremely controlled conditions.

The Myanmar political situation still unfolds, but we do not need to know the end here. The point in our recounting this sequence of political events is to illustrate the activist ethical role assumed by the Buddhist clergy. Two quotes, taken from *Associated Press* coverage, from Burmese spokespersons support how their fellow citizens say they understand the lay-clergy nexus in terms of engaged Buddhism:

A spokesperson of the National Council of the Union of Burma:

"When the monks take the leading role, the people will follow."

A young woman interviewed at a demonstration:

"The monks are the ones who give us courage."

But there is an addendum to this story of Buddhist compassion under violent circumstances in Myanmar. In May 2008 a vicious cyclone swept over Myanmar, devastating whole regions of the countryside and leaving almost 100,000 dead and tens of thousands more missing. (The number of injured could not even be estimated.) Initially the military junta (for its own reasons) shunned foreign aid, claiming it had relief matters under control while forbidding experienced international relief aid workers even to enter the country. In many of the hardest hit areas no government forces or representatives ever showed up, and drowned unburied bodies, along with fears of serious dehydration, starvation, exposure, and disease mounted throughout Myanmar. Eventually foreign aid and relief workers were permitted into the country after world opinion railed against the intransigent junta (whereupon the government did an about-face and "slammed" the allegedly inadequate aid from the same countries that had ships and supplies waiting offshore for delivery all the while the junta arrogantly rejected it).

Most importantly in this narrative, the Buddhist monks played an invaluable role in ministering to victims during and after the cyclone. Many citizens sought refuge in monasteries, first for shelter during the storm itself and then after for the basic necessities of life while the junta refused outside international assistance. Monasteries functioned as soup kitchens, hospitals, and refugee camps. Seeing the politically embarrassing fall-out of the monks' humanitarian efforts, military forces reportedly broke into monasteries and forced persons to leave on threat of being jailed if they received assistance from the monks. The *Los Angeles Times* reported ("Cyclone Misery Compounded by Junta's Cruelty," 5/24/08) that 1,500 survivors were evicted from one monastery alone.

As matters stood by June 2008 the junta regime's reluctance to admit the true proportions of the national disaster by default left addressing the humanitarian problems much of the time to the Buddhist monks. The ironic result (for the regime) was that the monks' post-mobilization for relief for the population provided them again common cause to regroup and galvanize their members and strength after the political persecution of the previous year. Monasteries again became "flash points" for popular opposition to the junta. The military regime's own inept handling of the post-cyclone catastrophe left a political and social vacuum in many areas of Myanmar, not to mention stimulating anger towards itself. Reports from the *Associated Press* began coming out of Myanmar in 2008 that some monks were even building clandestine stashes of make-shift weapons. Whether the latter efforts were *Dharmic* under the oppressive circumstances (i.e., were in keeping with Precept norms rebuking the taking of life or even self-defense) is perhaps a matter best left for Buddhist scholars and theologians to sort out.

Environmental Activism

Traditional: Hindu and Primitive Buddhist

It is a defensible generalization that Western religions, unlike the religions of South and Far Eastern Asia, foster an anthropocentric view of nature. The subject-object consequences of language help remove human beings from much direct, intuitive experience with inanimate nature and many "lesser" animate creatures, of course, but the presuppositions of Judeo-Christian scriptures, in particular, are more explicit in making the disconnect. As Harvard theologian Harvey Cox argued in *The Secular City* several decades ago, the very creation story of Genesis displays "the disenchantment of nature." Unlike the early polytheistic rivals of early Judaism, the Hebrew scriptures deny that the natural world of weather, streams, fields, forests, and mountains is filled with magical entities and enchanted spiritual personifications. The non-Hebrews of the time generally thought, in the term used by Frankfort, Frankfort, Wislon, and Taccbben (1968), in *mythopoeic* frameworks.

The Genesis account radically changed such frameworks. Or rather, the creator-god Yahweh did. The creation, according to Genesis, separated nature from God and distinguished man from nature.... Yahweh the creator, whose being is centered outside the natural process, who calls it into existence and names its parts, allows man to perceive nature itself in a matter-of-fact way. (Cox, 1965: 22-23)

Thus, the moon, sun, and stars were no longer semi-divine entities. Such phenomena became part of a larger natural order, which (at best) existed for humanity to logically comprehend and cultivate with wise stewardship or (at worst) to use as short-run expediency would suggest. Observes Cox (1965: 23) of Judeo-Christian creation:

Just after his creation man is given the crucial responsibility of naming the animals. He is their master and commander. It is his task to subdue the earth.

In a parallel analysis, Watts (1958b: 28) sees an inherent bias in Judaic-Christian thought privileging the socially-constructed human environment over the rest of creation. Therefore

The nearest thing in the physical world to supernatural beauty is the beauty of the human being and more especially of the human mind. Christianity suggests the urban rather than the rural atmosphere because in the former we are surrounded by the works of the mind.

Contrast the Genesis version of human hegemony over the natural world with the following brief description of Taoism concerning nature:

To Taoists, man, living creatures, the earth, and the cosmos have always comprised one "living, breathing, organism" through which ch'i flows and pulses. The art of Feng Shui, literally wind and water, is concerned with those currents as they flow through the earth and as their results affect the fate of man. (Page, 1988: 72)

Taoism emphasizes the condition of harmony with, not subjugation and conquest of, nature. Likewise, Japanese Zen exponent D. T. Suzuki (1955: 181) acknowledges that "to treat Nature as something irrational and in opposition to human 'rationality' is a purely Western idea..."

Just as Zen is a sect, or offshoot, of the Buddhist trunk, so (Primitive) Buddhism in its first several centuries could be considered a Hindu sect (Coomaraswamy, 1943: 45-49). Certainly the intellectual worldview of Primitive Buddhism was distinctly South Asian, and its understanding of human beings' ethical relation to nature must be located in its Hindu roots.

Dharma conduct in traditional Hinduism was not simply equated with ritualistic moral and social duty nor was it only the abjuring of narrowly selfish interests. Rather, as exhorted repeatedly in *The Mahabharata*, *The Bhagavadgita*, and other writings, following the *Dharma* in the larger sense was to act to ensure the equilibrium among society, nature, and the cosmos. This meant that when human beings interfaced with the rest of the natural world there was no sharp point of demarcation between them as suggested in the Judeo-Christian scriptures. In a review of what classic Hindu writings have had to say about humans' obligations to the environment, Rao (2000: 24, 26) points out:

> A fundamental feature of the Hindu tradition is that there is no dividing line between the sacred and the secular. There is no area of life that is alien to spiritual influence: secular and sacred concerns are inextricably interwoven.... [Thus] nature owes its significance to a transcendent principle whose mind is reflected in it.... The physical world, both animate and inanimate, is a manifestation of the ultimate reality.

That ultimate reality is God, or the Supreme Being, or Brahma as Hindus have understood the concept. This means, according to O. P. Dwivedi (2000: 5) that God is immanent in *everything*, that "all this universe and every object in it has been created as an abode of the Supreme God; it is meant for the benefit of all; individual species must therefore learn to enjoy its benefits by existing as part of the system, in close relationship with other species and without permitting any one species to encroach upon the others' rights."

This perspective of the natural world was coupled with the belief in reincarnation or transmigration of soul (*atman*) essence (more than what Zennists regard as *karmic* rebirth). That meant that all species, as potential or past human beings or even God incarnate, were deserving of reverence and respect. For this reason, "Duty toward humanity and God's creation is an integral part of Hindu ecology and *dharma*" (Dwivedi, 2000:13).

Primitive Buddhists, not surprisingly, as Indians shared the legacy of this cosmic worldview regarding nature (including reincarnation). In the *Jataka Tales* (Stryk, 1969) which tell of the Buddha's youth and 550 previous incarnations, *animal and human*, nature played an enormously important role. Many of the Buddha's sermons dealt in parables and metaphors with compassion toward forest and domestic animals, some of which explicitly involved his past lives. Moreover, just as the early Buddhist community developed an ethic of devaluing professions that involved the killing of animals or the trading in their products (for instance, butchers and leather/hide workers) and advocated the prohibition against eating meat, its first habitations were rural (fields, forests, mountains and caves), not in towns and cities. This fact, claims Kabilsingh (1996: 141), "cultivated great respect for the beauty and diversity of their natural surroundings." This author even cites the early Buddhist monastic canon (the *Vinaya-pitaka*, or "Basket of Discipline," a set of rules and regulations for Indian Buddhist monks and nuns) as encouraging water conservation and discouraging the pollution of rivers and streams with waste. There were even instructions for the first generations of followers as to how and where to build toilets and dig wells (Kabilsingh, 1996). Later, in Indian, Chinese, and Japanese Mahayana Buddhism, with their more inclusive theologies as to who and what ultimately could achieve salvation (Enlightenment, or Buddhahood) environmental concerns and compassion expanded beyond the hierarchy of animals to other life forms, from insects to plants and trees (LaFleur, 1992).

Thus, it was as a direct consequence of Hindu monism that early Buddhists, who partook of the same assumptions about the *Dharmic* unity of all beings and reincarnation as well as mindfulness of the illusion of separateness between self and others—any others—in the *Dharmakaya*, laid the ethical foundation for the environmental group movements organizations of contemporary Buddhism.

Contemporary: Green Buddhists

Authentic (traditional) Zen Buddhism (not the iconoclastic "Beat Zen" of stoned-out poetry and countercultural lifestyles) began its modest ascendency in the United States during the 1960s about the same time as a variety of social movements emerged. Some movement organizations were spiritual in a radically non-theistic or non-Western sense, such as the myriad of groups in what was loosely termed New Age, from flying saucer cults to Native American/non-Western healers to spirit channellers. Some drew on old scriptures and renewed communal lifestyles, such as the Children of God (now The Family) in the Jesus Movement; some were messianic, such as the Unification Church of the Reverend Sun Myung Moon; or not-so-new imports of Asian religious traditions, such as ISKON (the Hare Krishnas); some were transcendent psycho-therapies and technologies, such as est and the Church of Scientology; and some were definitely secular, such as those anti-war, pro-animal rights, and various "liberation" efforts on behalf of children, women, and racial/ethnic/aged/physically-challenged subpopulations. Much has been published in the half-century since, analyzing the "real" reasons for their inspiration, formation, and varying popularities (for example, Needleman, 1972; Bellah, 1976; Wuthnow, 1976; Foss and Larkin, 1979; Rudin and Rudin, 1980; Robbins, 1988) and, of course, the multitudinous agenda behind the counter-movements that arose in response (Shupe and Bromley, 1980; Shupe and Darnell, 2006).

But receiving less attention during the "new religions/deprogramming" controversy was the place of Zen Buddhist activist in the environmental movement (a lacuna lately being admirably filled in by Buddhist writers). Zennists and their fellow Eastern religionists, along with many more Americans and Europeans, have been rightfully concerned with such inseparable, planet-wide deleterious effects of overpopulation, the harmful consequences of gross economic inequality, dwindling availability of clean water/air/arable land, deforestation, species extinction (land and marine), pollution of rivers and oceans, global warming-induced destruction of the Arctic/Antarctic/Greenland/Alaskan ice-sheets and glaciers, and pesticide pollution of soil and water, to name some issues.

Thus, Buddhists make such critiques as that of Devall (1996: 181, 186):

> During the past few centuries, almost every ecosystem and primal culture on Earth has been disrupted, and in many cases totally despoiled, by aggressive human beings.... Dwelling in harmony means dwelling as if life in the broadest sense, not just human life, really matters. It means liberating our minds from the shallow and anthropocentric attitudes drilled into us by a consumer culture that rewards the desire to manipulate others for selfish purposes; violence as a way to solve problems; egocentric individualism; and an intense fear of nature.

Some, like Joanna Macy (1996a: 175), locate much of the problem ultimately in the arch-nemesis of all Buddhism, human beings' delusion of *their selves*: "The crisis that threatens our planet, whether seen from its military, ecological, or social aspect, derives from a dysfunctional and pathological notion of the self." To paraphrase her point as regards the environment and our group movement responsibility toward its predicament, we humans (particularly Buddhists) must transcend the blinders of short-run self-interest, remembering that "what the Buddha taught was detachment from ego, not detachment from the world" (Macy, 1996b: 154).

This environmental ravaging would be merely ironic were it not so self-destructive, agree two famous modern *Rinzai* Zennists from different generations and cultures. They remind us that human beings most literally and materially are constituted of the same natural planet-stuff that the former seem to be so aggressively despoiling. The venerable D. T. Suzuki (1955: 128) stated: "... Man himself is not Man-made but Nature-made, as much as anything we regard as of Nature," while some years later Vietnamese monk Thich Nhat Hanh (1996: 167) concurred that "since we humans are made of non-human elements, to protect ourselves we have to protect all of the non-human elements."

The very concept of an ecosystem calls forth to Zennists their *Dharmic* obligation to protect human beings within their realistically interwoven and ideally balanced natural context. Kaza (2000: 160, 167), reviewing this obligation, notes:

> Acting with compassion in response to the rapidly accelerating environmental crisis can be seen as a natural fruit of Buddhist practice.... Because the web of interdependence includes not only the actions of all beings but also their thoughts, the intention of the actor becomes a critical factor in determining what happens.

Zen, along with Tibetan and other forms of Buddhism, has made a series of "natural interface" connections with other environmentalists through spiritual conferences, academic and popular "teach-ins" and workshops, and multi-target countercultural retreats. One important stimulus for this activism, from the Zen standpoint, is Zen's insistence of "mindfulness" of the web of mutual causality and the non-duality of the *Dharmakaya*. These activists have become generally known within the United States (and increasingly elsewhere) as "Green Buddhists." Their compassionate inclusive worldview is symbiotic with such planetary reinterpretations as James Lovelock's (1979) *Gaia* hypothesis: that Gaia (the Earth) is normally a self-regenerating, self-regulating, integrated system (of which human beings are an inextricable part) akin to a living organism, and that a dualistic humanity-nature stance is destructive to all, if not suicidal.

There may also be in such activism something of the pragmatic American character. Recalls Peter Matthiessen (1998: 398):

> I love *zazen*, but somehow sitting on that black cushion and straining toward the absolute while in the relative world, where there was so much misery and poverty, didn't make much sense. I don't think Americans were ever really geared for sitting only, and I think there was always a schism between American students and Japanese teachers for this reason.

Of course, there has been a similar understanding urged by non-Buddhist secular environmentalists. For instance, Nobel Peace Prize winner, former U.S. Senator and former Vice-President Al Gore, in *Earth in the Balance* (1992: 2), has written:

> The ecological perspective begins with a view of the whole, or understanding of how the various parts of nature interact in patterns that tend toward balance.... But this perspective cannot treat the earth as something separate from human civilization, we are part of the whole too, and looking at it ultimately means also looking at ourselves.

Biologist Barry Commoner (1990: 8) similarly has stated: "One of the basic laws of the ecosphere can be summed up as 'Everything is connected to everything else.'" Parallel sentiments can also be found in distinctly (if non-mainstream) Christian treatments of the environmental crisis (such as Meyer and Myer, 1991; Linzey, 1994) and in the earlier cited works of German philosopher Arthur Schopenhauer as well (Schirmacher, 1996). Green Buddhists have had no trouble discovering allies.

Looking historically as to an aesthetic sense as well, there is a rich tradition in both Chinese and Japanese art reaching back well over a thousand years, expressing the simultaneous unity and diversity of *sunyata*, or Ultimate Reality. Particularly in feudal Japan the underspoken Zen motif can be found in the subtlety of Zen landscaping, ceramic art, scenery paintings, music, drama (the *Noh* theater), poetry (*haiku*) and calligraphy, and in what Hoover (1978: 213-23) terms "private Zen," i.e., flower arranging (*ikebnana*) and food presentation (See also Suzuki, 1959; Binyon, 1963).

Kaza (2000: 170-73), within her review of ways in which Green Buddhism has emerged, from protests over logging of ancient redwood trees to stopping or delaying shipments of dangerous nuclear materials to finding more efficient methods of recycling, discerns three distinct (though sometimes overlapping) patterns to this group movement activism: (1) immediate "holding actions," or protests, sit-downs, and demonstrations to halt immanent local destruction; (2) more long-term structural analysis and creation of "green visions" grounded in Buddhist ethics; and (3) broader cultural transformation, by which she means education and actual implementation of alternative ecological models.

There is no space here or in any single chapter to detail the many events and episodes of the above-mentioned strategies, though they are covered in sources already provided here. Green Buddhism in action is frequently local and idiosyncratic as much as the awareness of individual Green Buddhist group movement measures seems so particularistic to assorted observers. What *is* readily apparent in the emerging literature of activists' reports, however, is the ethically driven nature of Green Buddhism and its this-worldly focus.

Empathy and Compassion in Zen Buddhism

In sociology's subdiscipline of deviant behavior there is a perspective called social control theory that asks not why people engage in non-conformist behavior but instead why more people do not. In other words, it

> assumes that norm violations are generally so attractive, exciting, and profitable that most people are motivated to violate norms. Thus, it is not necessary to explain deviant motivation; rather, it is necessary to explain why so few people act upon their deviant motives and violate norms. (Liska, 1981: 89-90)

Probably the most famous social control theorist, Travis Hirschi (1969), sees the answer to this question in what binds persons to their normative culture. He posits that four kinds of bonds serve to keep most persons acting in law-abiding ways most of the time: *belief* (that certain kinds of behavior are considered wrong and proscribed); *attachment* (the sensitivity to the opinions of others, perhaps influential others); *commitment* (self-interest seeks the rewards that come from obeying rules); and *involvement* (persons busily engaged in conventional behavior have less time to consider deviant or non-conformist activities).

Zen Buddhism also emphasizes bonds and asks why more people do not realize their linkages to one another as well as to the natural world, i.e., why do more people not engage in group movements once the illusion that our separate selves exist apart from others' imputed selves is broken? After all, our fates and interests are interwoven in the *Dharmakaya*. Why do more people not wake up to the Reality of our mutually dependent health, freedom, and safety in a world that is only artificially conceived as divided?

What the examples of Buddhist monk involvement in the 2007 Myanmar protests against a repressive military dictatorship and current pro-ecology activism by American Buddhists essentially illustrate are what Harvard's Christopher S. Queen (1996: 11) terms a "distinctive shift of thinking" among some Buddhists: *from the transmundane to the mundane*. That is, there has emerged a turning away from solitary detached monastic asceticism of the type portrayed by nineteenth-century German sociologist Max Weber toward engaged activism (as there always was at intervals) on behalf of laypersons' social, economic, and political concerns. It is about outcomes that matter to the latter within their lifetimes in this world. (It also may help explain for one of us during a year's fieldwork in rural Japan during the early 1970s why Zen Buddhists displayed higher voting rates and other forms of political engagement compared to other Buddhists—See Shupe, 1977.)

This activism is squarely within the Mahayanist Buddhist tradition that makes much of the *karuna* (compassion) displayed by *bodhisattvas*. Adds Queen (p. 31):

A tradition may be transformed without being betrayed, and heresies may enrich and broaden a cultural heritage while leaving behind those elements—beliefs, practices, institutional forms, public roles—that no longer meet the needs of living communities in a changed world.

King (1996b: 406) offers one of the two philosophically core Buddhist ethical justifications for intervention illustrated by both the Myanmar and environmental examples: "The Buddhist principle of interdependence is probably the most powerful concept used by the social activists to understand, express, and justify their perspective." And there is a second one: out of interdependence flows the auxiliary notion of not-self (*anatman*), one of the Buddha's major insights. Not-self, the rejection of a distinct, permanent, personal identity, means that there is a non-separation from the causes and sufferings of others. In the obligatory sense, empathy then is compassion.

Queen (1996: 10), in explaining the new mundane level of engaged Buddhist concerns (both clerical and lay), refers to the empathy engendered through suffering as a logical extension of not-self, "a new awareness of the social and institutional dimensions of suffering and the liberation from suffering that has contributed to the rise of contemporary Buddhist liberation movements."

In short, empathy as an emotion is a consequence of achieving (or even approaching) *sunyata*, or *satori*, for all the reasons reviewed. Compassion for others' suffering—for their sufferings are really ours, too—is the more activist expression of empathy. As a world religion, Buddhism makes up only about six or seven percent of all living religionists on the planet. But in societies where it has gained a foothold, if not close to a majority, it portends a new future of social engagement in concert with existing secular group movements.

5

Putting Constructs in Their Place

Zen, we began as our description, is beyond being described as just a religion, philosophy, or a type of human inquiry; *it is a way of liberation* to achieve actualization of human spiritual and mental potential. The great American epistemological philosopher F. S. C. Northrop, in generically coming to grips with differences between Oriental (or Asian) "ways of liberation" and Western historical religions, observed in his book *The Meeting of East and West* (1979: 403) of any of the former that "their religion is best thought of by Westerners as something nearer to what the West regards as aesthetics than it is to what the West has regarded as religion." This is a profound generalization, and in a penetrating, thorough comparison of Eastern and Occidental religions at the level of their epistemological assumptions, Northrop allots nearly a quarter of his considerable book to just that subject: the differing (but comprehensible) aesthetic characters of the two cultural spheres.

It should be apparent that Zen Buddhism and Western social psychology do share some mutually important features. Foremost is that Zen respects the reality of consciousness. Indeed, consciousness (or mind, or cognitive thought) presents a constant factor in all human beings and is the main focus of efforts in both social psychology and Zen. That is, Zen readily admits the psychological existence of emotions, ideas, expectations, and memories in every mind. It agrees with social psychology that these elements for the most part are subtly conditioned or taught within primary groups or in institutional secondary group contexts.

However, the language of Zen, militant and even hostile to the effects of socialization, as it has to be to "shake up" taken-for-granted assumptions about social reality, might lead one to believe otherwise. While social psychology views the cognitive products of socialization as often non-problematic, it is the very fact of their being so smoothly internalized and usually unexamined that subverts the mental transcendent, non-discursive clarity sought by Zen. Awakening, or *kensho* or *satori*, cannot be realized within any culture without first offering a major critique of that construct-laden culture. As eighteenth-century proto-social psychologist David Hume (1956: 24-5) observed of the limited self-reflection of the average person, "the more regular and uniform, that is, the more perfect nature appears, the more is he familiarized to it, and the less inclined to scrutinize and examine it." Considering Zen's critique of language and taken-for-granted social constructions of the everyday world, Hume's statement is Zen's point of departure.

That is why Zen Buddhism is ultimately countercultural *in every culture*. In fact, Zen's message of liberation (that is to say, at its heart) is anti-authoritarian, as Thurman (1998: 462-464) suggests, despite the authoritarian nature of the cultural "baggage" brought over to the United States by the first two generations of Japanese masters, steeped as they were in Confucian ethics.

As Chapter 2 examined in some detail, the self-concept or individual identity is the mainstay concept of social psychology. In Zen (and all) Buddhism, however, the notion of a permanent self is worse than a mere conceit; it is the primary source of most interpersonal and many macrosocietal problems. Once we deal at the level of a relative self, however, that is undeniably part of the everyday phenomenal world—once, that is, when the metaphysical rhetoric of there being or not being an essential self or even individual soul is dismissed—then the two perspectives are basically in accord.

True, social psychology, aided by statistics, has at times reified the self and its close psychological "cousin construct" personality in ways unimagined by Zen *roshis*. Consider the case of psychologist Raymond B. Cattell and his studies of personality during the 1960s. Cattell became enamored with the (then) new multivariate statistical technique of factor analysis made more readily accessible by high-speed computers. Factor analysis takes a group of presumably related variables and, employing the logic of what is known as the maximum likelihood estimation, assembles streams or clusters of weighted interrelationships among them. These clusters of interrelated variables are termed factors.

Cattell was a "trait" theorist, seeking to break "personality" down into its component dimensions. After a while his research became a testimony to psychometrics carried to an extreme. Early on Cattell claimed he has isolated thirty-three dimensions, or factors, of personality. To complicate things further he began factor analyzing the factors themselves, no longer working with raw data taken from human beings but instead with the adjusted algebraic averages, averages of other algebraic averages, and so forth, producing factors of the second order, third order, and so on. These he diagramed into what he called "lattices." Cattell's lattices looked as much like an artist's depiction of the neurons and connecting synapses in a section of the brain as anything else. After a time even the discipline itself became somewhat disheartened at this hyper-reification. As two prominent psychologists politely summed up Cattell's statistical excess: "The essence is that the derived factors are not psychologically meaningful" (Hall and Lindzey 1970: 411).

Nor for that matter would classical Zen masters agree with the work of cognitive development theorists who conclude that human morality is a progressive sequence of developments from the absolute zero stage of the youngest amoral child to the lofty heights (for some) of universal spirituality. The work of psychologist Lawrence Kohlberg (1984) is most famous for its three-stage/six sub-stage moral development schema of an initial "preconventional morality" stage based on the external physical consequences, in operant conditioning terms, of actions for appropriate behavior; then a more sophisticated exchange of good behavior for symbolic social approval and an appreciation for the benefits of social order in the "conventional morality" stage; and finally (where, Kohlberg admits, most persons do not ever reach) a "postconventional morality" level that appreciates individual rights and responsibilities and ultimately can evolve to universal ethical principles beyond a single creed adhered to by the individual.

Kohlberg's development scheme has been criticized for a number of reasons (See DeLamater and Myers, 2007: 76-77 for a review) that are irrelevant to Zen, for Zen maintains that we are each born with an inherent Buddha nature, our own essence shared with the Dharmakaya, that is stainlessly pure in the sense it is beyond the dualities of good versus bad or moral versus immoral. That essence is what has become corrupted during socialization. Zen turns Kohlberg's moral development sequence on its head. From birth onwards, unless there is Awakening, we really regress rather than progress. That Buddha nature, says Zennist author Peter Mathiessen (1985: ix), is

> that natural religion of our early childhood, when heaven and a splendorous earth were one. But soon the child's clear eye is clouded over by ideas and opinions, preconceptions and abstractions. Simple free *being* becomes encrusted with the burdensome armor of the eye.

Later in life, Mathiessen goes on to say, we become more mired in the relative world and spiritually compartmentalized:

... we are filled with yearning for that paradise that is lost when, as young children, we replace with words and ideas and abstractions—such as merit, such as past, present, and future—our direct, spontaneous experience of the thing itself, in the beauty and precision of this present moment. We identify, label, and interpret our surroundings as abstract concepts, quite separate from yet another concept, which is our own separate identity and ego. Even holiness is removed from us, a Heaven up there with a God in it. (1985: 8)

But again these are matters more of a nature-versus-nurture debate, which philosophers, psychologists, and sociologists have tossed about for several centuries. Zen's rather strident and admittedly theological views on human nature may be forgiven or ignored and should not obviate its many other commonalities with Western social psychology. Readily admitting the entire scientific corpus of work on socialization, Zen Buddhism is really a process-oriented system designed to at least temporarily undo the effects of social, cultural, and psychological conditioning in order to reestablish an original mental clarity that, it maintains, has been obscured but never really lost. It is sometimes difficult to put aside the rather blunt and "shock-value" language of Zen to see that it is actually not trying to throw the baby out with the bathwater. Zen is about *liberation* from cultural and linguistic baggage that it asserts weighs us down and distorts our purported true nature. But Zennists have to live everyday in a world where children must be exposed to language, schooled, taught morality, and cultivate personal identities. Thus, when the eminent Columbia University Tibetan scholar Robert A. F. Thurman (1998: 452), in offering a general definition of what all Buddhism is and aims to be, claims that

Buddhism, of course, first and foremost probably, is a therapy. It's a therapy that Buddha elaborated for demented human beings...

"demented" should not be interpreted to mean that Zen makes no distinctions between the findings of social psychology and abnormal psychology. The sometimes eccentric teaching styles of classic Zen masters like Lin-chi or Ma-tsu do not indicate that there is no distinction between bizarreness in demeanor or etiquette, on the one hand, and the suffering caused by mental/emotional illnesses, on the other.

And, of course, Zen's version of liberation (or therapy in Thursman's sense) involves coming to appreciate that the relative difference of culture, geography, gender or race that seem to separate us as human are only superficial. We all share a common essence that in reality makes our apparently separate lives and fates indivisible. Otherwise, a psychology of atomized individual differences is a gross distortion of human life, and in fact the realization that a psychology squarely located within the influences emanating from a social context is precisely why the social psychological subdiscipline developed out of work by analysts like James, Cooley, and Mead in the first place. As eighteen-century British philosopher David Hume (1956: 26) expressed this unity:

> All things in the universe are evidently of a piece. Every thing is adjusted to every thing. One design prevails throughout the whole.

Thus, for Zen there are simultaneously differences extant in unity, or in The Dharma, or in The Tao. Or as philosopher F. S. C. Northrop (1979: 354) observed in seeking an intellectual *rapprochement* between Eastern and Western styles of conceptualizing reality in both particularistic and universalistic forms: "The Buddhist merely reminds one of the equally realistic and positivistic, immediately apprehended fact that the self and all things are not merely the many distinguishable and different transitory differentiations, but also the all-embracing, indeterminate aesthetic continuum of which the transitory factors are the temporary differentiation." Multiplicity and unity cannot exist apart. Form and emptiness (in the Zen sense) only reflect each other. American Zennist Robert Aitken (1996a: 87) put it succinctly in a dual analogy:

> ... without the photon, there is no wave of light. Without the frame, there is no movie.

In the remainder of this chapter we consider the sociological and social psychological issues that confront a Zen Buddhism now evolving within Western contexts, a process its first Asian missionaries could afford to ignore a century ago but which now confronts it more than ever.

Zen and Its Constructs

Zen's ruthless analysis of the ways in which we all become figuratively prisoners within arbitrarily constructed social and physical realities—the Platonicity of our lives—can also be turned somewhat on itself. Indeed, this critique applied to Zen is as much warranted as it is applied to every other ism, ideology, and macro-perspective, for Zen must be considered as any other alternative perceptual schema if its practitioners are to avoid promoting the erroneous dualism of "superior" versus "inferior" world-views. Modern Zen Buddhism, insofar as it has expanded to encounter non-Asian cultures, must face the challenge of acculturation into narrow social realities just as it simultaneously must consider the dangers of being trapped in the linguistic cage of its own constructs. For example, it must adapt the essence of its liberation techniques to new situations and populations without dogmatic attachment to its past culture-laden forms. Otherwise it risks an idolatry and fossilization of these same forms.

Zen in the West has come to a fork in the road, to put it metaphorically, and choices must be made. One path leads eventually to sterile, anachronistic marginalization; the other path will demand innovation and creative adaptation. This overarching issue of Zen's acculturation to societies beyond Asia prompts a number of questions about the continued practice, even existence, of its way of mental liberation. Three loom most significantly:

1.   What will be Zen Buddhism's evolving mythology beyond the deeds and "crazy-wise" anecdotes of its ancient predecessors grounded in remote cultures in times long past? Another way of asking this question is: How much of Zen must be transplanted before an indigenous tradition in new circumstances becomes cultivated and accepted?

2.   How will Zen's traditional authoritarian teacher-pupil (master-disciple) roles change as Zen is transplanted to more egalitarian lay populations where most persons want little to do with a strictly monastic lifestyle? What will be its new social psychology of authority and adjustment of power in learning situations?

3.   How will the undeniable presence of women—not just educated, professional women who are already politically and legally liberated and who are also often wives and mothers—be assimilated as practitioners and leaders? This is not merely a feminist issue but is also a sociological reality that currently is being addressed in an *ad hoc* manner in all Western Buddhism; in Zen it is acute.

We address these issues in a tentative, not futuristic, way.

Zen, the Paradox of Language, and Zen Mythology

As argued in Chapter 1, language is at the heart of the cultural "snare" from which the Zennist seeks mental liberation. Language is the purveyor of and vehicle for constructs. *Therefore it is something of a paradox that in order for a Zen teacher to push (or lead) a student to go beyond thinking to an intuitive "transmission of the Dharma," the former must necessarily use language (among other tools) to do it.*

Of course, much of that language use is in non-linear terms, i.e., metaphoric, allegoric, even illogical. (Sometimes the masters even shouted at an opportune time in training: *Kwan! Katsu! Kwatz!* were apparently favorite Chinese outbursts eleven hundred years ago.) Comments Suzuki

(1961: 89-90) on the paradoxical Zen use of language in the form of what Buddhists refer to an *upayaic* (skillful) means:

> ... the idea of the masters is to show the way where the truth of Zen is to be experienced but not in and through the language which they use and which we all use, as the means of communicating ideas. Language, in case they resort to words, serves as an expression of feelings, of moods or inner states, but not of ideas, and therefore it becomes entirely incomprehensible when we search its meaning in the words of the masters as embodying ideas.... Language is then with the Zen master a kind of exclamation or ejaculation as directly coming out of their inner spiritual experience. No meaning is to be sought in the expression itself, but within ourselves, in our own minds which awaken to the same experience.

Likewise, Wu (1996: 13) stresses the emotive nature of language when used by teachers:

> The language used by Zen is therefore in some sense an antilanguage, and the "logic" of Zen is a radical reversal of philosophical logic. The human dilemma of communication is that we cannot communicate ordinarily without words and signs, but even ordinary experience tends to be falsified by our habits of verbalization and rationalization.... We quickly forget how to simply see things and substitute our words and formulas for the things themselves, manipulating facts so that we see only what fits our convenient prejudices. *Zen uses language against itself* to blast out these preconceptions and to destroy the specious "reality" in our minds.... [Emphasis ours]

That is why parables and stories of the original Ch'an masters from the Chinese T'ang (618-907) and Sung (960-1279) Dynasties seem to us moderns often so bewildering and downright bizarre. The teachers did not preach concepts; rather, they sought to awaken the minds of their students in unpredictable, sometimes violent, and seemingly irrational ways. And it should be remembered that these students had been psychologically prepared by arduous mental exercises to bring them close to a point where a radical breakthrough of consciousness would be possible. We often need expert interpretation of these ancient techniques for them to retain their relevance.

For example, consider the following series of encounters between Lin-chi I Hsuan (in Japanese, *Rinzai*) and his famous Zen master Huang Po (nicknamed for a mountain in China):

> Halfway through the summer retreat, I Hsuan climbed Huang Po mountain where he saw the master reading a sutra. He said: "I thought you were one of our kind, but you are only an old monk whose black beans are covered by his hands." After staying a few days, he bade farewell to Huang Po who said: "You have broken the summer retreat to come here, why did you not wait until its end before leaving?" I Hsuan replied: "I only came here to pay reverence to the Venerable Sir." Thereupon, Huang Po struck him (with his staff) and drove him out. After walking a mile or so, a doubt arose in the mind of the disciple who then returned to the monastery. After the summer retreat, he again took leave of Huang Po who asked: "Where are you

going?" I Hsuan replied: "If it is not to the north, it will be to the south, riverbank." Thereupon Huang Po struck him with the staff. I Hsuan caught hold of it and slapped the master's face. Laughing loudly, Huang Po called his attendant: "Bring me my late master Pai Chang's Ch'an ruler and desk." I Hsuan called: "Attendant give me fire." Huang Po said: "No, no, just go away and later you will sit on and twist the tongues of men all over the country." (Yu, 1960: 89-90)

A major stumbling block in making contemporary sense of such narratives is literally in its translation. As Blofield (1958: 26) observes, the euphemisms and even profanity found in the *Goroku* tales (in Chinese, *Yu-lu*, or "recorded sayings" of the Ch'an masters) were transcribed in colloquial archaic Chinese for Zennists over a millennium ago. Such a passage as just cited "here and there employs a sort of T'ang Dynasty slang, the meaning of which has to be guessed from the context." Suzuki (1961: 111) further comments on this "literary" style, noting that the Ch'an masters "found colloquialism a better and more powerful medium for the utterance of their inner experiences."

Well and good, but it leaves us moderns somewhat confused. Thus the translator of the previous passage concerning the Huang Po-I Hsuan "dialogue," Lu Kuan Yu (Charles Luk), in his essay entitled "Stories of the Founders of the Five Ch'an Sects" (Yu, 1960: 55-228), has to expend many more words and considerable space in his book deciphering the original meanings encoded in the story, such as:

the assumed sectarian superiority of Zen (over other schools) in stressing direct intuitive Dharma transmission over Buddhist *sutra* (scripture) reading; (I Hsuan criticized Hung Po for studying a Buddhist scripture.) violations of age-old monastic rules; "black beans" instead of seeing eyes, signifying ignorance and futility; clever *double-entendre* word traps set by Master Huang Po to trick/test his pupil; final praises from the master (the prediction of 'twisting the tongues of men') that I Hsuan's powers of dialectic persuasion will conquer minds and win converts (Yu, 1960: 90);

and so forth.

These sorts of anecdotes, used as teaching vignettes, have pedagogic value as learning templates (once adequately explained), but many of them fall short as accurate renderings of historical persons or events. Moreover, particularly when they portray alleged early conflicts and rivalries they can even foster false constructs that are dualistic and counterproductive and construct misleading mythologies. Scholars have established that much of the early history of Zen's origins, as we presented in the "official" version in Chapter 1, may be somewhat dubious. Many alleged encounters and meetings between Bodhidharma and others may have been contrived or grossly embellished. The story of the supposed tension between Northern and Southern schools of Ch'an, for example, is largely an elaboration selectively reconstructed by writers of a later era when such perceived sectarian divisions were real to them in *their* time. And the supposed rivalry between the rustic, unlettered Hui-neng and the literate Shen-hsiu for the Sixth Patriarchy of Zen was probably the invention of later writers seeking to establish the *Dharma* genealogy of both Bodhidharma as a bonafide patriarch tracing his legitimacy to the Buddha Gautama and Hui-neng as a *Dharma* heir in the same lineage.

McRae (1988: 138) concludes that Hui-neng's counterpart, Shen-hsiu, was (in the seventh and eighth centuries) well-known and easily authenticated, but that Hui-neng, a real figure to be sure but about whom little was known, became a useful literary vehicle for later writers promoting their own sectarian agenda:

> The attraction of Hui-neng was that he was the antithesis of everything that upper-class society cherished: he was from the far South; he had no education or social standing; and he was not even a monk. The figure of Hui-neng represents a prototypic religious anti-hero, a legendary image that could develop only because Hui-neng's actual biography was almost entirely unknown.

Like many folk heroes, writers could graft onto Hui-neng's legend and into his sayings and sermons the germane issues and perspectives they wished (and imagined) such a person would say. McRae likens the images of classic Zen masters conjured by Zen's own historiographers to a string of pearls. With the string of pearls, or sequence of embellished or exaggerated "snapshot" profiles of the masters, a seemingly beautiful coherent necklace is obtained. But, as McRae (1988: 138-139) warns:

> Alas, from the standpoint of history we find that the pearls are illusory and the necklace only a convenient fiction. There is virtually nothing known about Ch'an during the seventh century that does not come down to us filtered through the perspectives of the eighth century or later periods.... Like Bodhidharma and Hui-k'o before him, and Ma-tsu and Lin-chi after him, Hui-neng is in part a creation of the collective Chinese religious inspiration.... [Their stories represent a] spiritual ideal generated from the aspirations of early Ch'an practitioners and embraced by subsequent generations.... [Bracketed insert ours]

A hazard in such historiography, of course, is that any sectarian disagreements or diversities in Zen, otherwise a fairly uniform approach to mental "liberation," albeit with technical differences in practice, become blown out of proportion. Historical mythologies are themselves nothing but sequences of constructs, dangerous when not recognized as such. In any case, their purpose should be to enlighten and edify, not be elevated as gospels. J. C. Cleary (1991: 5, 14) terms such mythological embellishments and creations "pseudo-history" and maintains that this type of approach simply transposes onto Buddhist history the set of human motivations and the limited range of human experiences considered normal or possible in our "modern world." ... Otherwise, if all we do is search for evidence of supposed sectarian rivalries, and labor to piece together questionable hypotheses about long-forgotten controversies among the ill-informed, we are using a conceptual sieve that keeps the chaff and disregards the grain.

This is the familiar social psychological problem with historical constructs and "narratives" becoming reified in Zen as if they had the same status as actual events. Zen, which goes to such efforts to castigate the appearances foisted on each of us by the constructed social reality around us and that so pervades our thoughts, cannot afford to do this to its own origins. These origins, incidentally, are largely irrelevant to Awakening now. There is some role for homage to be paid in any spiritual tradition, but not idolatry of a past that stimulates any modern divisiveness.

Meanwhile, American Zennists like Steven Hagen (2003, 1997), Ruben L. F. Habito (2004), and Ezra Bayda (2003) analyze, teach, and present the Zen *Dharma* for the modern reader in the absence of much reference to the Ch'an and early Zen teaching vignettes. They use instead appropriate contemporary examples and situations to provide social psychological insight in the colloquial language and aphorisms of this era. Perhaps out of their anecdotes, or from the dialogues between the late Roshi Philip Kapleau and his pupils, such as those published in *Zen Dawn in the West* (1979) will emerge a new set of teaching vignettes. (We believe that is what Kapleau's conversations with students and various professionals in his several books really are.) These anecdotes will survive minus the unsettling shouts, slaps, and long forgotten puns of ancient Chinese, but that will make them all the more relevant, if less dramatic. The following brief contemporary exchange between a student and Roshi Kapleau can stand alongside any comeback by a ninth-century Chinese Ch'an master to a pupil:

QUESTIONER: Roshi, I am not satisfied with your demonstration. You have shown us something that I am not sure I understand. It must be possible to *tell* us what Zen is.

ROSHI: If you insist on words, Zen is an elephant copulating with a flea. (Kapleau 1979: 8-9) [Emphasis in the original]

Roshi Kapleau's reply is vintage Zen. The student wishes a discursive psychological explanation of Zen's goals and format. The Roshi responds in a way every bit as blunt, vivid, and absurd as any Ch'an master could have done.

A parting thought: what will be interesting to see in *Rinzai* Zen is the first compilation of twenty-first century *koans*, a sort of Western version of the much older Japanese *Momunkan* collection (Sekida and Grimstone, 1977).

Detoxing from Zen's Exotic Allure

One of us recalls beginning the earnest study of judo in a Mid-American city during the early 1960s. The black belt *senseis* were either Japanese (with a few Koreans) or ex-GIs who had brought judo back to the United States after their military service in places like Japan and Okinawa. In practicing "the gentle way" there was an unmistakable sense of the somewhat mysterious *Oriental* appeal of strange clothing (the *gi* and *obi*); learning how to bow and then count in Japanese for exercises and ranks (*rokkyu, gokkyu, yonkyu, sankyu, nikkyu, ikkyu, shodan, nidan*, and so forth); understanding Japanese commands (*Kiotsuketei, Rei!, Matte!*); the terminology for competition, sparring workouts, and techniques (*shiai, randori, o-soto-gari, harai-goshi, shime-waza*, and so forth); and a new appreciation for the *samurai bushido* code (or martial arts philosophy). This co-author remembers as a high school student being infatuated with the "Asian-ness" that all seemed so exclusive and transcendingly *exotic*!

One meaning of the word exotic (from the Greek *exotikos*) is for something to have the fascination or charm of the unfamiliar. Indulging in the exotic understandably provides the thrill of novelty and a sense of subcultural identity and belonging (which ideally does not evolve into smugness). To be exotic means to be alluring.

Zen practice often has all that. Zen, at least in its North American form, also offers a commercial panoply of accessories and appurtenances associated with meditation and the wider Buddhist lifestyle. A perusal of 2008 issues of the glossy North American Buddhist magazines *Shambhala Sun* or *Buddhadharma* (and in the catalogues that follow when one subscribes to either), for example, includes a wide variety of books, tapes, and opportunities to attend workshop retreats held in gorgeous geographic locales (often in mountain areas) presented by Eastern and Western Buddhist/Hindu (occasional Native American) adepts; the classified and full-page advertisements promote a wide variety of costumes, such as meditation robes and stylish Asian recreational wear; the ads offer meditation mats, rugs, and cushions along with clock timers, Asian furniture and room decorations, incense urns and pots, wall tapestries and reproductions of classic Eastern paintings; and they make available Buddha and bodhisattva statues and statuettes of every conceivable cost and size for home and garden as well as jewelry decorated with Buddhist and Taoist symbols.

In a Japanese Zen Buddhist temple one could find only a few of these items. Perhaps the fact that Americans do much of their Zen practice at home or outside a Zen center means that such items serve a function as aids to mindfulness. Sociologically, of course, they help reaffirm Zen members' spiritual uniqueness in a largely Judeo-Christian society; social psychologically these accoutrements reinforce a practitioner's identity as part of a deviant (i.e., non-conforming and marginal) religionist path.

But we must look further. Are all these physical appurtenances that one can order and pay for online merely a part of spiritual Zen's accommodation to North American culture where religion in many ways has joined the economic marketplace every bit as much as sports, education, and political advertising? Or are magazines and catalogues simply trading on the lure of the exotic, pandering to the thrill of its novelty? Might such examples of commercial Zen actually be diversions and therefore forms of regressive attachments? Are they indicative of an immature Zen movement with a mixed identity, having one foot yet in traditional Asian forms and another firmly planted in a capitalist retail culture?

Past Zennists had negative things to say about becoming "hung up" on *sutra*-knowledge, excessive devotion of or "obsessing" on doctrines, and enlarging the inevitable ritual practices growing up around this emerging branch of Buddhism. In the *Lin-chi Lu* (*The Recorded Sayings of Ch'an Master Lin-chi*), which translator Burton Watson (1993) and others consider to be a fairly authentic account of the iconoclastic Chinese master's sayings, there are unmistakable admonitions against attaching to concepts, doctrines, artificial goals and symbols of enlightenment, Buddhas and bodhisattvas, rituals, and even patriarchs. The *Lin-chi Lu* is replete with Lin-chi condemning temporary attachments to all these things because they waylay Awakening. For example, according to Lin-chi in a *teisho* (sermon):

> Followers of the Way, the true Buddha is without form, the true Dharma is without characteristics. You are striking poses and donning attitudes because of a new phantom. (Watson, 1993: 49) ... there is no Buddha to be gained, and the Three Vehicles, the five natures, the teaching of the perfect and immediate enlightenment are all simply medicines to cure diseases of the moment. None have any true reality. Even if they had, they would still all be mere shams, placards, proclaiming superficial matters so many words lined up, pronouncements of such kind. (Watson 1993: 49, 76)

According to Burton Watson, Lin-chi is driving at the natural human tendency to become attached to doctrines and rituals and all that flow out of them *and* why such attachment is addictive folly in Ch'an (Zen). It is ironic that such warnings are necessary in the one spiritual path that strives to liberate human beings from the infatuation of just such bonds and trends. Says Watson (1993: xxii) of Lin-chi: "What he is saying, and what the Ch'an masters all say in the end, is that one should not become unduly preoccupied with the scriptures and tenets of Buddhism, nor with the rules of conduct and devotional practices that are believed to lead one step by step along the path of spiritual advancement." Huang Po, Lin-chi's ninth century *Dharma* master, also argued the same case against "forms, practices and meritorious performances" (Blofield 1958: 30). Such attachments, which are anathema to Zen, are to be expected by social psychology.

In Zen, words and concepts are the constructions of Mind (and for each of us, the relative mind) ever much as are rituals and physically-related objects. They are what Japan's fourteenth century Zen master Bassui referred to as "the dharma of existent phenomena" (Braverman 1989: 30). Bassui was critical of those he termed "ordinary people," i.e., those persons caught up in the rituals and metaphysically intricate doctrines of his time, thereby missing the point that the real significance of these things was not inherent in them but rather illusory, all created by Mind. Said Bassui:

> There is no dharma outside the mind. Even the temporary formal practices are examples which point to the truth of seeing into your own nature, devised for the edification of ordinary people. Ordinary people misunderstand this and pursuing these examples they take them for reality. They delude themselves and become attached to form. (Braverman, 1989: 51)

There is an interesting and illustrative anecdote described by Robert Aitken (1996a: 10) in which Roshi Nyogen Senzeki, an early Zen missionary who began teaching Zen to Americans on the West coast during the 1920s, came to meet his old monk friend Roshi Furukawa Gyodo when the latter arrived by boat from Japan at a dock. Furukawa was now Abbot of Japan's prestigious Zen Enkakuji temple. According to Aitken, the Zen abbot received an "unpleasant surprise" and was "not amused" by his former friend's "laid-back" American persona:

> There was the roshi at the rail, resplendent in his robes, and there was Senzaki on the dock, dressed in work pants and shirt open at the neck. Running along the dock and waving his arms, Senzaki shouted up to his old friend happily, "Do San!" using the abbreviation of Gyodo Roshi's name that he had always used when they were monks together. It was not the formal greeting that the distinguished roshi had learned to expect.

Pretentiousness in elites, as political sociologist Robert Michels (1959) wrote about in his theory of "the iron law of oligarchy," is one of the accompaniments of the centralization of power and office, something that Lin-chi had warned about a long time ago. A more modern example can be found in Soto Zen Master Kosho Uchiyama who discourages use of the *kyosaku* stick (used to tap participants on the shoulders to keep them awake and mindful while meditating) during the often week-long *sesshin* meditation retreats. He regards the *kyosaku* as having a latent dysfunction in inhibiting *samadhi* and distracting meditators by keeping them more aware of the stick than their actual meditation:

> When the *kyosaku* is carried around, it becomes a toy and people start to play around with it. For example, someone may be sitting quietly and hear the *kyosaku* being carried around. They begin to think about how perfect their posture is and why there is no reason for them to get hit. Or else they may think about how long afternoon hours are and how they can arrange to get hit just to pass the time. (Uchiyama, 1993: 80)

Zen masters Lin-chi, Bassui, and Uchiyama concur: the mind unattended creates the relative world around us as we interpret it through discriminations and invests parts of it with importance, even sacredness, by developing attachments. These attachments, symbolic or otherwise, are "natural" in that they accompany believers in every religion. They also tend to accumulate. As happens periodically in religions such as Christianity, there is the dialectic of an inevitable Reformation (in Christianity, against Roman Catholicism) that in turn sets in motion a Counterreformation (internal reforms by Catholicism), and the dynamic process of internal change continues. Zen itself was a counter-scriptural reformation movement within Buddhism, seeking a return to the original intuitive enlightenment experience of the Buddha. American commercialism may stimulate yet another counterreformation effort in Zen as it establishes itself in North American culture. After all, what group better than Zen to recognize the tendency to cultivate cultural accretions ultimately irrelevant to Awakening as well as the need to safeguard against them?

Zen and Authority

Power and authority are two crucial constructs in sociology and important issues in the group processes studied by social psychology. A pragmatic set of definitions for these terms would be, first, that power is the ability to influence persons, events, and policies, though to say that one actor is powerful does not necessarily mean that, in some zero-sum fashion, less powerful actors are without influence themselves. In the event that less powerful actors create alliances, they may more than additively generate greater power. Clearly power is relative.

Second, authority is *legitimate* power; authorities are acknowledged as having the right or prerogative in the view of a group to exercise power. Authority is a part of social reality, a construct pure and simple. Thus, the State in most modern societies (operating through a variety of agents, such as the courts, police, or in the United States, the Internal Revenue Service) has the authority to enforce, interpret, and sometimes alter laws and exact punishments on those who refuse to abide by its authority.

In Western societies, such as the United States and Canada, where there exists religious pluralism, any religious institution or group has only the moral authority freely given it by its believers. There can be no religious authority (much less coercion) toward any persons unless they freely acknowledge it. And they can withdraw that authority at any time.

This is the situation of contemporary Zen in North America. When an older spiritual tradition is imported from societies historically more authoritarian in relationships into a society with a more recent legacy of resisting or being suspicious of authoritarian relationships, they are bound to develop issues of cultural accommodation and adjustment.

In terms of *external* authority relations in North America, this has not been a great problem, nor will it likely be in the future. Primitive Buddhism at times made the successful transition from being a minority countercultural religion into an establishment majoritarian religion, as it did in India when the Emperor Asoka converted to Buddhism during the third century B.C.E. or when the missionary Buddhist faith moved into Tibet. Zen underwent the same transition and rose as a predominant "establishment" religion first in China and later in Japan. True, Buddhism absorbed many indigenous spiritual ideas and cultural forms at the same time it was transforming these societies, but all this occurred in ancient or feudal societies where distinctly traditional authority relations among men and between men and women were assumed (for example, Das, 1998; Thurman, 1998; Gethin, 1998; Wright, 1959). In pluralist, largely Judeo-Christian North America, however, the scene is much different. Zen (as well as any other) Buddhism will never repeat its Asian ascendency in tandem with political power.

More important to consider, therefore, are the challenges of *internal* authority accommodation that Zen faces in the traditional master-disciple/teacher-pupil relationship. Since so much Zen has arrived in North America *via* Japanese teachers, and is now settling into this Western culture with the first generation of their advanced students, we will focus on the Japanese-North American nexus (though there are admittedly Korean and Chinese Zennist masters here as well). There are three issues of the authority construct to be considered:

Monastic versus Laicization

The first issues of the authority construct derives from the reality that for much of Japanese Zen history (as well as for the Ch'an experience) Zen Buddhism has been monastic, at least as far as its leadership and serious practitioners were concerned. The contemporary situation in North America is far different. Here, statistically speaking, true *roshis* are relatively rare; most Zennists are laypersons. North America has Zen centers, not monasteries. North American context Zen Buddhism is going through a transformation akin to what Roman Catholicism experienced during the 1960s after a series of papal councils in Rome (1962-1965) referred to as Vatican II. The result was a *laicization* of the church in many ways, involving laity in many activities formerly privileged for only the ordained clergy (Gibson, 2004). What this means is that in Zen Buddhism the tradition of the Three Jewels or Treasures (the Buddha, the *Dharma*, and the *Sangha*, this last a community of monastic devotees), particularly the *Sangha*, is having to be rethought. Says Robert Aitken (1996b: 234), one of the first generation of Japanese master-taught American spokespersons for Zen:

> As Western Buddhists we acknowledge our monastic heritage but tend to consider ourselves beyond that archaic, restrictive, and exclusive way of religious practice. Most of us are not ordained monks or nuns. Our Buddhist centers are not monasteries in any traditional sense.

In many other Mahayana Buddhist traditions and centers in North America, the situation is similar: laity as well as ordained clergy practice together, and the "ecclesiastical distance" between the two levels is blurred if not broken down. Laity are thereby empowered within the tradition in subtle ways. Meanwhile, modern Zennists of all ages and backgrounds, priests included, may and often do marry.

And, one could ask, why not? Many practicing (but not ordained) North American Zennists are married and have nuclear households of their own, career responsibilities, and so forth outside their centers. This is not the stuff reclusive monks and nuns are made of, however serious they are about practicing Buddhism on their own terms. The change sociologically is more inevitable than regrettable. After all, as Kenneth Kraft (1998: 180) asks:

> Was Zen meant only for the few who could dedicate themselves to an intensive ten-or-twenty-year course of training? Or should the teaching be made accessible to as many people as possible, even if that entailed certain compromises of rigor or purity?

Indeed, Kraft writes that

> If Western Zen cannot survive as a lay movement it may not survive at all. Thus there is a continuous struggle to establish Zen as a lifetime religious way rather than a narrowly goal-oriented practice. (p. 186)

This monastic-versus-laity lifestyle (and practice) issue was significant as analyzed by novelist/journalist Michael Downing in his book *Shoes Outside the Door*. His meticulous review of the "growing pains" of San Francisco Zen Center, the mixed efforts of which resulted in a major "meltdown" in the 1980s of this significant effort to transplant Japanese (*Soto*) Zen Buddhism in the United States, found a critical cultural disconnect between the Japanese Zen tradition and its emerging U.S. counterpart. In Japan Zen clerical novitiates train under strict monastic (or, analogously, "seminary") conditions, but then Zen priests return to secular life. They go on to maintain households as they marry and have children and perform "parish work" among laity in roughly the same way as do many Protestant ministers. However, American Zennists on the West Coast during the 1960s-1980s sought to carry monastic training practices into their lay lives and did not seem to acknowledge or anticipate an eventual transition. Recalls Downing (2001: 135):

> But seen from Japan, the Zen Center model might have looked like backwards Buddhism.... What distinguished the Americans from the Japanese was their determination to maintain the intensity of monastic practice after they left the monastery.

To paraphrase the prognosis of Zennist Peter Mathiessen (1998: 397), himself a product of that original cohort of Japanese Zen masters in North America, the first great wave of Japanese teachers was already arrived and finished: no more will likely come. The baton is now passed into the hands of their "*Dharma* transmission" disciples.

Vertical versus Horizontal Relationships

The Japanese Zen masters brought with them a Zen steeped in monastic tradition but also a religion more broadly based on *vertical* relationships in society. It was a social system cultivated over 2,500 years ago. Confucianism, the product of a real man named Kung Fu-tzu who lived and died in the fourth century B.C.E., emphasized the harmony of the whole of society and the ethical role of each person in preserving that harmony by acting appropriately. It is still a system of top-down authority, from emperor to subject (or president/prime minister to citizen), with all the administrative levels in between, and from parent to child, husband to wife, brother to sister, and so forth. It was gradually introduced into ancient Japan along with Chinese writing and Buddhism and became officially promulgated during the seventh century with the *Taika* (Great Reform) in 645. The Japanese emperor installed it to impose a Chinese system of government and taxation but also intended it as a "vast system of coordinated knowledge and belief" to trickle down into private life. It eventually had a profound effect on Japanese comportment generally in ways so minute as to be difficult for Westerners to imagine (Tsunoda, De Bary, and Keene, 1964: 53). Most importantly for a transformed Confucian Japan, more emphasis was put on the individual's obligations and responsibilities than on his or her rights. As British military historian and journalist Malcolm Kennedy (1963: 54) summarized it: "Rights were negligible, duty everything."

Modern Japanese social relationships, based on the Confucian ethical system, have been reflected in Japanese Zen. The dichotomous relations between feudal lord/retainer or master/servant have remained in the more modern secular *oyabun/kobun* or *sempai/kohai* relationships of superior/inferior. Likewise, in the traditional dyad of *roshi*-master and *deshi*-disciple the latter submitted himself unconditionally to the superior's instructions, even if they were (from the disciple's standpoint) erratic, seemingly nonsensical, extreme, or even abusive. The master, after all, presumably possessed the larger picture and superior knowledge, *and* kept the devotee's ultimate benefit in mind. No matter what "crazy-wise" pedagogy (Feuerstein, 1991), the prescribed role of the learner in the pair was to obey, endure, and accept unhesitatingly on faith what he was told to do. (The consequences of this system, among other things, fill the *Goroku* tales with anecdotes of masters trying to educate through slaps, nose-tuggings, ear-tweakings, and so forth.)

North American societies, however, are more based on *horizontal* or egalitarian relationships, particularly during the past four decades. While in the short run the initial uniqueness of "submitting" oneself to something like paramilitary discipline from a person supposedly imbued with superior spiritual knowledge, impressed as the novice is with the promise of unusual achievement and the novelty of the exotic, is almost intoxicating, in the longer run wears on the thrill factor, particularly in the face of hard, even arduous work. To complicate things, the old Confucian vertical dyad of master/disciple was *covenantal* in nature. That is, covenantal relationships are diffuse, with no set limits of obligation or duration, often in what become emotional contexts. Horizontal relationships, at least as most American have known them, are more likely to be *contractual*, with specified limits and durations and default conditions for exit (Bromley and Busching, 1988). Many North American Zen practitioners have probably not been prepared for the intense covenant that seriously working with a *roshi*, *Rinzai* or *Soto* entails.

Thus the traditional Zen mode of vertical authority, grounded in Confucianism, met in a collision of sorts with North American students. Observes Kraft (1988: 187):

> Zen was nurtured in a cultural context that valued vertical relationships: the person below was supposed to be loyal to the person above, and the person above was supposed to be responsible for the one below. The seniority system in Zen monasteries affects nearly all aspects of monastic life.... In contrast, Westerners increasingly expect their religious communities to embody the ideal of egalitarianism. This principle is frequently invoked among the students themselves, and sometimes it is even extended to the teacher-student relationship.

Probably worse for some students and centers in the subtle or deliberate rush to embrace the exotic, was the natural but destructively uncritical elevation of teachers to pedestals, which some were apparently not able to assume without traditional Confucian controls. Collcutt (1988: 203) rejects this eager adulation of students toward Zen teachers.

> Part of the problem here is that individuals and groups, even normally skeptical people, sometimes invest Zen teachers with an almost divine aura. They assume that anyone in the role of Zen master must be a person of deep spiritual insight and compassion and that such a person can do or say no wrong.... Aspiring trainees would be wiser to maintain some of their natural skepticism.

One Southern Baptist minister (Bratcher, 1984) has termed this uncritical tendency to elevate spiritual leaders of any sectarian persuasion to unjustifiably lofty heights as a "walk-on-water syndrome" that invariably sets up many church members for disillusionment and their leaders for relative failure. This is apparently what happened more than once during the 1980s when the North American Zen world was stunned by scandals of *roshis'* inappropriate sexual (and other lifestyle) behaviors with students in Zen centers. Some of it was plain sexual promiscuity, though it sometimes involved married ordained priests, therefore adultery. Much of the behavior belied the Buddha's Second Noble Truth and Buddhism's clear Third Precept against misuse of sex. Mentionings about the scandals at both east and west coast Zen centers, some more specific than others, can be found in Kraft (1988: 180); Ives (1992: 111-113); Tworkov (1994: 14; 1998: 533); Aitken (1996a: 160-170), Kapleau (1997: 150-151); and even an entire book by Downing (2001).

Downing's (2001) analysis, in fact, presents a quintessential case of what sociologists term "clergy malfeasance." Zen Roshi Shunryu Suzuki, a somewhat iconoclastic master in the sense that he wanted to mission-ize North America, nevertheless was firmly rooted in the Japanese Zen tradition. Selecting as the sole recipient of his "Dharma Transmission" a disciple named Richard Baker, Suzuki gave Baker essentially *carte blanche* authority to implement the mundane details of construction, finances, and fundraising, and executive operating procedures of a grow-ing ecclesiastical fiefdom. Baker went on to abuse his authority. In the course of San Francisco Zen Center's multi-operational growth, Baker (then married) became a voracious womanizer and involved himself in numerous affairs; he was a spendthrift on personal acquisitions and lifestyle, ignoring the Zen Center's board of directors as his follow-ers lived in accommodations ranging from squalid to modest; and as a spiritual leader he was plagued by self-pity, hubris, and a serious lack of capacity for introspection. At one point, as Baker drove away from one of the Zen Center's rural properties in his personal BMW car, he had dozens of followers in black robes stand in rows and bow to his de-parting vehicle (reminiscent of an earlier parallel in the Bhagwan Shree Rajneesh in Antelope, Oregon). Recalling that he did not know at the time of Baker's ongoing affair with a particular female Zen member, a member reminisced about the BMW departure incident and Baker's flamboyant lifestyle:

> What offended me was that Dick was turning it into an imperial presidency. I don't like that style, and I don't like to see it in Buddhism. He had become the Dick Nixon of Zen. (Downing 2001: 39)

Concludes Downing (p. 35) about Baker's material "appurtenanc-es":

> Bowing to the teacher was not bothersome for most practitioners; it tallied with many students' sense of the egoless ideal of Zen Buddhism. In effect, they were bowing to the dharma. More troubling was the knowledge that they had bowed to that car.

The fundamental problem, a microcosm of the larger North American Zen authority issue, was that the vertical relationship in a spiritual context, fraught with the possibility of emotional transference by a naive and/or impressionable student to an authoritative teacher, occurred in a largely horizontal relationship society. Models of authority were in collision. The students were unprepared, and the entire upshot was to create what criminologists call *opportunity structures* wherein human frailty, hero worship, or predatory motives could prevail. Neither teachers nor students had expectations or guidelines for what normal moral boundaries should be set for this type of authority in a spiritual relationship.

However, this is no problem unique to Zen, for it has afflicted religious bodies more established in North American societies. Since the mid-1980s there has been an (as yet unending) avalanche of revelations about sexually and economically predatory, exploitive, and abusive Roman Catholic priests, Protestant ministers and free-wheeling evangelists, and Jewish rabbis (See, e.g., Sipe, 1995; Shupe, 2008, 2007, 1998, 1995; Schwab, 2002). All analyses of these parallel cases emphasize the same issues as those that set up the Zen situations for scandals: religious hierarchies made up of elevated leaders who abused the fiduciary trusts placed with them by well-meaning but somewhat naive or awed congregants.

Clearly North American Zen's challenge, however, is to demote authority as some kind of supreme construct and disimbue its leadership accordingly with less of it. The ongoing pressures to laicize may accomplish this end in any event.

The Role of Women Practitioners

A third issue concerning the authority construct in Zen is the emerging role of female Zennists. In virtually every Western society, sociology has found that women display higher rates of religious behavior, or religiosity, than men. They pray more often, read Scriptures more, attend worship services more, and take greater responsibility for teaching moral values to their children compared to males. Therefore it is not surprising that North American Zennists would include a considerable (if not precisely known) number of women.

Though the Buddha initially resisted sharing his teaching of the *Dharma* with women, he did relent and allowed women to become cloistered nuns, but

> Even then the female order of Bhikkhunis was founded only under strict and humiliating rules, and the Buddha is reported to have said that their admission would materially shorten the life of the Buddhist religion. (Humphreys, 1951: 38)

The Buddha later taught that if a woman disciplined herself according to the Noble Eightfold Path, she could (possibly) achieve liberation in her own lifetime, thus avoiding as an Enlightened female having to be reborn as a Brahman male in Hinduism (Ives, 1992: 71).

Zen Buddhism inherited this sort of Eastern, vertical, patriarchal cultural "baggage," and the Confucian bias against women has been evident until recently. Kraft (1988: 186) recounts how the Japanese monk Eisai, who brought Lin-chi's "sudden awakening" brand of Zen from China to Japan, lumped Buddhist nuns in with women in general and "evil people" as those who should not be given shelter overnight in an all-male monastery. But there were some bright lights, such as Japan's thirteenth-century promulgator of *Soto* Zen, Dogen Kigen, who included in his immediate circle of disciples a variety of ages, social class backgrounds, and women along with men (Ives, 1992: 55). In Dogen's classic treatise on *Soto* Zen, *Shobogenzo Zuimonki*, he acknowledges that women, both ordained and lay, could achieve enlightenment (Masunaga, 1971: 49). In that overtly sexist age and society, Dogen's comments and actions were far from trivial.

Kraft (1988: 186-188) has dealt explicitly with the concerns and activities of women Zen practitioners in North America. They have begun to experience increasing ordinations, publish books and magazines, and are energetic speakers and authors at conferences and in edited books about Buddhists (for example, Macy, 1996a, 1996b; Halifax, 1998; Kaza, 2000; Moon, 2000). Unfortunately they have inherited a truly wretched second-class status from Japanese Zen. Faulk (1988: 158) has observed that as of the mid-1980s Zen Buddhist women in Japan made up a relatively tiny (single digit) percentage of the clergy in *Soto*, *Rinzai*, and *Obaku* sects. He writes concerning women in Zen vocations

> of a long history of discrimination against nuns in Japanese Zen (as well as in other traditional schools of Japanese Buddhism). It is only in the post-war era that nuns have managed to gain, on paper at least, rights and privileges equal to those of their male counterparts in the Zen establishment. Soto nuns, after a long struggle, first won the rights to ordain disciples and give Dharma transmission in 1951, and since 1970 they have been allowed to serve as the head priests of low-ranking branch temples. The official status of Japan's Rinzai and Obaku nuns lags even further behind that of Soto nuns, since their numbers are too small to be influential. Another way in which discrimination has manifested itself, ironically, is in a refusal to accept the propriety of marriage for nuns. Men are granted the privilege of modifying the Buddhist precept that forbids sexual activity for ordained clergy, but women are not.

This is the sociological legacy that female Zennists must work within as they address constructs surrounding authority. However, that Japanese pattern of sexual discrimination is unlikely to continue or be "transmitted" along with the *Dharma* into North American Zen. Female Zennists are numerically too large a presence, their Buddha natures truly in horizontal relations (literally often side by side) in Zen centers with men and engaged visibly and vocally as representatives of Zen faith and practice. As argued here and by others, the very construct of Zen authority is currently in transition. And more than any other element of authority, sexism is being challenged or, in fact, more than challenged. By default and in Western feminist fashion, women Zennists are simply bypassing it.

Last Word: The *Dharma* and the Game

The *Dharma* simply is, without form or discursive understanding. There have been various paths seeking its appreciation. The *Dharma* is the Tao of Lao-tzu. It is the Ultimate Reality behind what the Hindus call Brahma, or God, and the plethora of popular personified deities. Zen Buddhism is but one other path to appreciate the *Dharma*. The Buddha happened to penetrate awareness of the *Dharma* during the sixth century B.C.E. as others undoubtedly had before and since, but one does not have to be a Buddhist or a Zennist or anything else to do so. Zen really is not about Buddhism, anyway. The *bohisattvas*, the constructs about *satori* and *sunyata*, the icons and statues and incense and sutras, along with the Four Noble Truths, are all window-dressings. Lin-chi was right: if one is on the road to Enlightenment and a Buddha steps in his or her way, crush the Buddha (as a distraction).

Life is a game. That is what Zen really teaches. Games are also something to which social psychology has devoted a lot of attention. The relative reality around us is transitory and arbitrarily understood by our culture. So are all our goals, efforts, and fears. That does not mean we should become fatalistic and abandon the game of living and sequester ourselves in a cave. Play the game. Play it with intensity, avoiding the losses and savoring the successes whenever possible. That is playing the game well. Only be mindful that our beloved projects, rivalries, annoyances, defeats, and on and on are part of playing.

Zennist Steven Hagen, in *Buddhism: Plain and Simple*, writes that we should not be misled or conned by the conceptualizations that others foist on us while we are playing the game. Because even within the game they often are playing their own private games as well. The game is full of delusions. Wisdom is to *transcend* any inherent importance others award to elements of the game. Says Hagen (1997: 137):

> After all, it's not conceptualization itself that's the problem, but getting caught up in it, mistaking our concepts for Reality. The Awakened may have thoughts and concepts just like anyone else. The difference is that they're aware that what they actually *see* differs from what they think. [Italics in original]

That is Right Wisdom, part of the Buddha's Noble Eightfold Path, a user's guide to the game. Play the game but do not attach too much to its consequences. See through it as *maya* (arbitrary illusion). Transcend the limited horizons focused on by the other players.

That is a life philosophy for serenity. It puts the mundane office politics, pressures, and petty squabbles of daily life in their place. One doesn't detach from life, one merely chooses not to attach too much to it. Or as Hagen (1997: 88) offers in his prescription for acting in the gaming world around us:

> Buddhas don't get rid of delusion; they just see it for what it is and are not taken in by it.

End

A Brief Working Glossary of Zen Terms

(Note: Sanskrit = Skt, Chinese = Ch, Japanese = Jp)

anatman (Skt) – Buddhist doctrine about the non-existence of the individual self or soul; often referred to as "no-self" or "not-self," it maintains that the concept of an individual self is an illusion.

anitya (Skt) – Buddhist doctrine of impermanence or flux of all things.

avidya (Skt) – ignorance of the interrelatedness of all reality and of desire for permanence in things (as the source of suffering).

Atman (Skt) – Hindu concept of the great Soul, of which each person has an individual atman, of the impersonal godhead Brahma.

bodhi (Skt) – intuitive realization of wisdom.

Bodhidharma (Skt) – proper name of the founder of Ch'an (Zen) Buddhism, part legend and likely also a historical figure; "officially" the Twenty-eighth Patriarch of Buddhism, third son of a Brahman king in South India, who brought his "intuitive realization" style of Buddhism to China purportedly in 520.

Bodhisattva (Skt) – in Buddhist tradition a compassionate enlightened person who delays his or her ultimate entry into nirvana for the sake of all sentient beings and who acts as a sort of "intercessory" to enlightenment in the manner of a Roman Catholic saint; in modern Zen, because all persons innately and originally possess a Buddha-nature, all students of the Way may be termed bodhisattvas.

Buddha (skt) – the historical enlightened teacher Siddhartha Gautama (personal and family names, respectively) of the Shakya clan in Northern India, born 563-died 483 B.C.E.; founder of Buddhism, he was believed by early Buddhists to be the product of numerous reincarnations in both human and animal forms, not the first Enlightened One to appear nor the last.

Buddha-nature (Skt-Eng) – the original uncorrupt self-nature or spiritual essence of each person before cultural discriminations are socialized; believed in Zen to be realized or "reawakened to" in satori or "self-realization."

buddhi (Skt) – intuitive awakening to or realization of the wholeness of Reality.

Ch'an (Ch) – archaic Chinese pronunciation of the Sanskrit word dhyana, meaning meditation (in the sense of the dissolution of dualistic subject-object discriminations); this school of Buddhism began "officially" when Indian Buddhist monk Bodhidharma arrived in China in 520; pronounced by first Japanese monks to have studied the system in China and brought it to their homeland during the twelfth and thirteen centuries as Zen.

ch'i (Ch) – according to Taoism a pervasive, invisible, formless energy in all things and persons, generated by the dialectic tension between the yin and yang principles; it can be harnessed through harmony with the Tao; in Japanese called ki, meaning spirit.

deva (Skt) – in Hindu "shining one," meaning a celestial being akin to a deity.

dharma (Skt) – in Hinduism the order and law of the universe or righteous conduct; in Buddhism the principles behind Reality and Awakening, which the Buddha taught and discovered through intuitive appreciation as well as recorded in the scriptures of his emerging religion.

Dharmakaya (Skt) – literally "Dharma body," one of three metaphysical aspects of the Buddha godhead, representing the aspect of the Buddha, which was his True Self-nature, i.e., the essence of the timeless universe; often used as equivalent to dharma.

dhyana (Skt) - as meant in Zen, meditation that is not "focused" but transcends subject-object dualisms.

dokusan (Jp) – the private interview a Zen master has with his pupil; in Rinzai Zen a meeting held between master and pupil to determine the student's koan understanding; in modern Zen often used interchangeably with sanzen.

dukkha (Skt) – suffering derived from frustrated desires.

Goroku (Jp) - Japanese pronunciation of Chinese Yu-lu, shortened title for "recorded sayings of the masters" in Ch'an.

karma/karman (Skt) - Hindu-Buddhist belief known as the law of actions' causes and effects, i.e., the effects of past behavior influences the present condition and present actions influence future conditions for individuals and groups; may or may not be tied to beliefs in personal reincarnation in Zen.

karuna (Skt) – compassion (with an action orientation).

kendo (Skt) – Japanese saber fencing, a modern sport derived from the older samurai kenjutsu.

kensho (Jp) – to look into one's self-nature, to appreciate one's unity with all of Reality.

koan (Jp) – a riddle (seemingly nonsensical) not answerable or resolvable with logic but instead relying on a flash in insight to appreciate deeper Buddhist truths of unity with Reality; used particularly by the Rinzai Zen sect, from the Chinese kung-an.

ksana (Skt) – the shortest imaginable moment or fragment of time.

kyosaku (Jp) – a light flattened stick (wood or bamboo) 75-100 cm in length, used in Soto Zen to strike meditators lightly about the shoulders and back during zazen meditation; it purportedly invigorates, helps refocusing, and inhibits dozing.

hara (Jp) – lower diaphragm; the abdomen or lower stomach where air is drawn in and expelled during breathing in Zen meditation and martial arts.

Hinayana (Skt) – Theravada Buddhism, or "the Lesser Wheel or Lesser Vehicle," one of the two general theological approaches in Buddhism, characteristics of a rift in Buddhism several centuries after the Buddha's death; maintains a distinction between samsara (the round of life and death) and nirvana (salvation or Enlightenment); found mostly in Southeastern Asian countries such as Myanmar, Vietnam, and Ceylon; its enlightened members are referred to as arhats.

Hua-yen (Ch) – literally the "flower garden" school; a Mahayana Buddhist approach emphasizing the holistic nature of Reality and total interdependence of all knowledge, beings, and nature; fully emerged during the T'ang Dynasty (618-907) along with Ch'an, though its teachers and scriptures had existed in China several centuries before (with its own system of patriarchs).

Lankavatara-sutra (Skt) – an important Indian Buddhist scripture, written perhaps in the early fourth century, which emerged from the Yogacara school and is considered to have synthesized aspects of Mahayana and Hinayana Buddhism.

Lao-tzu (Ch)- legendary founder of Taoism living in anywhere from fifth to seventh century B.C.E.; Chinese literally means "Old Man," or "old Master;" recognized at least nominally as author/compiler of the classic Tao Te Ching.

Mahayana (Skt) – "the Greater school or Greater Vehicle" theological approach in Buddhism; began in India several centuries after the Buddha's death and spread to Tibet, China, and Japan (among other countries); includes Ch'an or Zen; emphasizes that samsara (the wheel of life and death) or phenomenal world is the same as nirvana (Enlightenment), which is the noumenal world; emphasizes the salvationary role of bodhisattvas.

maya (Skt)- Hindu (Vedic) and Buddhist notion of illusion, i.e., the world as we ordinarily perceive it is actually a social construction; culturally conditioned thoughts that mislead us.

Mu (Jp) – "Not!'" name of a famous Ch'an koan that is meant to provide a single non-specific answer to a double-barreled question as to whether a dog has a Buddha-nature or doesn't have one.

mushin (Jp) – "no mind;" the same as wu-nien in Chinese Taoism; mental detachment from dualism in acting or meditating; not to be confused with mushinjo, a self-inducted trance that is not satori.

nen (Jp) – thought impulse or feeling sense; immediate impression of a sensation unfiltered through interpretation.

Nirmanakaya (Skt) – the physical body, brain, etc. of the historical man Buddha Gautama who participated in Enlightenment.

nirvana (Skt) – literally "extinguishing of a flame," it is Enlightenment; complete accord with the Dharma; it is not mental, physical, or spiritual extinction.

Noble Eight-fold Path – the Buddha's prescription, path, or methodology for behavior that will lead to nirvana, or Enlightenment.

prajna (Skt) - literally "primordial knowing" (jna) and awakened (pra); the original ways of apprehending the world around us before cultural conditioning; a non-dualistic, intuitive appreciation of Reality.

Rinzai (Jp) – both the Japanese pronunciation of the name of Lin-chi, ninth-century Ch'an master and of the Zen approach emphasizing sudden awakening and koans.

samadhi (Skt) – meditative state wherein dualistic thinking is transcended, eventually leading to satori.

sanzen (Jp) – See dokusan.

Satipatthana (Skt) – in Ceylon a retreat training center for Hinayana Buddhist meditative devotion, often lasting for six weeks or longer.

Sambhogakaya (Skt) – one of three aspects in the godhead principle of Buddha; the essence of the Buddha that was his realization of prajna and entrance into nirvana not separated from his compassionate connection to the world.

satori (Jp) – an equivalent to nirvana; enlightenment or awakening to prajna; in Rinzai Zen it is sudden; in Soto Zen it is more progressive and usually referred to as kensho.

sesshin (Jp) – intensive twenty-four-hour meditative retreat often lasting a week to ten days.

shikantaza (Jp) – "just sitting" in meditation; used in Soto Zen; believed to eventually lead to Awakening; emphasis on mental serenity and exact breathing; developed methodologically and conceptually by Dogen Kigen (1200-1253), founder of Soto Zen school in Japan.

Soto (Jp) – both the Japanese pronunciation of the name of the Ch'an Buddhist Ts'ao-Tung school (an amalgamation of two ninth-century Ch'an masters Tung-shan Liang-Chieh and Ts-ao-shan Pen-chi); one of the two major surviving approaches in modern Zen.

sunyata (Sktd) – the Plethora, Void, Ultimate Reality, or Dharmakaya, which is all of undifferentiated existence.

sutra (Skt) – scripture, either Hindu or Buddhist.

Tao (Ch) – "the Way," the undifferentiated Reality that must be intuited, not discursively or logically described or even named; it is all, permeates all, and Taoists seek to live in harmony with it.

Tariki (Jp) – forms of Buddhism, such as Jodo, Judo-Shin-shu, or Nichiren-sho-shu, that are "salvationist" i.e., putting faith in sutras, teachers, or bodhisattvas (often employing sacred mantras or chants) for Enlightenement.

Tathata (Skt) – "thusness" or "suchness" of reality as it is; the state of prajna and sunyata, where realization of Reality is unfiltered through any cultural lens.

teisho (Jp) – formal lecture, exposition of teachings, etc. given by a Zen master.

Tetsugaku (Jp) – modern Japanese word coined in the nineteenth century to describe Western philosophy.

tsu-jen (Ch) – Taoist principle of just growing or naturally emerging, without being created.

upaya (Skt) – skillfull (practical, realistic) means to teach the Dharma and principles of Buddhism.

vijnana (Skt) – ordinary linear, logical knowledge and learning; opposite of prajna.

wu-nien (Ch) – "no-mind"; in Taoism the mental state free of linear discursive apprehensions and limitations.

wu-wei (Ch) – acting to be in harmony with the Tao; yielding to the Tao so as to act more effectively in a situation.

Yang (Ch) – in Taoism the assertive male principle complementary with Ying; their dialectic interaction creates ch'i, the active force or power permeating all reality and which can be harnessed.

Yin (Ch) – the passive female principle complementary with Yang; their dialectic interaction creates ch'i, the active force or power permeating all reality and which can be harnessed.

zazen (Jp) – Zen meditation posture and/or activity; usually knees bent, sitting either on the heels or in the folded-leg lotus position; can also be performed laying down or sitting in a chair.

References

Zen Buddhism References

Abe, Masao (Editor). 1986. *A Zen Life: D. T. Suzuki Remembered.* New York: Weatherhill.

Aitken, Robert. 1996a. *Original Dwelling Place.* Washington, DC: Counterpoint.

Aitken, Robert. 1996b. "Precepts and Responsible Practice." Pp. 234-237 in *Engaged Buddhist Reader,* edited by Arnold Kotler. Berkeley, CA: Parallax Press.

Austin, James H. 1999. *Zen and the Brain.* Cambridge, MA: MIT Press.

Barnes, Nancy J. 1996. "Buddhist Women and the Nuns' Order in Asia." Pp. 259-294 in *Engaged Buddhism: Buddhist Liberation Movements in Asia,* edited by Christopher S. Queen and Sallie B. King. Albany, NY: State University of New York Press.

Bayda, Ezra. 2003. *Being Zen: Bringing Meditation to Life.* Boston, MA: Shambhala Publications.

Bhikshu, Cheng Chien. 1992. *Sun Face Buddha: The Teachings of Ma-tsu and the Hung-chou School of Ch'an.* Berkeley, CA: Asian Humanities Press.

Binyon, Laurence. 1963. *The Spirit of Man in Asian Art.* New York: Dover Publications.

Blofeld, John (Translator). 1958. *The Zen Teaching of Huang Po: On the Transmission of Mind.* New York: Grove Weidenfeld.

Braverman, Arthur (Translator). 1989. *Mud and Water: A Collection of Talks by the Zen Master Bassui (Wadeigassui).* San Francisco, CA: North Point Press.

Brown-Simmer, Judith. 2000. "Speaking Truth to Power: The Buddhist Peace Fellowship." Pp. 67-94 in *Engaged Buddhism in the West,* edited by Christopher S. Queen. Boston, MA: Wisdom Publications.

Cabezon, Jose Ignacio. 1996. "Buddhist Principles in the Tibetan Liberation Movement." Pp. 295-320 in *Engaged Buddhism: Buddhist Liberation Movements in Asia,* edited by Christopher S. Queen and Sallie B. King. Albany, NY: State University of New York Press.

Cleary, Christopher (Translator and Editor). 1977. *Swampland Flowers: The Letters and Lectures of Zen Master Ta Hui.* New York: Grove Press.

Cleary, J. C. (Translator). 1991. *Zen Dawn: Early Zen Texts from Tun Huang.* Boston, MA: Shambhala.

Cleary, Thomas (Translator and Editor). 1978. *Sayings and Doings of Pai-chang.* Los Angeles, CA: Center Publications.

Cleary, Thomas. 1983. *Entry into the Inconceivable: An Introduction to Hua-Yen Buddhism.* Honolulu, HI: University of Hawaii Press.

Cleary, Thomas. 1988. *Awakening to the Tao by Liu I-ming.* Boston, MA: Shambhala Publications.

Cleary, Thomas. 1994. *Instant Zen: Working Up to the Present.* Berkeley, CA: North Atlantic books.

Cleary, Thomas. 1997. *The Five Houses of Zen.* Boston, MA: Shambhala Publishing.

Cleary, Thomas. 2000. *Zen Essence: The Science of Freedom.* Boston, MA: Shambhala Publications.

Collcutt, Martin. 1988. "Epilogue: Problems of Authority in Western Zen." Pp. 199-207 in *Zen: Tradition and Transition,* edited by Kenneth Kraft. New York: Grove Press.

Commoner, Barry. 1990. *Making Peace with the Planet.* New York: Pantheon.

Conze, Edward. 1959. *Buddhism: Its Essence and Development.* New York: Harper & Row.

Conze, Edward. 1967. *Buddhist Thought in India.* Ann Arbor, MI: Ann Arbor Paperbacks.

Coomaraswamy, Ananda K. 1943. *Hinduism and Buddhism.* New York: Philosophical Library.

Coomaraswamy, Ananda K. 1957. *The Dance of Shiva.* New York: the Noonday Press.

Corless, Roger. 2000. "Gay Buddhist Fellowship." Pp. 269-279 in Engaged Buddhism in the West, edited by Christopher S. Queen. Boston, MA: Wisdom Publications.

Cox, Harvey. 1965. *The Secular City.* New York: Macmillan.

Das, Lama Surya. 1998. "Emergent Trends in Western Dharma." Pp. 450-468 in *Buddhism in America,* edited by Al Rapaport and Brian D. Hotchkiss. Rutland, VT: Charles E. Tuttle.

Deshimaru, Taisen Roshi. 1979. *The Voice of the Valley: Zen Teachings,* edited by Philippe Coupey. Indianapolis, IN: The Bobbs-Merrill Company.

Devall, Bill. 1996. "Ecocentric Sangha." Pp. 181-188 in *Engaged Buddhist Reader,* edited by Arnold Kotler. Berkeley, CA: Parallex Press.

Downing, Michael. 2001. *Shoes Outside the Door: Desire, Devotion, and Excess at San Francisco Zen Center.* Washington, DC: Counterpoint.

Dwivedi, P. P. 2000. "Dharmic Ecology." Pp. 3-22 in Hinduism and Ecology, edited by Christopher Key Chapple and Mary Evelyn Tucker. Cambridge, MA: Harvard University Press.

Eisai. 1958. "Propagation of Zen for the Protection of the Country." Pp. 235-237 in *Sources of Japanese Tradition. Vol. 1,* edited by Ryusaku Tsunoda, William Theodore De Bary and Donald Keene. New York: Columbia University Press

Evans-Wentz, W. Y. 1969. *The Tibetan Book of the Great Liberation.* London, England: Oxford University Press.

Faulk, T. Griffith. 1988. "The Zen Institution in Modern Japan." Pp. 157-177 in *Zen: Tradition and Transition,* edited by Kenneth Kraft. New York: Grove Press.

Feuerstein, Georg. 1991. *Holy Madness: The Shock Tactics and Radical Teachings of Crazy-Wise Adepts, Holy Fools And Rascal Gurus.* New York: Paragon House.

Fromm, Erich, 1960. "Psychoanalysis and Zen Buddhism." Pp. 197-203 in *The World of Zen,* edited by Nancy Wilson Ross. New York: Vintage Books.

Gethin, Rupert. 1998. *The Foundations of Buddhism.* New York: Oxford University Press.

Glassman, Roshi Bernard Testsugen. 1998. "Zen Lessons in Living a Life That Matters." Pp. 427-439 in *Buddhism in America,* edited by Al Rapaport and Brian D. Hotchkiss. Rutland, VT: Charles E. Tuttle9.

Goleman, Daniel. 2003. *Destructive Emotions: How Can We Overcome Them?* New York: Bantam Books.

Gore, Al. 1992. *Earth in the Balance.* New York: Houghton Mifflin.

Green, Paula. 2000. "Walking for Peace: Nipponzan Myohogi." Pp. 128-156 in *Engaged Buddhism in the West,* edited by Christopher S. Queen. Boston, MA: Wisdom Publications.

Green, James (Translator and Editor). 1998. *The Recorded Sayings of Zen Master Joshu.* Boston, MA: Shambhala Press.

Grigg, Ray. 1994. *The Tao of Zen.* Edison, NY: Alva Books.

Habito, Ruben L. F. 2004. *Living Zen, Loving God.* Boston, MA: Wisdom Publications.

Hadden, Jeffrey K. and Anson Shupe. 1988. *Televangelism: Power and Politics on God's Frontier.* New York: Henry Holt.

Hagen, Steve. 1997. *Buddhism Plain and Simple.* New York: Broadway Books.

Hagen, Steve. 2003. *Buddhism Is Not What You Think.* San Francisco, CA: HarperSanFrancisco.

Halifax, Joan. 1998. "Being with Dying." Pp. 373-393 in *Buddhism in America,* edited by Al Rapaport and Brian D. Hotchkiss. Rutland, VT: Charles E. Tuttle.

Hanh, Thich Nhat. 1967. *Vietnam: Lotus in a Sea of Fire.* New York: Hill and Wang.

Hanh, Thich Nhat. 1995. *Zen Keys.* New York: Doubleday.

Hanh, Thich Nhat. 1996. "The Sun My Heart." Pp. 162-170 in *Engaged Buddhist Reader,* edited by Arnold Kotler. Berkeley, CA: Parallex Press.

Haskel, Peter (Translator). 1984. *Bankei Zen: Translations from the Record of Bankei.* Edited by Yoshito Hakeda. New York: Grove Press.

Hoover, Thomas. 1978. *Zen Culture.* London, England: Routledge.

Humphreys, Christmas. 1951. *Buddhism.* Baltimore, MD: Penguin Books.

Humphreys, Christmas. 1986. "Dr. D. T. Suzuki and Zen Buddhism in Europe." Pp. 81-89 in *A Zen Life: D. T. Suzuki Remembered,* edited by Masao Abe. New York: Weatherhill.

Ives, Christopher. 1992. *Zen Awakening and Society.* Honolulu, HI: University of Hawaii Press.

Kapleau, Philip (Roshi). 1979. *Zen: Dawn in the West.* Garden City, NY: Anchor Press.

Kapleau, Philip (Roshi). 1989. *The Wheel of Life and Death.* New York: Doubleday.

Kapleau, Philip (Roshi). 1997. *Awakening to Zen: The Teachings of Roshi Philip Kapleau.* Edited by Polly Yong-Eisendrath and Rafe Martin. New York: Scribner.

Kaza, Stephanie. 2000. "To Save All Beings: Buddhist Environmental Activism." Pp. 159-183 in *Engaged Buddhism in the West,* edited by Christopher S. Queen. Boston, MA: Wisdom Publications.

Kennedy, Malcolm. 1963. *A Short History of Japan.* New York: The New American Library.

King, Sallie B. 1996a. "Thich Nhat Hanh and the Unified Buddhist Church of Vietnam: Non-Dualism in Action." Pp. 321-363 in *Engaged Buddhism: Buddhist Liberation Movements in Asia,* edited by Christopher S. Queen and Sallie B. King. Albany, NY: State University of New York Press.

King, Sallie B. 1996b. "Conclusion: Buddhist Social Activism." Pp. 401-436 in *Engaged Buddhism: Buddhist Liberation Movements in Asia,* edited by Christopher Queen and Sallie B. King. Albany, NY: State University of New York Press.

Kohn, Michael H. (Translator), 1991. *The Shambhala Dictionary of Buddhism and Zen.* Boston, MA: Shambhala.

Kraft, Kenneth. 1988. "Recent Developments in North American Zen." Pp. 178-198 in *Zen: Tradition and Transition,* edited by Kenneth Kraft. New York: Grove Press.

Kabilsingh, Chatsumarn. 1996. "Early Buddhist Views on Nature." Pp. 140-144 in *Engaged Buddhist Reader,* edited by Arnold Kotler. Berkeley, CA: Parallex Press.

Kyi, Aung San Suu. 1995. *Freedom from Fear, Revised Edition.* New York: Penguin Books.

LaFleur, William R. 1992. *Liquid Life: Abortion and Buddhism in Japan.* Princeton, NJ: Princeton University Press.

Linssen, Robert. 1958. *Living Zen.* New York: Grove Weidenfeld.

Linzey, Andrew. 1994. *Animal Theology.* Urbana, IL: University of Illinois Press.

Loori-Sensei, John Daido. 1998. "Lotus in the Fire: Prison, Practice, and Freedom." Pp. 304-314 in *Buddhism in America,* edited by Al Rapaport and Brian D. Hotchkiss. Rutland, VT: Charles E. Tuttle.

Lovelock, James E. 1979. *Gaia: A New Look at Life on Earth.* New York: Oxford University Press.

Macy, Joanna. 1996a. "The Greening of the Self." Pp. 171-180 in *Engaged Buddhist Reader,* edited by Arnold Kotler. Berkeley, CA: Parallex Press.

Macy, Joanna. 1996b. "World as Lover, World as Self." Pp. 150-161 in *Engaged Buddhist Reader,* edited by Arnold Kotler. Berkeley, CA: Parallex Press.

Maezumi, Taizan and Bernie Glassman (Editors). 2002. *On Zen Practice: Body, Breath, Mind.* Boston, MA: Wisdom Publications.

Malone, Rev. Kobutsu. 1998. "Prison Zen Practice in America: Life and Death on the Razor's Edge." Pp. 440-447 in *Buddhism in America,* edited by Al Rapaport and Brian D. Hotchkiss. Rutland, VT: Charles E. Tuttle.

Masunaga, Reiho (Translator). 1971. *A Primer of Soto Zen: A Translation of Dogen's Shobogenzo Zuimonki.* Honolulu, HI: University of Hawaii Press.

Mathiessen, Peter. 1985. *Nine-Headed Dragon River.* Boston, MA: Shambhala Publications.

Mathiessen, Peter. 1998. "The Coming of Age of American Zen." Pp. 396-406 in *Buddhism in America,* edited by Al Rapaport and Brian D. D. Hotchkiss. Rutland, VT: Charles E. Tuttle.

McClellan, Janet. 2000. "Social Action among Toronto's Asian Buddhists." Pp. 280-303 in *Engaged Buddhism in the West,* edited by Christopher S. Queen. Boston, MA: Wisdom Publications.

McRae, John R. 1988. "The Story of Early Ch'an." Pp. 125-139 in *Zen: Tradition and Transition,* edited by Kenneth Kraft. New York: Grove Press.

Meckel, Daniel J. and Robert L. Moore (Editors). 1992. *Self and Liberation: The Jung-Buddhism Dialogue.* New York: Paulist Press.

Merton, Thomas. 1967. *Mystics and Zen Masters.* New York: Dell.

Merton, Thomas. 1968. *Zen and the Birds of Appetite.* New York: New Directions Publishing.

Merzel, Dennis Genpo. 1991. *The Eye Never Sleeps: Striking to the Heart of Zen.* Boston, MA: Shambhala Publications.

Metraux, Daniel A. 1996. "The Soka Gakkai: Buddhism and the Creation of a Harmonious and Peaceful Society." Pp. 365-400 in *Engaged Buddhism: Buddhist Liberation Movements in Asia,* edited by Christopher S. Queen and Sallie B. King. Albany, NY: State University of New York Press.

Meyer, Art and Jocele Meyer. 1991. *Earth-Keepers.* Scottdale, PA: Herald Press.

Mipham, Sakong. 2008. "Which Part Is Me?" *Shambhala Sun,* May: 19-22.

Mizuno, Kogen. 1980. *The Beginnings of Buddhism.* Translated by Richard Gage. Tokyo, Japan: Kosei Publishing Co.

Moon, Susan. 2000. "Activist Women in American Buddhism." Pp. 246-268 in *Engaged Buddhism in the West,* edited by Christopher S. Queen. Boston, MA: Wisdom Publications.

Northrop, F. S. C. 1979. *The Meeting of East and West: An Inquiry Concerning World Understanding.* Woodbridge, CT: Ox Bow Press.

Page, Michael. 1988. *Understanding the Power of Ch'i.* London, England: Hammersmith.

Palmer, Martin. 1991. *The Elements of Taoism.* Rockport, MA: Element Books.

Powell, Robert. 1961. *Zen and Reality: An Approach to Society and Happiness on a Non-Sectarian Basis.* New York: The Viking Press.

Powers, John, 2000. "The Free Tibet Movement: A Selective Narrative." Pp. 218-244 in *Engaged Buddhism in the West*, edited by Christopher S. Queen. Boston, MA: Wisdom Publications, pp. 218-44.

Price, A.F. and Mou-lam Wong (Translator). 1990. *The Diamond Sutra and The Sutra of Hui-neng*. Boston, MA: Shambhala Publications.

Queen, Christopher. 1996. "Introduction: The Shapes and Sources of Engaged Buddhism." Pp. 1-44 in *Engaged Buddhism: Buddhist Liberation Movements in Asia*, edited by Christopher Queen and Sallie B. King. Albany, NY: State University of New York Press.

Queen, Christopher, 2000. "Glassman Roshi and the Peacemaker Order: Three Encounters" Pp. 95-127 in *Engaged Buddhism in the West*, edited by Christopher S. Queen. Boston, MA: Wisdom Publications.

Queen, Christopher and Sallie B. King (Editors). 1996. *Engaged Buddhism: Buddhist Liberation Movements in Asia*. Albany, NY: State University of New York Press.

Rao, K. I. Seshagiti. 2000. "The Five Great Elements (Pancamahabhuta): An Ecological Perspective." Pp. 23-38 in *Hinduism and Ecology*, edited by Christopher Key Chapple and Mary Evelyn Tucker. Cambridge, MA: Harvard University Press.

Rosenbaum, Robert. 1999. *Zen and the Heart of Psychotherapy*. New York: Taylor & Francis.

Schirmacher, Wolfgang (Editor). 1996. *Arthur Schopenhauer: Philosophical Writings*. Translated by E. F. J. Payne. New York: Continuum.

Sekida, Katsuki. 1985. *Zen Training: Methods and Philosophy*. New York: Weatherhill.

Sekida, Katsuki (Translator) and A.V. Grimstone (Editor). 1977. *Two Zen Classics: Mumokan and Hekiganroku*. New York: Weatherhill.

Shaku, Soyen. 1993[1913]. *Zen for Americans*. Translated by D.T. Suzuki. New York: Barnes & Noble Books.

Shattock, E. H. 1958. *An Experiment in Mindfulness*. New York: Samuel Weiser, Inc.

Shupe, Jr., Anson D. 1977. "Conventional Religion and Political Participation in Postwar Rural Japan." *Social Forces*, 55(3): 613-29.

Shupe, Anson. 1986. "Militancy and Accommodation in the Third Civilization." Pp. 235-253 in *Prophetic Religions and Politics*, edited by Jeffrey K. Hadden and Anson Shupe. New York: Paragon House.

Shupe, Anson. 1991. "Globalization versus Religious Nativism: Japan's Soka Gakkai in the World Arena." Pp. 183-199 in *Religion and Global Order*, edited by Roland Robertson and William R. Garrett. New York: Paragon House.

Shupe, Anson. 1993. "Soka Gakkai and the Slippery Slope from Militancy to Accommodation." Pp. 231-238 in *Religion and Society in Modern Japan*, edited by Mark R. Mullins, Shimazono Susumu and Paul L. Swanson. Berkeley, CA: Asian Humanities Press.

Shupe, Anson and Jeffrey K. Hadden. 1989. "Is There Such a Thing as Global Fundamentalism?" Pp. 109-122 in *Secularization and Fundamentalism Reconsidered*, edited by Jeffrey K. Hadden and Anson Shupe. New York: Paragon House.

Snelling, John. 1991. *The Buddhist Handbook*. New York: Barnes & Noble Books.

Stevens, John. 1993. *Three Zen Masters: Ikkyu, Hakuin, and Ryokan*. New York: Kodansha International.

Stryk, Lucien. 1969. *World of the Buddha: A Reader—from the Three Baskets to Modern Zen*. New York: Anchor Books.

Sutton, Florin Giripescu. 1991. *Existence and Enlightenment in the Lankavatara-Sutra*. New York: State University of New York Press.

Suzuki, Beatrice Lane. 1959. *Mahayana Buddhism*. New York: Macmillan.

Suzuki, Daisetz Teitaro. 1955. "The Role of Nature in Zen Buddhism." Pp. 176-206 in *Studies in Zen Buddhism,* edited by D. T. Suzuki. New York: Dell.
Suzuki, Daisetz Teitaro. 1959. *Zen and Japanese Culture.* Princeton, NJ: Princeton University Press, Bollingen Series LXIV.
Suzuki, Daisetz Teitaro (Translator and Editor). 1960. *Manual of Zen Buddhism.* New York: Grove Press.
Suzuki, Daisetz Teitaro. 1961. *Essays in Zen Buddhism.* New York: Grove Press.
Suzuki, Daisetz Teitaro. 1964. *An Introduction to Buddhism.* New York: Grove Press.
Suzuki, Daisetz Teitaro. 1969. *The Zen Doctrine of No-Mind.* York Beach, ME: Samuel Wiser, Inc.
Suzuki, Daisetz Teitaro. 1970a. *Shin Buddhism.* London, England: George Allen & Unwin, Ltd.
Suzuki, Daisetz Teitaro. 1970b. *The Field of Zen.* New York: Harper & Row.
Thurman, Robert A. F. 1998. "Toward An American Buddhism." Pp. 450-468 in *Buddhism in America,* edited by Al Rapaport and Brian D. Hotchkiss. Rutland, VT: Charles E. Tuttle.
Tsunoda, Ryusaku, William Theodore De Bary and David Keene. 1964. "Chinese Thought and Institutions in Early Japan." Pp. 52-60 in *Sources of Japanese Tradition, Volume I,* edited by Ryusaku Tsunoda, William Theodore De Bary and David Keene, eds. New York: Columbia University Press.
Tworkov, Helen. 1994. *Zen in America.* New York: Kodansha International.
Tworkov, Helen. 1998. "Buddhism in the Media: A Panel Discussion." Pp. 529-542 in *Buddhism in America,* edited by Al Rapaport and Brian D. Hotchkiss. Rutland, VT: Charles E. Tuttle.
Uchiyama, Kosho. 1993. *Opening the Hand of Thought: Approach to Zen.* Translated by Shohaku Okumura and Tom Wright. New York: Arkana.
Watson, Burton (Translator). 1993. *The Zen Teachings of Master Lin-chi (Lin-chi Lu).* Boston, MA: Shambhala.
Watts, Alan W. 1957. *The Way of Zen.* New York: Vintage Books.
Watts, Alan W. 1958a. *The Spirit of Zen.* New York: Grove Press.
Watts, Alan W. 1958b. *Nature, Man and Woman.* New York: Vintage Books.
Watts, Alan W. 1961. *Psychotherapy East and West.* New York: Ballantine Books.
Watts, Alan W. and Al Chung-liang Huang. 1975. *Tao: The Watercourse Way.* New York: Pantheon.
Wei, Henry. 1982. *The Guiding Light of Lao Tsu: A New Translation and Commentary on the Tao Te Ching.* Wheaton, IL: The Theosophical Publishing House.
Wong, Eva (Translator). 1992. *Cultivating Stillness.* Boston, MA: Shambhala Publications.
Wood, Ernest. 1962. *The Dictionary of Zen.* New York: Citadel Press.
Wright, Arthur F. 1959. *Buddhism in Chinese History.* Stanford, CA: Stanford University Press.
Wu, John C. H. 1996. *The Golden Age of Zen, Second Edition.* New York: Doubleday.
Yu, Lu Kwan. 1960. *Ch'an and Zen Teachings.* Berkeley, CA: Shambhala Publications.

Social Psychology References

Adler, Alfred, 1954[1927]. *Understanding Human Nature.* Translated by W. Beran Wolfe. New York: Fawcett Books.
Adorno, T. W., Else Frankel-Brunswick, Daniel J. Levinson and R. Nevitt Sanford. 1950. *The Authoritarian Personality.* New York: W. W. Norton.
Albarracín, Doloris, Blair. T. Johnson and Mark P. Zanna (Editors). 2005. *The Handbook of Attitudes.* Mahwah, NJ: Erlbaum.

Allport, Gordon W. 1954. "The Historical Background of Modern Social Psychology." Pp. 3-56 in *The Handbook of Social Psychology*, edited by Gardner Lindzey. Cambridge, MA: Addison-Wesley Publishing.

Allport, Gordon W. 1967. "Attitudes." Pp. 1-13 in *Readings in Attitude Theory and Measurement*, edited by Martin Fishbein. New York: John Wiley & Sons.

Allport, Gordon W. 1968. "The Historical Background of Modern Social Psychology." Pp. 1-80 in *The Handbook of Social Psychology, 2nd Edition*, edited by Gardner Lindzey and Elliot Aronson. Reading, MA: Addison-Wesley Publishing.

Allport, Gordon W. 1979. *The Nature of Prejudice: Twenty-Fifth Anniversary Edition.* Reading, MA: Addison-Wesley.

Alwin, Duane F. 1995. "Quantitative Methods in Social Psychology." Pp. 68-89 in *Sociological Perspectives on Social Psychology*, edited by Karen S. Cook, Gary Alan Fine and James S. House. Boston, MA: Allyn and Bacon.

Ansbacher, Heinz L. and Rowena R. Ansbacher, eds. 1964. *The Individual Psychology of Alfred Adler.* New York: Harper and Row.

Azjen, Icek and Martin Fishbein. 2005. "The Influence of Attitudes on Behavior." Pp. 173-222 in *The Handbook of Attitudes*, edited by Dolores Albarracin, Blair T. Johnson and Mark P. Zanna. Mahway, NJ: Lawrence Erlbaum Associates.

Becker, Howard S. 1968. "The Self and Adult Socialization." Pp. 194-208 in *The Study of Personality: An Interdisciplinary Approach*, edited by Edward Norbeck, Douglass Price-Williams and William M. McCord. New York: Holt, Rinehart and Winston.

Bellah, Robert N. 1976. "New Religious Consciousness and the Crisis in Modernity." Pp. 333-352 in *The New Religious Consciousness*, edited by Charles Y. Block and Robert N. Bellah. Berkeley, CA: University of California Press.

Blumer, Herbert. 1969. *Symbolic Interaction: Perspective and Method.* Englewood Cliffs, NJ: Prentice-Hall.

Bollen, Kenneth A. 1989. *Structural Equations with Latent Variables.* New York: Wiley.

Boutilier, Robert G., J. Christian Roed and Ann C. Svendsen. 1980. "Crises in the Two Social Psychologies: A Critical Comparison." *Social Psychology Quarterly*, 43(1): 5-17.

Bratcher, Edward B. 1984. *The Walk-on-Water Syndrome.* Waco, TX: Word Books.

Brim, Orville G. Jr. 1966. "Socialization Through the Life Cycle." Pp. 1-49 in *Socialization After Childhood*, edited by Orville G. Brim, Jr. and Stanton Wheeler. New York: John Wiley and Sons.

Bromley, David G. and Anson D. Shupe, Jr. 1979. "'Just a Few Years Seems Like a Lifetime': A Role Theory Approach to Participation in Religious Movements." Pp. 159-185 in *Research in Social Movements, Conflicts, and Change, Volume 2*, edited by Louis Kriesberg. Greenwich, CT: JAI Press.

Bromley, David G. and Bruce C. Busching. 1988. "Understanding the Structure of Contractual Covenantal Social Relations: Implications for the Sociology of Religion." *Sociological Analysis*, 49: 15-32.

Brown, J. A. C. 1967. *Freud and the Post-Freudians.* Middlesex, England: Penguin Books.

Canary, Daniel J. and David R. Seibold. 1984. *Attitudes and Behavior: An Annotated Bibliography.* New York: Prager.

Cardinal, Rudolf N., John A. Parkinson, Jeremy Hall and Barry J. Everitt. 2002. "Emotion and Motivation: The Role of the Amygdala, Ventral Striatum, and Prefrontal Cortex." *Neuroscience and Biobehavioral Review*, 26: 321-352.

Chaplin, James P. 1959. *Rumor, Fear, and the Madness of Crowds.* New York: Ballantine Books.

Clausen, John A. 1968. "A Historical and Comparative View of Socialization Theory and Research." Pp. 18-72 in *Socialization and Society*, edited by John A. Clausen. Boston, MA: Little, Brown and Co.

Charon, Joel M. 2004. *Symbolic Interactionism: An Introduction, an Interpretation, an Integration, Eight Edition.* Upper Saddle River, NJ: Pearson.

Cleve, Felix M. 1969. *The Giants of Pre-Sophistic Greek Philosophy.* The Hague: Martinus Nijhoff.

Cooley, Charles Horton, 1962[1909]. *Social Organizations: A Study of the Larger Mind.* New York: Schocken Books.

Cooley, Charles. H. 1964[1902]. *Human Nature and Social Order.* New York: Schocken Books.

Cunningham, William A. and Philip David Zelazo. 2007. "Attitudes and Evaluations: a Social Cognitive Neuroscience Perspective." *Trends in Cognitive Sciences,* 11(3): 97-104.

Cunningham, William A., Philip David Zelazo, Dominic J. Packer and Jay J. Van Bavel. 2007. "The Iterative Reprocessing Model: A Multi-level Framework for Attitudes and Evaluations." *Social Cognition,* 25: 736-760.

Cytowic, Richard E. 1996. *The Neurological Side of Neuropsychology.* Cambridge, MA: MIT Press

Darrow, Charlotte and Paul Lowinger. 1970. "The Detroit Uprising: A Psychosocial Study." Pp. 117-125 in *The Upright Society,* edited by Howard Gadlin and Bertram E. Garskof. Belmont, CA: Brooks/Cole.

Davies, James C. 1962. "Toward A Theory of Revolution." *American Sociological Review,* 27: 5-19.

Davis, Michael. 1992. "The Role of the Amygdala in Conditioned Fear." Pp. 255-306 in *The Amygdala: Neurobiological Aspects of Emotion, Memory and Mental Dysfunction,* edited by John P. Aggleton. New York: Wiley-Liss.

DeLamater, John D. and David J. Myers. 2007. *Social Psychology, 6th Edition.* New York: Thomson Wadsworth.

Deutscher, Irwin. 1966. "Words and Deeds: Social Science and Social Policy." *Social Problems,* 13: 235-254.

Dorman, Jeffrey P. 2001. "Associations Between Religious Behavior and Attitude to Christianity Among Australian Catholic Adolescents: Scale Validation." *The Journal of Social Psychology,* 141(5): 629–639

Eagly, Alice H. and Shelly Chaiken. 1993. *The Psychology of Attitudes.* Orlando, FL: Harcourt Brace Jovanovich.

Fine, Gary A., James S. House and Karen S. Cook. 1995. "Introduction." Pp ix-xii in *Sociological Perspectives on Social Psychology,* edited by Karen S. Cook, Gary Alan Fine and James S. House. Boston, MA: Allyn and Bacon.

Fishbein, Martin. 1967. "Attitudes and the Prediction of Behavior." Pp. 477-492 in Attitude Theory and Measurement, edited by Martin Fishbein. New York: John Wiley & Sons.

Fishbein, Martin and Icek Ajzen. 1975. *Belief, Attitude, Intention and Behavior: An Introduction to Theory and Research.* Reading, MA: Addison-Wesley.

Foss, Daniel and Richard W. Larkin. 1979. "The Roar of the Lemming: Youth, Postmovement Groups, and the Life Construction Crisis." Pp. 264-285 in *Religious Change and Continuity,* edited by Harry M. Johnson. San Francisco, CA: Jossey-Bass.

Frankfort, Henri, H. A. Frankfort, John A. Wilson and Thorkild Jacobsen. 1968. *Before Philosophy: The Intellectual Adventure of Ancient Man.* Baltimore, MD: Penguin Books.

Freud, Sigmund. 1936. *The Problem of Anxiety.* Translated by Henry Alden Bunker. New York: W. W. Norton.

Freud, Sigmund. 1947[1923]. *The Ego and the Id.* London, England: The Hogwarth Press.

Garrison, Vivian. 1974. "Sectarian and Psycho-Social Adjustment: A Controlled Comparison of Puerto Rican Pentecostals and Catholics." Pp. 298-329 in *Religious Movements in Contemporary America,* edited by Irving I. Zaretsky and Mark P. Leon. Princeton, NJ: Princeton University Press.

Gecas, Viktor. 1982. "The Self-Concept." *Annual Review of Sociology,* 8: 1-15.

Gecas, Viktor. 1989. "Rekindling the Sociological Imagination in Social Psychology." *Journal for the Theory of Social Behavior,* 19(1): 97-115.

Gecas, Viktor. 1991. "The Self-Concept as a Basis for a Theory of Motivation." Pp. 171-187 in *The Self-Society Dynamic; Cognition, Emotion, and Action,* edited by Judith A. Howard and Peter L. Callero. New York: Cambridge University Press.

Gibson, David. 2004. *The Coming Catholic Church, Revised Edition.* San Francisco, CA: Harper San Francisco.

Glock, Charles E. 1964. "The Role of Deprivation in the Origins and Evolution of Religious Groups." Pp. 24-36 in *Religion and Social Conflict,* edited by Robert Lee and Martin E. Marty. New York: Oxford University Press.

Goffman, Erving. 1959. *The Presentation of Self in Everyday Life.* New York: Doubleday.

Gordon, Cyrus H. 1982. *Forgotten Scripts, Revised Edition.* New York: Dorset Press.

Greene, A. L. and Elizabeth Reed. 1992. "Social Context Differences in the Relation Between Self-Esteem and Self-Concept During Late Adolescence." *Journal of Adolescent Research,* 7(2): 266-282.

Gulliksen, Harold. 1950. *Theory of Mental Tests.* New York: Wiley.

Gurr, Ted Robert. 1970. *Why Men Rebel.* Princeton, NJ: Princeton University Press.

Hall, Calvin S. 1954. *A Primer of Freudian Psychology.* New York: New American Library.

Hall, Calvin S. and Gardner Lindzey. 1970. *Theories of Personality, Second Edition.* New York: John Wiley & Sons.

Henerson, Marlene, Lynn L. Morris and Carol T. Fitz-Gibbon. 1987. *How to Measure Attitudes.* Newbury Park, CA: Sage.

Hertzler, Joyce O. 1965. *A Sociology of Language.* New York: McGraw-Hill.

Hewitt, John P. 2000. *Self and Society: A Symbolic Interactionist Social Psychology, Eighth Edition.* Boston, MA: Allyn and Bacon.

Hill, Terrence and Christopher Bradley. 2010. "The Emotional Consequences of Service Work: An Ethnographic Examination of Hair Salon Workers." *Sociological Focus,* 43(1): 41-60.

Hine, Virginia. 1974. "The Deprivation and Disorganization Theories of Social Movements." Pp. 646-661 in *Religious Movements in Contemporary America,* edited by Irving I. Zaretsky and Mark P. Leon. Princeton, NJ: Princeton University Press.

Hirschi, Travis. 1969. *Causes of Delinquency.* Los Angeles, CA: University of California Press.

Hochschild, Arlie R. 1979. "Emotion Work, Feeling Rules, and Social Structure." *The American Journal of Sociology,* 85(3): 551-575.

Hochschild, Arlie R. 1983. *The Managed Heart: Commercialization of Human Feeling.* Berkeley, CA: University of California Press.

Hoffer, Eric. 1963[1951]. *The True Believer.* New York: Time Incorporated.

Holstein, James A. and Jaber F. Gubrium. 2000. *The Self We Live By.* New York: Oxford University Press.

Horney, Karen. 1966. *New Ways in Psychoanalysis.* New York: W. W. Norton.

House, James S. 1977. "The Three Faces of Social Psychology." *Sociometry,* 40(2): 161-177.

Hume, David. 1956[1757]. *The Natural History of Religion.* Edited by H. E. Root. Stanford, CA: Stanford University Press.

Hume, David. 1978 [1739-1740]. *A Treatise of Human Nature.* Second edition by P. H. Nidditch. Analytical index by L. A. Selby-Bigge. Oxford, England: Oxford University Press.

Hyman, Herbert H. and Eleanor Singer. 1971. "An Introduction to Reference Group Theory and Research." Pp. 66-77 in *Current Perspectives in Social Psychology, 3rd Edition,* edited by Edwin P. Hollander and Raymond G. Hunt. New York: Oxford University Press.

Irvine, Leslie. 2004. "A Model of Animal Selfhood: Expanding Interactionist Possibilities." *Symbolic Interaction,* 27(1): 3–21.

Jaccard, James and Hart Blanton. 2005. "The Origins and Structure of Behavior: Conceptualizing Behavior in Attitude Research." Pp. 125-172 in *The Handbook of Attitudes,* edited by Dolores Albarracin, Blair T. Johnson and Mark P. Zanna. Mahway, NJ: Lawrence Erlbaum Associates.

James, William. 1929[1902]. *The Varieties of Religious Experience.* New York: The Modern Library.

James, William. 1985[1892]. *Psychology: The Briefer Course.* Notre Dame, IN: University of Notre Dame Press.

James, William. 1993[1890]. "The Self and Its Selves." Pp. 157-162 in *Social Theory: The Multicultural and Classic Readings,* edited by Charles C. Lemert. Boulder, CO: Westview Press.

Jary, David and Julia Jary. 1991. *HarperCollins Dictionary of Sociology.* New York: HarperPerennial.

Johnson, Norris R. 1987. "Panic at 'The Who Concern Stampede': An Empirical Assessment." *Social Problems,* 34: 362-73.

Jones, Edward E. 1985. "Major Developments in Social Psychology During the Past Five Decades. Pp. 47-108 in *The Handbook of Social Psychology, 3rd Edition,* edited by Gardner Lindzey and Elliot Aronson. New York: Random House.

Katovich, Michael A., Dan E. Miller and Robert L. Stewart. 2003. "The Iowa School." Pp. 119-139 in *Handbook of Symbolic Interaction,* edited by Larry T. Reynolds and Nancy J. Herman-Kinney. New York: Roman and Littlefield.

Kelley, Harold H. 2000. "The Proper Study of Social Psychology." *Social Psychology Quarterly,* 63(1): 3-15.

Kemper, Theodore D. 1981. "Social Constructionist and Positivist Approaches to the Sociology of Emotions." *American Journal of Sociology,* 87(2): 336-62.

Kiesler, Charles A., Barry E. Collins and Norman Miller. 1969. *Attitude Change.* New York: John Wiley & Sons.

Kohlberg, Lawrence, 1984. *The Psychology of Moral Development: Moral Stages and the Life Cycle.* San Francisco, CA: Harper & Row.

Kraus, Stephen J. 1995. "Attitudes and the Prediction of Behavior: A Meta-Analysis of the Empirical Literature." *Personality and Social Psychology Bulletin,* 21(1): 58-75.

Krosnick, Jon A., Charles M. Judd and Bernd Wittenbrink. 2005. "The Measure of Attitudes." Pp. 21-76 in *The Handbook of Attitudes,* edited by Dolores Albarracin, Blair T. Johnson and Mark P. Zanna. Mahway, NJ: Lawrence Erlbaum Associates.

Kuhn, Manford H. and Thomas S. McPortland. 1954. "An Empirical Investigation of Self-Attitudes." *American Sociological Review,* 19: 68-76.

Kuhn, Thomas. 1962. *The Structure of Scientific Revolutions.* Chicago, IL: University of Chicago Press.

LaBarre, Weston. 1968. "Personality from a Psychoanalytic Viewpoint." Pp. 65-87 in *The Study of Personality: An Interdisciplinary Appraisal,* edited by Edward Norbeck, Douglas Price-William and William M. McCord. New York: Holt, Rinehart and Winston.

Lange, C. G. 1922. "The Emotions: A Psychophysiological Study." Pp. 33-90 in *The Emotions,* edited by C. G. Lange and William James. Baltimore, MD: Williams and Wilkins.

LaPiere, Richard. 1934. "Attitudes versus Actions." *Social Forces,* 13: 230-37.

LeBon, Gustvae. 1982[1895]. *The Crowd: A Study of the Popular Mind.* Atlanta, GA: Cherokee Publishing Company.

LeDoux, Joseph. 1996. *The Emotional Brain: The Mysterious Underpinnings of Emotion Life.* New York: Simon and Schuster Paperbacks.

Leach, Colin Wayne and Larissa Z. Tiedens. 2004. "A World of Emotion." Pp. 1-18 in *The Social Life of Emotions,* edited by Larissa Z. Tiedens and Colin Wayne Leach. Cambridge, UK: Cambridge University Press.

Leidner, Robin. 1993. *Fast Food, Fast Talk: Service Work and The Routinization of Everyday Life.* Berkeley, CA: University of California Press.

Likert, Renis. 1932. "A Technique for the Measurement of Attitudes." *Archives of Psychology,* 140: 5-55.

Likert, Renis. 1967. "The Method of Constructing an Attitude Scale." Pp. 90-95 in *Readings in Attitude Theory and Measurement,* edited by Martin Fishbein. New York: John Wiley & Sons.

Likert, Renis. 1970. "A Technique for the Measurement of Attitudes." Pp. 149-158 in *Attitude Measurement,* edited by Gene F. Summers. Chicago, IL: Rand McNally and Company.

Linton, Ralph. 1945. *The Cultural Background of Personality.* New York: Appleton-Century-Crofts.

Liska, Allen E. 1981. *Perspectives on Deviance.* Englewood Cliffs, NJ: Prentice-Hall.

Locher, David K. 2002. *Collective Behavior.* Upper Saddle River, NJ: Prentice-Hall.

MacLean, Paul D. 1990. *The Triune Brain in Evolution: Role in Paleocerebral Functions.* New York: Plenum.

MacKay, Charles. 1980[1841]. *Extraordinary Popular Delusions and the Madness of Crowds.* New York: Three Rivers Press.

Massey, Douglas S. 2002. "A Brief History of Human Society: The Origin and Role of Emotion in Social Life." *American Sociological Review,* 67(1): 1-29.

Maxim, Paul S. 1999. *Quantitative Research Methods in the Social Sciences.* New York: Oxford University Press.

McCarthy, John and Mayer N. Zald. 1977. "Resource Mobilization in Social Movements: A Partial Theory." *American Journal of Sociology,* 82: 1212-1241.

McClendon, McKee J. 1994. *Multiple Regression and Causal Analysis.* Itasca, IL: F. E. Peacock Publishers.

McDougall, William. 1908. *Introduction to Social Psychology.* London, England: Methuen & Co. Ltd.

McGuire, William J. 1969. "The Nature of Attitudes and Attitude Change." Pp. 136-314 in *The Handbook of Social Psychology, 2nd Edition,* edited by Gardner Lindzey and Elliot Aronson. Reading, MA: Addison-Wesley.

McPhail, Clark. 1991. *The Myth of the Madding Crowd.* Hawthorne, NY: Aldine de Gruyter.

Mead, George H. 1962[1934]. *Mind, Self and Society.* Edited by Charles W. Morris. Chicago, IL: University of Chicago Press.

Meltzer, Bernard N., John W. Petras and Larry T. Reynolds. 1975. *Symbolic Interactionism: Genesis, Varieties and Criticism.* Boston, MA: Routledge and Kegan Paul.

Michels, Robert, 1959[1915]. *Political Parties.* New York: Dover Books.

Moser, Karin S. 2007. "Metaphors as Symbolic Environment of the Self: How Self-Knowledge is Expressed Verbally." *Current Research in Social Psychology,* 12(11): 151-178.
Mueller, Daniel J. 1970. "Physiological Techniques of Attitude Measurement." Pp. 534-552 in *Attitude Measurement,* edited by Gene F. Summers. Chicago, IL: Rand McNally and Company.
Mueller, Daniel J. 1986. *Measuring Social Attitudes: A Handbook for Researchers and Practitioners.* New York: Teachers College Press.
Needleman, Jacob. 1972. *The New Religions.* New York: Pocketbooks.
Ochsner, Kevin N. and Matthew D. Liberman. 2001. "The Emergence of Social Cognitive Neuroscience." *American Psychologist,* 56(9): 717-734.
Pals, Daniel L. 1996. *Seven Theories of Religion.* New York: Oxford University Press.
Pampel, Fred C. 2007. *Sociological Lives and Ideas: An Introduction to the Classical Theorists.* New York: Worth.
Panksepp, Jaak. 1998. *Affective Neuroscience: The Foundations of Human and Animal Emotions.* New York: Oxford University Press.
Phelps, Elizabeth A. 2004. "Human Emotion and Memory: Interactions of the Amygdala and Hippocampal Complex." *Current Opinion in Neurobiology,* 14: 198–202.
Plato. 1928. *The Republic.* New York: Charles Scribners Sons.
Pollak, Lauren Harte and Peggy A. Thoits. 1989. "Processes in Emotional Socialization." *Social Psychology Quarterly,* 52(1): 22-34.
Porier, Gary W. and Albert J. Lott. 1970. "Galvanic Skin Responses and Prejudice." Pp. 489-496 in *Attitude Measurement,* edited by Gene F. Summers. Chicago, IL: Rand McNally and Company.
Prus, Robert. 2003. "Ancient Forerunners." Pp. 19-38 in *Handbook of Symbolic Interaction,* edited by Larry T. Reynolds and Nancy J. Herman-Kinney. New York: Roman and Littlefield.
Ridgeway, Cecilia L. 1994. "Affect." Pp. 205-230 in *Group Processes: Sociological Analyses,* edited by Martha Foschi and Edward J. Lawler. Chicago, IL: Nelson-Hall Publishers.
Riesman, David. 1950. *The Lonely Crowd: A Study of the Channing American Character.* New Haven, CT: Yale University Press.
Robbins, Thomas. 1988. *Cults, Converts, and Charisma.* Beverly Hills, CA: Sage.
Robinson, James P. and Phillip R. Shaver. 1970. *Measures of Social Psychological Attitudes.* Ann Arbor, MI: University of Michigan Institute for Social Research.
Rohall, David E., Melissa A. Milkie and Jeffrey W. Lucas. 2007. *Social Psychology: Sociological Perspectives.* Boston, MA: Pearson.
Rosenberg, Morris. 1979. *Conceiving the Self.* New York: Basic Books.
Rosenberg, Morris. 1990. "Reflexivity and Emotions." *Social Psychological Quarterly,* 53(1): 3-12.
Rosenberg, Morris, Carmi Schooler, Carrie Schoenbach and Florence Rosenberg. 1995. "Global Self-Esteem and Specific Self-Esteem: Different Concepts, Different Outcomes." *American Sociological Review,* 60: 141-156.
Ross, Edward Alsworth. 1915[1908]. *Social Psychology: An Outline and Sourcebook (Eighth Printing).* New York: The Macmillan Company.
Rudin, A. James and Marcia R. Rudin. 1980. *Prison or Paradise? The New Religious Cults.* Philadelphia, PA: Fortress Press.
Sapir, Edward. 1949. *Culture, Language and Personality: Selected Essays.* Edited by David G. Mandelbaum. Berkeley, CA: University of California Press.
Schachter, Stanley and Jerome Singer. 1962. "Cognitive, Social, and Physiological Determinants of Emotional State." *Psychological Review,* 69: 379-99.

Schachter, Stanley and Ladd Wheeler. 1962. "Epinephrine, Chlorpromazine, and Amusement." *Journal of Abnormal and Social Psychology,* 65: 121-28.

Schuman, Howard. 1995. "Attitudes, Beliefs, and Behavior." Pp. 68-89 in *Sociological Perspectives on Social Psychology,* edited by Karen S. Cook, Gary Alan Fine and James S. House. Boston, MA: Allyn and Bacon.

Schwab, Charlotte Rolnick. 2002. *Sex, Lies, and Rabbis: Breaking a Sacred Trust.* Bloomington, IN: 1st Books.

Schweingruber, David and Ronald Wolstein. 2005. "The Maddening Crowd Goes to School: Myths about Crowds in Introductory Sociology Textbooks." *Teaching Sociology,* 33: 136-153.

Seggar, John and Philip Kuntz. 1972. "Conversion: Evaluation of a Step-like Process for Problem-Solving." *Review of Religious Research,* 13(Spring): 178-184.

Sewell, William H. 1989. "Some Reflections on the Golden Age of Interdisciplinary Social Psychology." *Social Psychology Quarterly,* 52(2): 88-97.

Shibutani, Tamotsu. 1962. "Reference Groups and Social Control." Pp. 128-147 in *Human Behavior and Social Processes,* edited by Arnold M. Rose. Boston, MA: Houghton Mifflin.

Shupe, Jr., Anson D. 1995. *In the Name of All That's Holy: A Theory of Clergy Malfeasance.* Westport, CT: Praeger.

Shupe, Anson. 2007. *Spoils of the Kingdom: Clergy Misconduct and Religious Community.* Champaign, IL: University of Illinois Press.

Shupe, Jr., Anson D. 2008. *Rogue Clerics: the Social Problem of Clergy Deviance.* New Brunswick, NJ: Transaction Publishers.

Shupe, Anson. 2009. "Religious Fundamentalism." Pp. 478-496 in *The Oxford Handbook of the Sociology of Religion,* edited by Peter B. Clarke. Oxford, UK: Oxford University Press.

Shupe, Anson D. (Editor). 1998. *Wolves within the Fold: Religious Leadership and Abuses of Power.* New Brunswick, NJ: Rutgers University Press.

Shupe, Jr., Anson D. and David G. Bromley, 1980. The New Vigilantes: Deprogrammers, Anti-Cultists, and the New Religions. Beverly Hills, CA: Sage.

Shupe, Anson and Susan E. Darnell. 2006. *Agents of Discord: Deprogramming, Pseudo-Science, and the American Anticult Movement.* New Brunswick, NJ: Transaction Publishers.

Shupe, Anson, William A. Stacey, and Lonnie R. Hazlewood. 1987. *Violent Men, Violent Couples.* Lexington, MA: Lexington Books.

Singer, Margaret Thaler. 1995. *Cults in Our Midst: The Hidden Menace in Our Everyday Lives.* San Francisco, CA: Jossey-Bass.

Sipe, A. W. Richard. 1995. *Sex, Priests and Power: Anatomy of a Crisis.* New York: Brunner/Mazel.

Smelser, Neil J. 1962. *Theory of Collective Behavior.* New York: The Free Press.

Smith-Lovin, Lynn. 1995. "The sociology of affect and *emotion.*" Pp. *118-148* in *Sociological Perspectives on Social Psychology,* edited by Karen S. Cook, Gary Alan Fine and James S. House. Boston, MA: Allyn and Bacon.

Smith-Lovin, Lynn and Linda D. Molm. 2000. "Introduction." *Social Psychology Quarterly,* 63(4): 281-283.

Snow, David A., E. Burke Rochford Jr., Steven K. Warden and Robert D. Benford. 1986. "Frame Alignment Processes, Micromobilization, and Movement Participation." *American Sociological Review,* 51(3): 464-81.

Spearman, Charles. 1904. "General Intelligence, Objectively Determined and Measured." *American Journal of Psychology,* 15: 201-293.

Spearman, Charles. 1910. "Correlation Calculated from Faulty Data." *British Journal of Psychology,* 3: 271-295.

Stacey, William A., Lonnie R. Hazlewood and Anson Shupe. 1994. *The Violent Couple.* Westport, CT: Praeger.

Stryker, Sheldon and Richard T. Serpe. 1994. "Identity Salience and Psychological Centrality: Equivalent, Overlapping, or Complementary Concepts?" Social Psychology Quarterly, 57(1): 16-35.

Taleb, Nassim Nicholas. 2007. *The Black Swan: The Impact of the Highly Improbable.* New York: Random House.

Thoits, Peggy A. 1989. "The Sociology of Emotions." *Annual Review of Sociology,* 15: 317-342.

Thurstone, Louis L. 1928. "Attitudes Can Be Measured." *American Journal of Sociology,* 33: 529-54.

Tourangeau, Roger, Lance J. Rips and Kenneth Rasinski. 2000. *The Psychology of Survey Response.* New York: Cambridge University Press.

Turner, Ralph H. 1969. "Role-Taking: Process Versus Conformity." Pp. 215-230 in *Readings in Social Psychology,* edited by Alfred R. Lindesmith and Anselm L. Strauss. New York: Holt, Rinehart and Winston.

Turner, Ralph H. and Lewis M. Killian. 1987. *Collective Behavior,* 3rd *Edition.* Englewood Cliffs, NJ: Prentice-Hall.

Turner, Ralph H. and Lewis M. Killian. 1993. "The Field of Collective Behavior." Pp. 5-20 in *Collective Behavior and Social Movements,* edited by Russell L. Curtis and Benigno E. Aguirre. Boston, MA: Allyn and Bacon.

Von Scheve, Christian and Rofl Von Luede. 2005. "Emotion and Social Structures: Towards an Interdisciplinary Approach." *Journal for the Theory of Social Behaviour,* 35: 303-328.

Wallace, Anthony F. C. 1968. "Anthropological Contributions to the Theory of Personality." Pp. 41-64 in *The Study of Personality: An Interdisciplinary Approach,* edited by Edward Norbeck, Douglass Price-Williams and William M. McCord. New York: Holt, Rinehart and Winston.

Weber, Max. 1964[1922]. *The Sociology of Religion.* Translated by Ephraim Fiscoff. Boston, MA: Beacon Press.

Weigert, Andrew J. and Viktor Gecas. 2003. "The Self." Pp. 267-288 in *Handbook of Symbolic Interaction,* edited by Larry T. Reynolds and Nancy J. Herman-Kinney. New York: Roman and Littlefield.

Whyte, William H. 1956. *The Organization Man.* Garden City, NY: Doubleday.

Wicker, Allan W. 1969. "Attitudes versus Actions: The Relationship of Verbal and Overt Behavioral Responses to Attitude Objects." *Journal of Social Issues,* 25: 41-78.

Woodmansee, John J. 1970. "The Pupil Response As a Measure of Social Attitudes." Pp. 514-533 in *Attitude Measurement,* edited by Gene F. Summers, ed. Chicago, IL: Rand McNally and Company.

Wuthnow, Robert. 1976. "The New Religions in Social Context." Pp. 267-293 in *The New Religious Consciousness,* edited by Charles Y. Glock and Robert N. Bellah. Berkeley, CA: University of California Press, pp. 267-93.

Yinger, J. Milton. 1946. *Religion in the Struggle for Power.* Durham, NC: Duke University Press.

Zeller, Richard A. and Edward G. Carmines. 1980. *Measurement in the Social Sciences.* Cambridge, MA: Cambridge University Press.

Index

For Product Safety Concerns and Information please contact our EU
representative GPSR@taylorandfrancis.com Taylor & Francis Verlag GmbH,
Kaufingerstraße 24, 80331 München, Germany

Batch number: 08158437

Printed by Printforce, the Netherlands